Sevenoaks

AN HISTORICAL DICTIONARY

Sevenoaks – looking north, early 20th century. This postcard offers a view north across Sevenoaks from the 90-foot tower of ***St Nicholas*** parish church. In the immediate foreground is ***Six Bells Lane***, to the left ***Rockdale***. Centre, almost on the skyline, is the spire of the new ***Methodist*** church built in The Drive in 1904.

Sevenoaks

AN HISTORICAL DICTIONARY

Compiled and edited by

David Killingray and Elizabeth Purves

for the Sevenoaks Historical Society

and the Sevenoaks Society

PHILLIMORE

2012

Published by

PHILLIMORE & CO. LTD

Andover, Hampshire, England

ISBN 978-1-86077-736-3

Contents

Acknowledgements

We are grateful to Roger FitzGerald for letting us use his watercolours on the front cover and elsewhere in the book. Other illustrations have been provided by Andrew Bamji, Andrew Beard, the Kent History and Library Centre, Paul Dunn, Eric Keys, David Killingray, Colin Miles, Richard Mitchell, Peter Moss, Tim Pearce, Jim Purves, Peter Rosling, St Nicholas parish church, Salmons, Sevenoaks Library, Sevenoaks Society, Sevenoaks Town Council, Ed Thompson and David Williams.

Funding for the book has come from a number of local organisations and bodies: Kent County Council Member's Fund, with thanks to Councillor John London; Sevenoaks District Council; Sevenoaks Town Council for two grants; the Kent Archaeological Society for grants from the Allen Grove Fund, and also from the Kent History Fund; the Sevenoaks Historical Society; and the Hollybush Residents Association.

We are also grateful to Chris Dance who compiled the index.

Contributors

This book has been a communal effort, and the editors are most grateful for the contributions made by: Anthony Akerman; Richard Aldrich; Brian Alleeson; Mark Ballard; Mike Bamforth; Andrew Bamji; Juliet Bankes; Susanne Beard; Chris Bell; Maureen Bennell; Les Best; Phyllis Black; Mike Bolton; Robert Brewer; Robin J. Brooks; Marjorie Brown; Elizabeth Cairns; Ian Campbell; Merilyn Canet; Janice Castle; Carol Cheeseman; Jim Cheeseman; Tony Clayton; Philip Clucas; Patrick Connelly; Lucile Corby; Heather Cornwell-Kelly; Roland Courtney; Neil Crabtree; David Cufley; Ed Diplock; Helen Doherty; Gill Draper; Katharine Draper; Paul Dunn; Margaret Durdant-Hollamby; Barbara Eastwood; Pauline Edwards; Mary Fagg; Avril Ferguson; Roger FitzGerald; Joan Gamble; Sue Gosling; Pat Harman; Michael Harrison; Gerry Hayward; Patricia Hayward; Philip Headley; Charles Hebert; Sue Henson; Ramon Higgs; Richard Hillary; Michael Hobbs; Chris Holgate; Margaret Holgate; Barbara Ide; John Ingram; Dan Jeffcote; Gillian Jones; Kate Kendell; Eric Keys; David Killingray; Jim Latheron; Di Latter; Deidre Le Faye; Sarah Lloyd; Keith Loney; Frank Marshall; Peter Mayes; Derek Medhurst; Colin Miles; Tina Milman; Penny Morrison; Peter Moss; Peter Mountfield; Diana Newall; Edward Oatley; Bob Ogley; Monty Parkin; Doreen Pascall; Tim Pearce; Iain Pearson; Deborah Petrick; Barbara Piper; Nick Polkinhorne; Henry Pound; Elizabeth Purves; Jim Purves; Sheila Reynolds; Adrienne Rogers; Evelyn Rogers; Peter Rogers; Susan Roome; Arthur Russ; Maureen Russ; Ray Russell; Robert Sackville-West; Charles Salmon; Jo Salmon; Jonathan Sargant; Rosemary Sassoon; Marigold Seal; Sevenoaks Town Council staff; Roger Sheldon; Denise Sims; Ann Slater; Harriette Smale; Terry Steley; Phyllis Styles; Chris Sutton; Magda Sweetland; Bill Taylor; Iain Taylor; Ed Thompson; David Toser; Graham Usher; Keith Wade; Ian Walker; Pam Walshe; Roger Walshe; Jill Webster; Alan Wilkinson; Claire Williams; David Williams; Michael Willsher and Peter Young.

Introduction

Sevenoaks: An Historical Dictionary
has been written by people of
Sevenoaks for the people of Sevenoaks.

More than 100 local residents have submitted research and illustrations for this history, which covers the great estates, buildings, trades, industries, occupations, transport, notable people, organisations, schools, churches, events and themes relating to our town and its environs.

Essentially the book is an A-Z of the area covered by the historic parish of St Nicholas (which stretched south from the river Darent to include Weald village), but is flexible in allowing for many people's modern mental maps of Sevenoaks. When we were planning the book one idea of a sub-title was 'Nearly everything you wanted to know about nearly everybody and everything in Sevenoaks in the past'. That would have been a near impossible task, resulting in a very long and unwieldy book. Our aims have been more modest: to raise and answer some of the questions that people curious about the locality have often asked; and to do so in the framework of a modern agenda of local history which, we hope, extends and challenges how the past is viewed.

So, how to use this book? The entries are alphabetically arranged. Within each entry other relevant entries are cross-referenced, indicated in ***bold italics***. At the end of many entries there are suggestions for further reading, indicated by a name and date in italics which refers to the bibliography at the end of the book. There is also a comprehensive index which enables the reader to find references throughout the book to people, places and topics which do not have individual entries.

A couple of final points are worth emphasising. This book has been the work of many contributors and two editors. All have striven hard to present an accurate account of Sevenoaks's past and we hope this will stimulate a wider interest in our local history. There might be errors in the Book. Please let us know, so that we can amend future editions of *Sevenoaks: An Historical Dictionary*. And if readers think that there should have been an entry on a place, person, topic or theme, why not write it and submit it for possible inclusion in a further edition.

Maps

Sevenoaks

AN HISTORICAL DICTIONARY

Entries

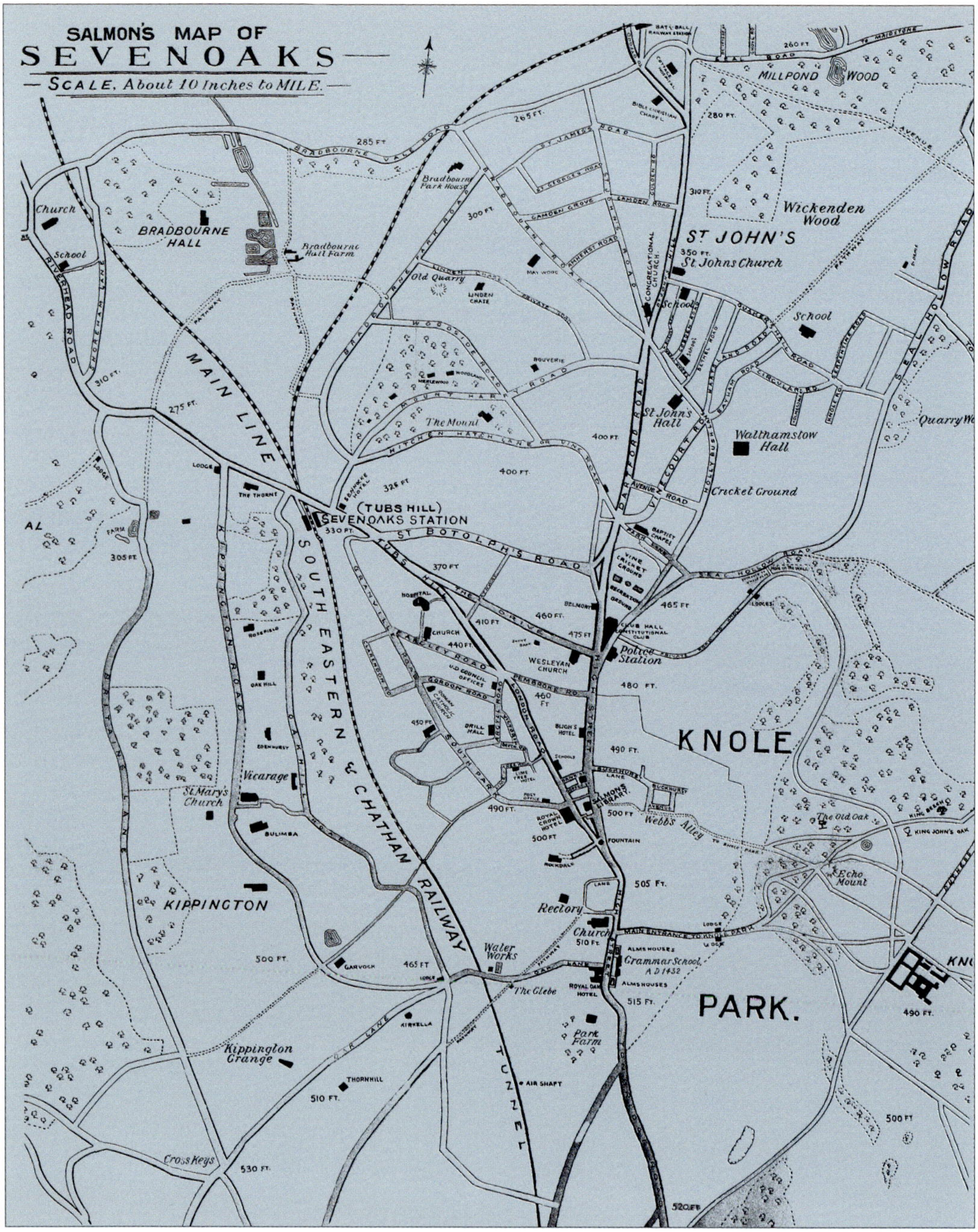

Map 1 Sevenoaks in 1903, from Salmon's Guide to the town. A small market town of large estates – Knole, Bradbourne, Montreal Park, Kippington and Wildernesse, but also a growing number of new 'gentry' houses, many of which are named on the map.

A

agriculture
Sevenoaks stands on the high ground of the greensand ridge, running gently down to the clays of the Vale of Holmesdale to the north and falling sharply to the wealden clays to the south. The greensand is not very fertile; much of it remains wooded or as parkland at Knole. The lighter soils on either side of the ridge have been cultivated over centuries for various crops. There are only patchy records; a useful overall snapshot is the ***Tithe Survey*** of 1841. But at different times wheat, oats, barley and hay, beans and peas, hops, apples, and soft fruits have been grown. Commercial woodlands, deciduous and in later years coniferous, have always occupied large areas, although the difficulty of transport meant that much heavy timber was used locally. Other trees were regularly coppiced, for basket making, hop-poles and housing. There was also much pasture land, particularly on the heavier soil which was difficult to plough; sheep were more common on the chalk downs to the north of Sevenoaks. Most of the produce went for local consumption, sold at Sevenoaks ***market*** because of high haulage costs on poor roads, although cattle were sometimes driven to London. After the arrival of the ***railway*** in 1862, access to wider markets became possible, so market gardening and soft fruit for London were added to local production.

Owen Aisher (1900-1993)
Builder, entrepreneur, and founder of Marley Ltd. In the 1920s Aisher and his father established a building materials firm producing cement roofing tiles. The Marley Tile Company began production at ***Riverhead*** in 1935, extracting sand from what became ***Chipstead Lake***. During the war, when house building was at a stand-still, Marley was involved in making prefabricated concrete Mulberry harbours for the D-Day landings in France. The company prospered with the post-war housing boom, also making plastic floor tiles and guttering and plumbing fixtures. Aisher was not sympathetic to trade unions in his plant. In 1968 he was one of the highest paid business executives in Britain, when Marley recorded its best ever profits of £4.5 million, and employed more than one hundred workers at the Riverhead factory. Aisher was knighted in 1981. He contributed to various local interests, most notably the Aisher Hall at ***Sevenoaks School***. Sand on the Riverhead site became exhausted in the 1980s and the tile plant closed in 1989, the land being sold for housing development and a Tesco ***supermarket***.
Wellings (1994)

allotments
Small allotments of land for the 'deserving labouring poor' to supplement their food supply were proposed from the late 18th century onwards. This became a statutory requirement for local authorities by the Allotments Act of 1887. In the 1890s Lord Hillingdon gave the local authority a plot of elevated land at Quakers Hall for allotments. In the early 1960s, ***Sevenoaks***

Urban District Council sold eight acres of the site for the development of housing which became Kennedy Gardens, the remaining 11 acres being leased to the Quakers Hall Allotment Association until 2016. A further three acres of land on the north side of Bradbourne Vale Road were purchased by the ***Sevenoaks Urban District Council*** in 1931 for allotments. Allotments formerly occupied land on the slope between Webbs Alley and Knole Park on land leased from the Knole estate, also on Crown Fields, and on land north of Bradbourne Park Road where Harrisons Way is now situated. During the ***Second World War*** temporary allotments were created from playing fields and waste land to encourage food production.
Burchardt (2002); Burchardt & Cooper (2010); Mills (1994), 11-12

almshouses
Almhouses were built as a charity and usually catered for the 'deserving poor'. The town almshouses, situated in the Upper High Street, owe their origin to a rich London merchant, ***William Sevenoke***, who made provision in his will of 1432 to endow a Grammar School for poor boys and an almshouse for 20 men and women 'in greatest want'. The first known almshouses were built in the late 16th century, but none of the original timber-framed cottages remain. The inmates were required to be elderly, of good character and to have resided in the Parish for 12 years. They received free accommodation and a weekly allowance and were expected to attend St Nicholas Church 'to hear divine service and sermons'. For centuries the school and the almshouses were administered jointly by a Corporation made up of two Wardens and four Assistants. Although close ties remain with the School, a separate group of trustees was established in 1967. They administer both the town almshouses, with its 16 elderly residents, and eight almshouse cottages in ***Weald*** which were a gift from ***Multon Lambarde*** in 1832. The Retreat almshouses, situated behind the ***Methodist*** church in The Drive, were built in 1904, paid for by ***Henry Swaffield*** who also provided an endowment fund. They were to house elderly people 'of limited means', not restricted to Methodists.

Amherst family
Jeffrey Amherst (1716-1797) was born at ***Brook's Place***, Riverhead; he was twice married, but both marriages were childless. As a young staff officer he enjoyed the patronage of the Dorset family. While serving in Europe during the War of the Austrian Succession, Amherst caught the eye of Field Marshal Ligonier who recommended him to be commander of an expedition to drive the French out of Canada. In skilfully directed campaigns in North America, Amherst defeated the French forces in 1758-60, for which he was knighted. Amherst continued as Commander-in-Chief in North America, but his policies angered many Native Americans who, led by Pontiac, fought the British in the mutually brutal frontier war of 1763-66. Historians continue to debate whether or not Amherst encouraged the use of smallpox infected blankets as a weapon against the Native Americans. In 1764, before the war was concluded, he was recalled to London under something of a cloud. Largely ignored in Britain, Amherst returned to Riverhead where he had built his new country seat ***Montreal***, partly

1 Sevenoaks almshouses. The Kentish rag-stone building, erected in 1731-32, was described as 'a Stone Building of 375 feet in Front, [built] under the direction of Mr Roger Morriss, Master Bricklayer of the Office of Ordinance'. The building follows a 'design for a school and forty almshouses' by Richard Boyle, 3rd Earl of Burlington. However, his plans were considerably altered and he left others to supervise its building. The two almshouse rows provided accommodation for 32 men and women 'in reduced circumstances due to unforeseen misfortune'.

using materials from the by then dilapidated Brooks Place. Amherst petitioned for a peerage which was eventually granted; he became Baron Amherst of Holmesdale in May 1776 and of Montreal in 1788. Although appointed C-in-C (then a Cabinet post) during the American war of independence, and again during the war with France in the early 1790s, these were not command positions. A plaque commemorating Amherst's achievements, erected by his second wife, is on the south wall of ***St Nicholas's church***. On Jeffrey's death his estate was inherited by his nephew, William Pitt Amherst (1773-1857), who became in 1836, 1st Earl Amherst and Viscount Holmesdale. After his first wife Sarah died in 1838, William married Mary Sackville, Dowager Countess of Plymouth, eldest daughter of the 3rd Duke of Dorset, who inherited ***Knole***. From 1839, until he died in 1857, the Amhersts lived at Knole. The 2nd and 3rd Earls lived at Montreal; the 4th Earl sold the ***Montreal estate***. Line and titles were extinguished with the death of the 5th Earl in 1993.
Nunnerley (2000)

Amherst obelisk
The obelisk was erected by Jeffrey ***Amherst*** in his ***Montreal Park***, estate in the mid-1760s; it is now in the garden of 81 Marlborough Crescent. It commemorates the reunion, in January 1764, of Amherst and two of his

2 The Amherst obelisk. The obelisk was dedicated to William Pitt, Earl of Chatham, who promoted Jeffrey Amherst from relative obscurity. It lists Amherst's victories, as army Commander-in-Chief, over the French in North America. Remedial work to halt the weathering of the obelisk was carried out in 2009 at the initiative of the Montreal Park Residents' Association supported by an English Heritage grant.

brothers, John (an Admiral) and William (later a General), following their return to Britain after the Seven Years' War (1756-63).

Amicable Society of Sevenoaks
The Amicable was a benefit or friendly society to assist members during a period of sickness. Its *Articles and Rules* were published in London in 1738.

Gordon Anckorn (1913-2005)
Photographer and journalist who worked for the *Sevenoaks Chronicle* for 50 years, retiring in 1978. He followed his father into journalism and learned photographic skills from his grandfather. During his years in Sevenoaks he not only took a large number of photographs but also collected many from different sources. The Anckorn Collection is held by Sevenoaks Library and the Sevenoaks Society. Two books with photographs selected from the Collection were published in 1979 and 1984.
Anckorn (1979), (1984)

architects
In the past 150 years several local architects have lived and worked in Sevenoaks. John Marshall Hooker (1829-1906) worked in the town 1866-89, designing ***St Mary's Kippington***, and the rectory of ***St Mary's Riverhead***. Edwyn Evans ***Cronk*** designed the ***Cobden Road School*** (1877) and the Free Public Library (1905). David Barclay Niven (1864-1942), a Scottish architect, designed several houses built in the early 20th century in Granville Road and South Park. In Bayham Road, three pairs of semi-detached houses, known as the Dutch houses, were designed by J. Leonard William, and built in 1899 for Hilder Daw of ***Quaker's Hall***. Thomas Potter and his son Percy undertook several commissions in the town: Percy was responsible for the Kings and Queens Halls built behind Bligh's Hotel in the 1920s, later used for book fairs, bazaars, dancing classes, and as a meeting place for local clubs; and the new ballroom for the hotel in 1936. In the 1930s he also designed ***Youngs*** store in the High Street.

art
The Sevenoaks Art Club was founded by Elsie Druce in 1901 for professional and amateur artists to meet and work together. Meetings were held in the ***Lime Tree*** Studios. By the 50th annual exhibition, several prominent artists were offering their works for show, including John Ward RA and Bernard Hailstone, a member of the Royal Portrait Society. Since 1951 the Club has welcomed a number of notable members including Gwen Bewsher, Ray Campbell Smith, and Joan Wyatt. The Sevenoaks District Arts Council was set up in 1974 and, with finance from ***Sevenoaks District Council***, it provided grants, loans and underwriting to groups with skills ranging from music, drama, dance, visual arts, and to camera clubs and historical societies.

artists
Sevenoaks and Knole were popular subjects for artists. John Bridgman, a steward at Knole, used his sketches to illustrate his slim volume on Knole (1821). George Richmond (1809-96), a disciple of William Blake and a

friend of ***Samuel Palmer***, often visited Sevenoaks and painted scenes in Knole Park. So also did William Knight (1812-1878) and his son John Buxton Knight (1843-1908), who painted scenes of Knole House, the park, and of the town, thus providing a contemporary pictorial record of Sevenoaks. Both Knights exhibited at the Royal Academy between 1840 and 1885. Richard Butler, another exhibitor at the RA, painted scenes of Knole and the park. An earlier water colourist, Robert Hills (1789-1844), preferred to paint the deer. ***Charles Essenhigh Corke***'s watercolour paintings were used by ***Salmon*** for their postcards and as illustrations in local guide books.
Bridgeman (1821)

Ashgrove
A large house on ***Sevenoaks Common*** shown on Andrews and Drury's map of 1769. It was built *c.*1760 by Captain John Smyth, a friend of Lord George Sackville. Land attached to Ashgrove was formerly part of Sevenoaks Common. Ashgrove had several owners including Multon ***Lambarde***. Eventually it was bought by ***William Haldimand*** who employed George Basevi to remodel the west half of the house in the 1820s. Haldiman's widow sold Ashgrove to Kirkman Hodgson, an M.P. who bought more land, including Cross Keys and Dransfield farms. ***Edward Kraftmeier*** bought the property in 1907 from Robert, son of Kirkman Hodgson. Private schools have used the house since 1932 when ***West Heath School*** moved there from London. Substantial damage by flying bombs during the ***Second World War*** led to major rebuilding and repairs after 1945.

Assembly Rooms
The Assembly Rooms in the London Road, shown on the Ordnance Survey map of 1869, contained the largest room in the town before the ***Crown Hotel*** was available; it was used for grand balls and political meetings. The building was also known as ***Oddfellows*** Hall. The Loyal Sevenoaks Lodge of the Oddfellows used to meet in the Hall.

Austen family
When John Austen of Horsmonden died in 1704 he left his widow Elizabeth in debt with seven children. She moved to Sevenoaks and took the post of housekeeper at the Grammar School. This enabled her to obtain free education for five of her sons. Francis (1698-1791), became a wealthy attorney, and bought the ***Red House*** in the High Street, and William (1701-37) became a surgeon and the grandfather of Jane Austen, the novelist. Francis became wealthy from his legal practice, from buying and selling land, and by marrying two wealthy widows who both predeceased him, and from whom he inherited an estate in West Wickham. His first wife died giving birth to their son, Francis Motley Austen (1747-1815) who in his turn became wealthier by inheriting not only his father's property but other extensive estates. In 1796 he bought ***Kippington House*** where he raised a family of 11 children. The eldest son, Francis Lucius (1773-1815), became mentally ill; Thomas inherited Kippington; another, John (1777-1851), became rector of nearby Chevening. When Thomas died without issue, John's

son John Francis (1817-1893) inherited Kippington which later he sold. In 1788, when she was 12, Jane Austen visited Sevenoaks with her mother and father and her sister Cassandra, staying with her great-uncle Francis at the Red House. There is little substance in the idea that ***Chevening House*** was the model for Rosings, and its rectory the model for Mr Collins' house in Jane Austen's *Pride and Prejudice*. Thomas Austen (1775-1859), the son of Francis, served under Wellington in the Peninsular War, and from 1813-17 acted as lieutenant-governor of Ireland and *aide-de-camp* to Charles Earl Whitworth, Viceroy of Ireland. Austen inherited Kippington in 1817. During the dispute between George IV and his wife Caroline, Thomas supported the King. Austen refused to take part in the pro-Caroline celebrations in Sevenoaks, and a mob supporting the Queen attacked Kippington and broke the windows. Thomas Austen subsequently became a justice of the peace and MP for West Kent from 1845 to 1847, breaking with Peel's government over the repeal of the Corn Laws. He died childless, leaving Kippington to his nephew John Francis Austen (1817-1893).
Keith-Lucas (1986); Le Faye (1989); Wilson (2001)

B

Baden F. S. Baden-Powell (1860-1937)
Professional soldier, a pioneer in the field of military aviation, and an inventor, who lived at Riverhead. He was brother of the founder of the Boy Scout movement, and local District Commissioner for Sevenoaks from 1918-25. A road in Riverhead is named after him.

bakeries
Baking bread was a common domestic activity using locally milled flour. In England the weight, quality, and price of bread publicly sold was first regulated by the Assize of Bread in the 13th century. David Durtnall 'of Seavenoke Baker' is mentioned in a late 17th-century will. By the 1830s there were several bakers in the area, some specialising in biscuits and gingerbread; in 1912 Sevenoaks had five main bakers, while Weald had one. Factory produced bread began in the late 19th century. Some local bakers and also supermarkets continue to bake their own bread today, one example being the Plaxtol Bakery, founded in 1963, which opened a shop in the High Street in 1976.

bandstand and town band
The Sevenoaks Town Band was founded in 1890 after a public meeting held at the ***Lime Tree Hotel***. The brass band aimed to provide a non-alcoholic way of keeping the working men's community together. Twenty-two men enrolled, each paying 15 shillings to the treasurer. ***Henry Swaffield*** paid for a bandstand on the ***Vine*** in 1894 and an adjoining band room on the ***Vine*** for practice in 1902. The Town Band, unable to attract enough members, disbanded in the 1990s.
West (n.d)

3 The bandstand in the Vine Gardens, the line of the North Downs on the horizon. Bands and bandstands were very popular in the late Victorian years. The Vine Gardens were open at specific hours in the day and local people could walk there and listen to the band playing. Bandstands could be bought ready to assemble; the Sevenoaks one came from a Glasgow firm.

Bank Street
This short street was formerly known as ***Black Boy Lane.***

banks and banking
Country banks were important as places to deposit money and to raise finance on mortgages for local farmers and business people. A private Sevenoaks Bank, which issued its own notes, was established in the town by 1820, as was also a Sevenoaks Trustee Savings Bank. The Sevenoaks Bank is listed among the Country Banks in 1822. A London newspaper in December 1821 recorded the 'Executor of Edward Jardine, late of Sevenoaks, Banker' and goes on to refer to 'Holders of Notes of the Sevenoaks Bank', the Bank's solicitors being the local firm of Austen and Claridge. A directory of 1828-29 lists 'Thos. Beeching & Sons' as bankers in the town. A will dated 1856 mentions 'the Sevenoaks Bank of Messrs Palmer'. A one pound note issued by the Sevenoaks Bank was discovered some years ago. The Surrey, Kent and Sussex Banking Company opened a branch in Sevenoaks in 1847. The London and County Banking Company was in the town by 1841 (in 1909 it merged with London & Westminster Bank), and 30 years later moved from Suffolk Place to new premises at 67 High Street. Lloyds Bank opened in the former house of the ***Salmon*** family in the Market Place in 1898. Lloyds was enlarged in 1929 with the purchase of the adjoining 85 High Street; in 1923 the Midland Bank built on the corner of London Road and the High Street.

Baptists
The earliest meeting place of Christians known as Baptists was in a house in the Bradbourne area in the mid 17th-century. At the time Baptists were persecuted and met in private. The first chapel built was at ***Bessels Green*** in 1716 (now ***Unitarian***), William Cox giving £40 towards the building and £60 towards buying the land. In 1766 John Stanger, a stocking weaver from Leicester, was appointed assistant preacher; he was a dynamic character and his preaching and sentiments soon roused controversy. Three years later he was dismissed on a charge that 'he was a Calvinist, in favour of Singing and Catholic communion'.

The congregation split and those who supported Stanger moved up the road and built a new Baptist chapel and manse in Bessels Green Road, opened in 1770. By then a Baptist chapel had been built in Sevenoaks on the east side of the London Road. This remained in use for just over 100 years; it still stands although hidden by shop fronts. The Sevenoaks Baptists bought a site on the edge of the ***Vine Court*** estate and moved to their new gothic style building in 1887. Vine Baptist was extended in 1924 when the chapel keeper's cottage and the Spurgeon Memorial Hall were built. In 2010 the building was remodelled with a new entrance, foyer, and meeting area. A small Baptist chapel was built in Bethel Road, ***Hartsland,*** in 1842. The ***Salvation Army*** used it for some time; latterly it belonged to the Jehovah's Witnesses. The Bethel Road graveyard is adjacent to the old chapel, one of the few green spaces in the Hartsland area. This patch of grass and trees, once the graveyard for the Baptist chapel, is now owned and maintained by ***Sevenoaks Town Council.***
Butterfield (1993); Newton (1948); Anon (1998)

barracks
Soldiers were stationed in Sevenoaks at various times. The Militia Act 1757 billeted troops in the town which led to unrest and a mob, believing the Rector complicit, besieged his home and the unfortunate cleric fled across the park to the safety of Knole. Barracks were built in the late 18th century on ***Gallows Common,*** standing where today Amherst Road and St John's Road intersect. A newspaper report of 1799 records that 'Captains Stehelin and Parrys of the 2nd [battalion]' are to march to Sevenoaks, 'and be quartered in the barracks there'. The area where Bradbourne Road and St John's Road meet the Dartford Road was for some time known as Barracks Corner.

John Bartholomew (d.1862)
Bartholomew was the last parish Beadle, the constable appointed by the ***Vestry*** to deal with minor acts of disorder. In 1858 he was reported as living 'near Brewery' in the High Street; the lock-up was on the site of 159 High Street. By the time of Bartholomew's death in 1862 his ***police*** duties had largely been taken over by the recently formed Kent Constabulary.

Bat and Ball
Area of north Sevenoaks, the name taken from a local pub at the junction of the A25 and Otford Road; the railway station is also thus named.

Albert Bath (1839-1917)
Born in Bexley, Bath became a tenant farmer in Shoreham and later at Colgate's Farm, Halstead. He was described in 1885 as 'a well-known local politician holding advanced radical views'. A member of the local ***Baptist*** church, he opposed paying tithes which went to local Anglican clergy, and also rates that supported Church schools. Thus Bath refused to pay hop tithe to the rector of Halstead and he was prominent in the passive resistance campaign during the 1902 Education Act which required local councils to support Church schools. He was also local leader of the Farmers' Alliance, an organisation representing the interests of tenant farmers. Bath never married, and in retirement he moved to live in Sevenoaks.

Bayham Road
The arrival of the ***railway*** at the Bat and Ball in 1862 and at Tubs Hill in 1868 inspired a flurry of speculative land purchase and building. ***Henry Owen***, a builder and contractor, built houses in Bayham, Serpentine, Knole and Holmesdale roads for hoped-for new commuters. *Salmon's Guide* (1881) states 'many good residences have been built on this estate and only await suitable tenants'. Bayham Road was named after the Sussex estate of the local landowner Lord ***Camden***, who was also Viscount Bayham.

Beacon School
Established as a boys' preparatory school in St John's Road in 1863 by Arthur Lockwood. It was taken over by Alice and John Norman in 1882. The school moved to a new home at Cross Keys in 1900. The site, Clenches Field, part of the ***Montreal estate***, was purchased from Lord ***Amherst*** and was where the ***Pest house*** had been situated. The new school, built by local builders Durtnells, was renamed The New Beacon School. The poet Siegfried Sassoon was a pupil there for several years.
Barty-King (2000)

Beechmont
Beechmont, in Gracious Lane, was probably constructed on family-owned land by ***Multon Lambarde*** II about 1830. On his death in 1836 William Lambarde III inherited, getting his father-in-law Sir John Nasmyth to design remarkable garden terraces. In 1866 Multon Lambarde III became the owner. The census of 1891 records that he was living there with his wife and five daughters, sustained by three footmen, a housekeeper, two lady's maids, a nurse, a cook, a coachman, two grooms, and 14 other inside servants. His son William Gore Lambarde inherited in 1896 but leased this large unattractive Gothic pile with its 800 acres and great avenue of monkey puzzle trees and magnificent gardens, as he chose to live in ***Bradbourne Hall*** (another Lambarde-owned property). After the sale of Bradbourne Hall, Lambarde moved back into a room at Beechmont until his death in March 1939. From 1906 to 1920 Beechmont had become a boys' prep school, run by the Rev. C.W. Bode who, according to the poet William Plomer educated there for three years, was 'a self righteous, mean and cold man' who, nevertheless, had 'a rare facility for teaching the classics and for awakening appreciation of the use of words in the poetry of Virgil and Horace'. Plomer appreciated, too, 'the wide lawns and fine trees – cedars, wellingtonias and copper beeches – and vast thickets of rhododendrons'. From 1920 Robert Scott (a Lambarde relative) and his family rented the property. His son Anthony C.M.B. Scott has left a vivid account of this period and much else.

The last of the Lambardes, Deborah Campbell, Lambarde's daughter, inherited the massive house on her father's death and, soon after, on the outbreak of the ***Second World War***, it was requisitioned by the army. The house was destroyed by a flying bomb in July 1944 and two women stationed there were killed. After the War the site remained derelict and overgrown until, in 1966-67, the new Beechmont, built in contemporary style of brick and cedar boarding, came under the ownership of John and Valerie Dunlop, who restored the grounds with energy and skill. New

4 Beechmont in its heyday as a private house in the late 19th century. This large gothic pile has been a home, a school, and also a military base. After Dunkirk, General Montgomery occupied it for some time. In 1944 a flying bomb hit the house directly utterly destroying it and killing two ATS women, part of a contingent maintaining vehicles in Knole Park. From the devastation the Lambarde portraits were saved, although damaged, and the enormous stone, carved with the arms of the Lambarde family, was rescued intact.

owners in 1984 soon faced the devastation of the great storm of 1987 but this, in turn, provided further opportunities for continuing planting and restoration.

Scott (1997); Plomer (1943); Alexander (1989)

bells

The most familiar bells in Sevenoaks were those of ***St Nicholas*** parish church. No details are recorded about the original bells although a bell casting pit was discovered near the tower. Before and after the Reformation parish church bells were considered to be the public sound of the community to call people to services and as an important means of expressing loyalty. The bells would have been rung when Queen Elizabeth visited ***Knole*** in 1573, and for the coming of age of the young George Sackville in November 1814. Church bells were also rung in times of emergency such as a fire. During the ***Second World War*** bells were silenced, being reserved for warning of invasion; they were rung to celebrate the end of both World Wars. The only surviving book of St Nicholas churchwardens' payments, dating from 1727, lists annual payments for eight ringing days. Throughout the country ringing days included Gunpowder Day (5 November), the King's and Queen's birthdays, Accession Day and Coronation Day. In 1966 the wooden frame of 1769 was found to be rotten and bells 6 and 8 cracked, and it was therefore decided to recast the whole ring as memorial bells. The

work was carried out at the Whitechapel foundry as it had been two hundred years earlier. Other Anglican churches also had bells. The regular ringing of ***Crawshay***'s two-ton bell at ***Bradbourne*** was widely heard, and annoyed some local people. However, few if any complaints were registered about the bell clock which from the 1870s has rung the hours from the stable block of ***Maywood***. A small clock bell hangs in the Clock House at Bradbourne. Smaller brass bells were used on fire engines, while hand bells were used by salesmen and in schools.
Rooker (1910); Love and Pickford (2002)

George Bennett (1900-1973)
Bennett was the Librarian of Sevenoaks ***Library*** from 1920-1965. In 1940 he set up the ***Citizens Advice Bureau*** in the old Library. Over 40 years (during the war years he served in India and Burma) he compiled the Kent Bibliography, a list of all books about Kent that are kept in Kent Libraries, and was the editor of the 1948 edition of the *Guide and Handbook to Sevenoaks*.

Thomas Jewell Bennett (1852-1925)
Conservative ***member of parliament*** for Sevenoaks 1918-23. After a period as a journalist Bennett went to Bombay in 1884, ten years later becoming editor and proprietor of *The Times of India*. He returned to Britain in 1901. In parliament he was among the first of the Tory backbenchers to endorse support for Lloyd George's Coalition government. He spoke sympathetically on Indian affairs and matters of race. In condemning General Dyer's massacre of Indians at Amritsar in 1922, Bennett incurred the anger of 'diehard' members of the Conservative party in Sevenoaks, although his stand was supported at a special meeting of members.

Bert Budgen's Sweet Shop
This was at 28 High Street, opposite ***Six Bells Lane***, and sold everything from sweets and fireworks to fruit and washing powder. It was used by the boys from ***Sevenoaks School*** as a tuck shop.

Bessels Green
The green is the remains of an area of common land, originally much larger which stretched across the Westerham Road. Pieces of this common land were enclosed, principally by the ***Polhills***, who incorporated the northern part into their estate. The name has been spelt in various ways over the years – Bedsells, Sessels, Vessels, and finally Bessels – but the origin of the name is not known. The oldest surviving building on the green is Southdown House, originally the Red Lion inn, and probably once the centre of a good deal of trading in the fish that went past its doors on the ***Rye road***; until the 1930s Southdown house still had a licence to sell wet fish on Sundays, though it lost or gave up its licence to sell alcohol about the time it was rebuilt in 1728. The oldest part of the Kings Head was in existence in 1686, as it was bequeathed in the will of William Durtnoll to his son at that time. The oldest house on the western side of the green is Heath Cottage, built between 1711 and 1733 by Thomas Reeve, a timber merchant, who sold the house and Bessels Green farm to David Polhill

in 1733. The present Vessels was built in 1814 by William and John Couchman; the present Bessels House, previously known as Prospect House, was built in 1819 by John Epps.

Bessels Green chapel

The original ***Baptist*** chapel in Bessels Green, now the ***Unitarian*** Old Meeting House, was built *c.*1715 on land probably owned by David ***Polhill***, owner of ***Chipstead Place***. One of the worshippers was Robert Colgate who denounced the policy of the Tory government and was threatened with arrest; however, Earl Stanhope arranged for Colgate and his son William to flee the country. In 1800 he settled in Maryland and started a soap and candle manufacturing business, which grew into the Colgate business of today. The church congregation split in 1769, partly over the question of the Trinity. A gallery was built in 1784 at a cost of £18 12s. but this was removed in 1882; the pulpit was moved from the west wall and the high box pews facing it and running the length of the building were removed.

5 Bessels Green. Roger FitzGerald's modern watercolour captures the cottages on the eastern side of the green which were built at different times. On the 1840 ***Tithe Map*** three cottages are shown on the southern end of Park Place, and probably date from the end of the 18th century. By 1851 the rest of Park Place had been built.

6 ***Bethlehem Farm.*** Names have come and gone. At one time it was called Bedlam Farm, a local corruption of 'Bethlehem Farm', a biblical name not uncommon for 18th-century farms. This gave rise later to the false belief that the Bethlem Royal Hospital in London had rented the property for use as a country home for its patients.

Richard Betenson (d.1786)
The Betensons were a Surrey family with commercial interests in India. Richard inherited ***Bradbourne Hall*** in 1761 by the will of a distant relative, Henry ***Bosville,*** who was childless. Richard improved the park but he also died without any children. By Bosville's will the house and estate went to Thomas Lane who died before 1820.

Bethlehem Farm
Formerly a farm in the High Street, and now the Oak Tree pub. From the mid-17th century until 1900 it was part of the ***St Botolph's*** estate. In 1852 the St Botolph's Vestry rented it out to Samuel ***Bligh*** (and it became Bligh's farm), who turned the farmhouse into a hotel, and bought the adjoining brewery (Brewery Lane preserves its memory). ***Bligh's Meadow*** at the back, now the car park, was sometimes used by visiting circuses, and became the site of an army camp in 1914. When the St Botolph's estate was broken up in the late 1890s, the hotel and brewery were bought by the Bligh family.

Samuel Bourne Bevington (1832-1907)
Bevington entered his father's leather tanning business in Bermondsey in 1851. He was a generous benefactor to the poor of Bermondsey and was elected the first mayor of the newly formed borough. He moved to Sevenoaks and lived at ***Merlewood.*** Among his many concerns was housing for the poor (he became a major shareholder of the Sevenoaks Artisans Dwellings Company), and he was active in the ***Sevenoaks volunteers.*** His house and six acres of wooded grounds in ***Mount Harry Road*** were often used for garden parties, for example in 1898 and 1902, when he invited 400 of his employees who arrived by special train from London Bridge and, led by a fife and drum band, marched to the house where they had a cooked lunch and tea, played games and explored the town.

bicycles

The modern steel framed bicycle developed in the late 19th century. By the 1890s bicycles were in common use for work and also for leisure, 'going for a spin' as it was commonly called. Local pubs were meeting places for cyclists – the White Hart, the Amherst Arms in ***Riverhead***, and also the ***Lime Tree Temperance Hotel***. Maps and guides were published specifically for cyclists, and cafes serving their needs were developed in and around the town. The growing number of bicycles, and also motor cars, resulted in improved metalled road surfaces. Cycle shops, selling and repairing bicycles, opened in Sevenoaks. In 1895 Richard Philpot was the agent for the 'celebrated Rudge cycle'; by 1912 there were at least four cycle shops in the town centre. At the entrance to Lime Tree Walk was the shop of a local bicycle maker, Mr Timberlake, who designed, built and sold cycles.

Bishop's House, Upper High Street.

An example of a late 15th- or early 16th-century timber framed house, the building is made of great oak beams carrying the weight of the upper floor and roof. The walls are faced with hanging tiles (now 19th century fish scale ones) or brick filling between the timbering of the lower floor. The foundations are of Kentish ***ragstone*** and fireproof material was used for hearths and chimney breasts. Within the building there was a fine Tudor fireplace with the coats of arms of Archbishop ***Chichele*** and of New College, Oxford, to which Archbishop ***Warham*** belonged, on its spandrills. The building is thought to have been the home and office of the archbishop's bailiff, his resident agent in Sevenoaks. In 1873 James ***Outram*** opened a leather goods shop there.

Black Boy Inn

This inn in Bank Street is thought to have been called after ***Richard Blackboy***. Bank Street used to be called Black Boy Lane. Behind the Inn, the gardens and orchards joined those of ***Bethlehem Farm***. In 1818 the ***Lady Boswell*** Charity Trustees purchased the garden of the Black Boy Inn and built their new school on it.

Box (1927)

Black Charles

In the medieval period, houses were often known after their owners' names and it is probable that Black Charles in ***Underriver*** is named after the Blakecherl family. Records mention John de Blakecherl (1292), Will Blakecherl (1313) and John Blakecherl (1327). The present house is based around a medieval wealden four-bay hall house, probably built around 1400 but on the site of an older one. Originally it had a large open hall with ground and upper rooms at each end. The massive brick chimney was added around 1500, and further additions and changes were made in the 17th to 18th centuries.

Ward (1931)

Black Death

In 1347-49 a catastrophic epidemic of plague, probably bubonic, swept across large areas of Asia, Europe, and North Africa, transmitted to people by fleas on rats. The Black Death arrived in England in August 1348, reaching west Kent in late 1348 to early 1349. Within a year England's

population was reduced by 20-40 per cent, with further outbreaks of plague later in the century involving many more deaths. There were major social and economic consequences: the labour force was reduced and wages increased; arable production fell; in Sevenoaks the rents from shops and stalls in the market fell by two-thirds, and local trade declined.
Mate (2010), 11-17

black people in Sevenoaks
The first recorded person of African origin and descent in Sevenoaks was John Morocco, a servant at ***Knole*** in the early 17th century. During the next century the occasional black, Indian or Chinese person (Hwang-a-Tung, a servant at Knole attended the Grammar School) is mentioned in local records, and black servants, such as Jack Beef, passed through Sevenoaks *en route* for Tunbridge Wells. In the late 19th century newspapers and court records occasionally reported a black person who fell foul of the law in the town.
Sackville-West (1922); Yorke (1931); Killingray (2003)

Richard Blackboy
In 1510, Richard Blackboy, along with William ***Pett***, William Potkin and others, purchased 15 acres of land at Hollybush, near the Vine as an endowment for ***Sevenoaks School***. The land was known as ***School Lands***.

Blackhall Manor
Blackhall belonged to the Tottisherst family from *c*.1360. An earlier occupant was Roger de Wybarn in 1274. The Tottishersts sold to the ***Bosvilles*** who never lived at Blackhall. The medieval manor based on what is now Blackhall Farm could well predate both ***Knole*** and ***Wildernesse***, but it is now but a fraction of the size it once was. In the late 18th century parts of the then Blackhall estate were bought by the Dorsets of Knole and added to their estate. In 1826, the Earl of Plymouth, who had married Mary, sister of the 4th Duke of Dorset and was then resident at Knole, divided the old Blackhall estate with the ***Camdens*** of Wildernesse and Blackhall Lane was established as the boundary between them. Subsequently a stone wall was built on the boundary of the Knole estate from ***Godden Green***, up ***Seal Hollow Road*** and into ***Sevenoaks***. At the gate into Knole Park at Godden Green there had been a tavern, the Stock Inn, marked on maps from the late 18th century, which was now swept away along with ***Locks Bottom Farm*** which had been in the valley below where the ***golf*** clubhouse now is. A plan by ***Sevenoaks Urban District Council*** in 1947 to build 400 council houses on 47 acres at Blackhall was refused by the Ministry of Town and Country Planning as it was ***Green Belt*** and would harm the amenity of Knole Park. Apart from a few private houses the land to the south, between Blackhall Lane and the stone boundary wall, is still part of the Knole estate.
Hasted (1797); Ward (1931), p. 109

John Samuel Bligh (1839-1919)
John was the son of Samuel Bligh (b. 1807), a hop planter and coal merchant who took a lease on the ***St Botolph's estate*** in 1852. He was born at the ***Rose and Crown Hotel*** where his father held the licence, and in 1862 he

purchased the old brewery and Holmesdale Tavern. He did well in business and by 1882 built a larger brewery, calling it the Holmesdale Brewery. Although primarily a brewer Bligh also owned some 27 ***public houses*** in and around Sevenoaks. Two oasts at the top of Pembroke Road were part of his ***Bethlehem Farm*** on which he grew hops to make beer. The farm in the High Street became Bligh's Hotel. In 1919 the oast houses and barns of Bligh's Farm were so derelict they were demolished and the land sold. ***Gordon Ward*** bought a plot and built a large brick house, Oastfield Court, for himself.

Michael Bligh (d.1794)
Minister of the Baptist church at Bessels Green in the early 1740s. His congregation split in 1746, some taking exception to his emphasis on salvation only through Jesus Christ. Bligh left the Bessels Green chapel, which eventually became ***Unitarian,*** and with a number of followers eventually established a Particular Baptist church in the London Road, Sevenoaks in 1754 where he was minister until his death.

Bligh's Meadow
One acre of land at Blighs Meadow was acquired in 1930 by ***Sevenoaks Urban District Council*** for a 'parking place' or car park and bus station. The car park eventually opened in 1935 and the bus station a year later. There was fierce disagreement within the town as to whether cars should be charged to park. In 1975 a large and unsightly brick-built social club and offices was opened on the north of the site. Further schemes to develop the 'meadow' in the 1980s were met by public objections and official uncertainty. Eventually the bus station was demolished in 1991 and, after numerous plans, delays and much controversy, the new town square with shops and car park eventually opened in 2000.

Bogs Island
A name given to the Pounsley Road area of ***Dunton Green*** where small insanitary huts were erected for the navvies and their families to live in whilst they were digging the ***railway tunnel*** at Polhill during the late 1860s.

Bonfire Night or Guy Fawkes Day
An annual commemoration of the failure of a plan organised by a handful of Roman Catholics to blow up the House of Lords and kill King James on 5 November 1605. Guy Fawkes, along with the other plotters, was arrested and executed. As the rhyme went: 'Remember, Remember, the fifth of November, Gunpowder, Treason, and Plot'. The commemoration, celebrated nationally with parades, fireworks and large bonfires on which a 'guy' was burned, became a focus of anti-Catholic sentiment. In Sevenoaks, as elsewhere, the Bonfire Committee organised a parade through the streets every 5 November, a local banner declaring 'Success to the Sevenoaks Bonfire Boys'. This continued until the early 20th century. At times effigies of local people who had annoyed the town, for example Lord Mortimer Sackville in 1884, were paraded and burned as guys on the town bonfire. By the 1950s many families or communities had their own bonfires, often in the backgarden. The sale and public use of fireworks was increasingly controlled, and by the 1980s a town bonfire was organised and regulated under proper controls.

booksellers
The earliest known booksellers in Sevenoaks were Bryan Holland in the 1750s, and Thomas Clout Jnr (1749/50-1813) who was also a printer. It was quite common in the 18th and early 19th centuries for books to be advertised by the publisher who might also be the printer. Wrightwick in the Market Square sold books in 1833, and J.T. Bowen, another bookseller, became insolvent in 1859. By 1895 there were two booksellers in the town and W.H. Smith had bookstalls at Tubs Hill station. In the mid-1930s Charles F. Corke owned a bookshop which was bought by John Richardson. The Sevenoaks Book Shop was established at 147 High Street in March 1948 when Basil and Frances Krish bought and renamed Richardson's ailing second-hand book business. By 1951 the Krishes were advertising 'a full selection of new books on all subjects'. On Krish's retirement in 1985 ownership of the business passed to Winifred Scott, and then in 2000 to Valerie Glencross and Sarah Webb-Wilson. The shop still uses the book and oak leaves logo designed in 1949 by Robert Ashwin Maynard, book illustrator and first Controller of the Gregynog Press in the 1920s.

boot and shoe makers
Until the late 19th century most people bought their shoes from local boot and shoe makers. Footwear was vital for the winter months and the condition of a person's shoes often indicated their social class and income. Most people owned a single pair of shoes or boots. As the population of Sevenoaks grew through the 19th century so the number of boot and shoe makers in the town increased: by 1895 there were 12 listed in the local directory, some of them selling factory produced boots and shoes. The number of shoe makers declined in the 20th century and only better-off people wore bespoke shoes.

Bosville family
In 1555 Ralph Bosville, Gentleman of Lincolns Inn, purchased the great estate of ***Bradbourne*** from the Crown. His son, also Ralph, inherited the estate from his father in 1592. By 1594 the estate consisted of 1,221 acres of land, ten smallholdings, 14 gardens, five orchards, two barns, three watermills, a stable, a dovecote and the manor of ***Blackhall***. Margaret (1595-1682) was the eldest of Sir Ralph's three children. In 1629 she married William, a distant cousin and scholarly diplomat, who spelt the family name as Boswell. When Margaret died, she left an endowment for a school to teach 15 of the poorest children of the parish, and provide two scholarships of £12 per year to Jesus College, Cambridge. The recipients were to come from Sevenoaks, or Tonbridge if none were suitable from Sevenoaks, and were to be 'learned and of the poorer sort'. The school when built was known as ***Lady Boswell's School***.
Lansberry (1988), 179-80

Botany Bay Bridge
The A25 road crossed the railway line from Tubs Hill to ***Bat and Ball*** by a bridge at the junction with Bradbourne Road. The sharp double bend formed a notoriously dangerous death trap to speeding and unwary motorists. In 1959, at a cost of £50,000, the old bridge was demolished,

and the road straightened so that modern drivers are barely aware that they have crossed the railway line.

bottle and mineral water manufacturers
There were many mineral water manufacturers working in and around the town in the mid-19th century. Vincer traded in Sevenoaks, as did Josiah Nash who had premises in the Old ***Post Office Yard*** in the early 1880s. Nash sold lemonade and practically all types of aerated mineral water including American soda water and kolas. Their bottles had a glass marble in the neck which could stop the flow of liquid. Nash's trademark incorporated an eagle sitting on a tortoise. Also in Sevenoaks were Alfred Pool, Horsleys, and the Sevenoaks Mineral Water Works who had premises in the High Street. The Chislehurst Mineral Water Works had a depot in Blackboys Yard, and R. Whites had a depot at the Bat and Ball station.

Thomas Bourchier (c.1411-1486)
Bourchier came from an aristocratic family but entered the church. He became bishop of Worcester, then of Ely, and served as Archbishop of Canterbury from 1454. He bought the manor of ***Knole*** in 1456 from William Fiennes, son of James ***Fiennes*** beheaded during ***Cade's rebellion***. At the time Knole was his private house but later he gave it to the See of Canterbury. It then became one of the many houses and palaces, including ***Otford Palace,*** belonging to later Archbishops until the Reformation. Bourchier lived at Knole for many years where, probably between 1454-64, he extended what was a manor house into a great archiepiscopal palace. The gate-tower between the Green Court and the Stone Court there bears his name. Bourchier may also have provided additions to the parish church of ***St Nicholas,*** Sevenoaks. Bourchier has been described as 'a mediator, probably by temperament and almost by profession', and this enabled him to remain a trusted councillor of several kings through the difficult years of the Wars of the Roses and after, and to remain as Archbishop until his death.

bowls
Bowls was the oldest outdoor pastime in England, next to archery. Biased bowls were introduced in the 16th century. Local bowling clubs developed in the 18th and 19th centuries. In Sevenoaks by 1906 the game was played on the lawn behind the ***Sennocke Hotel***. In 1911 players met at the ***Lime Tree Hotel*** and decided to form the Sevenoaks Bowling Club. ***Frank Swanzy,*** its president, got the ***Sevenoaks Urban District Council,*** which had just taken over the Hollybush Recreation Ground, to provide there a four-rink bowling green. The first pavilion was built in 1928, an open barn-like building with walls and ceilings lined with creosoted matchboarding, with a thatched roof and lit by gas. The Club flourished and, in 1929, the UDC provided a new six-rink bowling green. In 1962, the Club, needing better changing facilities, replaced their old pavilion with a new timber one. An Indoor Bowls Club had also been formed and this had an eight-rink purpose built bowls centre at Hollybush Recreation Ground built by ***Sevenoaks District Council*** in 1990.

Brad
A stream rising in ***Whitley Forest*** that flows north-east to ***Brittain's Farm*** and then to the ***Bradbourne*** lakes, from where it flows under the A25 and into the ***Darent***. Until the early 20th century the Brad flowed mainly through open country; with urban development it was culverted from Brittain's Lane to the Bradbourne lakes.

Bradbourne chapel
In 1614, Sir Ralph ***Bosville*** sought permission for a chapel at Bradbourne on the grounds that the parish church of ***St Nicholas*** was over a mile from the house, and was difficult for his wife and children to reach in bad weather. The Archbishop of Canterbury's approval included mention of 'a chapel . . . of great antiquity' on Sir Ralph's property, possibly a reference to the old chapel of ***St John*** which, until the Reformation, had stood at ***Greatness***, part of the Bosvilles' estate. The chapel was consecrated in January 1615, the sermon being preached by the Rector of Sundridge. Although the chapel was primarily intended for the use of the Bosville family, it appears that other local people may have attended some of the services and had children baptised there. In 1614, the Bosvilles were still living in the medieval house at Bradbourne and it now seems likely that Sir Ralph Bosville's chapel was situated within this building. It would thus have been demolished to make way for William Bosville's new mansion, which would explain why no baptisms or other references to the chapel occur after the 1680s.

Bradbourne Clock House
For many years, Sevenoaks historians have asserted that the Clock House was the Bradbourne chapel built by Sir Ralph ***Bosville***. However, in 1983, Anthony Stoyel made a study of the building and concluded that it was built in the mid-18th century as a pair of cottages for estate workers but was disguised on the two sides visible from the mansion to look like a small gothic church (see ***Bradbourne chapel***). William Bosville built the new mansion in the late 17th century, and his son Henry was responsible for the ornamental lakes laid out in the next century. It would have been entirely in accord with the landscape ideals of the time to have built this *trompe d'oeil*, as Anthony Stoyel described it, as a feature on the low hill visible from the main rooms of the new mansion and its park. The timber belvedere, on top of the stone tower, was probably added by ***Francis Crawshay***.
Stoyel (1998)

Bradbourne estate
Bradbourne originated as a farm within the manor of Otford and, as such, was owned by the Archbishops of Canterbury during the Middle Ages. It was leased to tenants, including the Robyn family, in the early 14th century and later to wealthier families – de Pevenly, Ashe and Isley – who built a more substantial house. In 1537 Archbishop ***Cranmer*** transferred the manor of Otford to Henry VIII and in 1555 the Crown sold Bradbourne to Ralph ***Bosville***, a lawyer and Clerk to the Court of Wards. Bosville was a wealthy man, and entertained Queen Elizabeth at Bradbourne when she visited the town in 1560. In 1563 he purchased ***Blackhall*** and, in 1571 ***Brittains***, making an estate that covered much of modern Sevenoaks.

7 Bradbourne House, the south side, with the assembled gentry ready to hunt, *c.*1905. William Gore ***Lambarde*** became huntmaster of the West Kent Hunt in 1904. After the Lambardes sold the estate, the great house was demolished in 1937. New roads and homes were laid out – Betenson Avenue, with its 19th-century lodge, following the line of the main road to the house. In 1935 three-bedroom detached bungalows built by New Ideal Homesteads were advertised for sale at £775. Numbers 16-22 Robyns Way now stand on the site of the old house.

He was followed by his son, Henry, and then his grandson, Sir Ralph, whose portrait hangs at Knole. During the ***Civil Wars***, Bradbourne, now owned by Sir Ralph's daughter Margaret and her husband Sir William Boswell, was sequestrated by the County Committee and in 1682 it was inherited by Lady Margaret's cousin, William Bosville. After the death of Henry Bosville in 1749, the estate passed to a distant cousin, Sir Richard Betenson, and for more than a century was owned by a string of unremarkable country squires. In 1826, the Blackhall lands were sold to the Marquis of ***Camden*** and the Earl of Plymouth and, following the construction of the ***railway*** in the early 1860s, further large areas were sold off to ***William Thompson*** and ***James German*** for development. By 1870, when Bradbourne was purchased by the eccentric Welsh ironmaster, ***Francis Crawshay***, the estate had been reduced to *c.*130 acres. The last owners were Multon ***Lambarde*** and his son William Gore Lambarde, the latter selling the house and remaining lands for development in 1927. The chain of artificial lakes and the seven-acre park were purchased by ***Sevenoaks Urban District Council*** for use as a public park and recreation ground in 1935.

Bradbourne farmhouse

The farmhouse, which stands to the north of the A25, was built in 1702 for Sir Charles ***Farnaby*** of Kippington House.

Bradbourne monoliths
The monolith standing near one of the gates to the Bradbourne park was originally one of many placed in the grounds of the ***Bradbourne estate*** by ***Francis Crawshay*** in the 1870s. An authority on Druids, Crawshay had huge stone monoliths erected in the grounds of the Hall which, according to his obituary, enabled him to indulge in midnight druidical practices. Denounced by a contemporary ethnologist as 'spurious imitations' which might mislead the unwary, the remains of some of these monoliths can still be found in local gardens. The tall Doric column of red Cornish granite, in the garden of 5 Pontoise Close, was listed by English Heritage in 1986.

Bradbourne Park Road
A new road cut in the 1870s along the then northern boundary of the Bradbourne estate to link the recently opened ***Tubs Hill*** station to the much older Bradbourne Road.

Bradbourne Riding and Training Centre
The Centre in Bradbourne Vale Road was founded in 1960 on a derelict farm by Peter Felgate from Knockholt with six horses. Since 1970 the Riding for the Disabled Association has made use of the facilities.

Brethren
The Brethren, sometimes known as the 'Plymouth Brethren', were evangelical Christians originating in the 1840s who sought to reclaim the simplicity of New Testament church life and worship. The Brethren began to worship in Sevenoaks in the 1860s in a hall, later known as 'The Room', at the top of St John's Road. As with many similar small religious groups, the Brethren split over matters of doctrine and personality, the major division in Sevenoaks leading to the 'open' and the 'closed' or exclusive brethren. From *c.*1870 the 'open brethren' met at Vine Hall, originally built as a hotel, now the Vine Evangelical Church. The 'closed' Brethren continued in 'The Room' which finally closed and was sold in the early 1990s.

breweries
Beer was commonly brewed within households and inns. Large houses such as ***Knole*** had a brewhouse, and so did many inns, at least 13 being mentioned in Sevenoaks inventories of the 1660s-70s, while smaller homes often possessed basic brewing equipment. The commercial production of beer increased from the mid-17th century and 200 years later local brewers were supplying ***public houses***. In the mid-19th century there were two breweries in Sevenoaks High Street. A good supply of clean water was essential. Robert Comfort (d.1847) converted the stables of ***Suffolk House*** into a brewery, its malting houses standing where now Suffolk Way meets the High Street. Mrs Comfort sold up and by 1865 the brewery was trading as James Smith and Company. Alfred Smith worked at the brewery in 1870 and assumed control in 1880, being joined by his son Percy. The brewery was enlarged, tied houses acquired and, by the turn of the century, they controlled 23 pubs in the Sevenoaks area. In March 1899 Percy Smith accepted an offer of £57,000 from Bushell Watkins and Company of the Black Eagle, Westerham, and brewing ceased in Sevenoaks in July 1899,

8 Cloth-capped workers at Bligh's brewery in the High Street, *c*.1900. Brewing required skilled workers as well as labourers: maltmasters, responsible for brewing the beer, coopers who repaired barrels, and draymen who made deliveries to pubs. The better dressed man is probably a clerk. In 1901 the nearly 60 pubs and three breweries in the Sevenoaks area employed a good number of people. It was not uncommon for brewery workers to have access to cheap beer offered by their employers, another concern of temperance campaigners in the town.

although a depot remained for several years. The Holmesdale brewery owned by John Allworth stood next to ***Bethlehem Farm***. It was bought by ***John Bligh*** in 1862. He altered and enlarged the brewery in 1882 and was recorded as the largest local grower of ***hops***. He sold the brewery and its tied houses in 1911 to the London brewers Watney Coombe Reid. The brewery closed in 1935. Goldings Brewery, built in 1901 in ***Cramptons Road***, had moved to Wrotham Heath by 1907.
Hetherington (1986)

brick and tile making
Local deposits of gault clay, common in the ***Vale of Holmesdale***, were used for making bricks and tiles. The Romans made bricks and tiles but they became a more common building material from the 16th century onwards. It was not uncommon for builders to seek a deposit of clay near the building site from which to make bricks, thus reducing transport costs. ***Railway*** construction required vast numbers of bricks, and the Weald brickworks, in Morley's Road, was developed in the 1860s and used by ***John Jay*** the railway contractor. Similarly, the St John's Brickyard to the east of the Otford Road (now the ***Vestry Estate***) was bought by ***Thomas Crampton*** with two kilns and a light railway that ran parallel to the Darent Valley railway to ***Bat and Ball*** Station. In 1876, *The Times* reported the brickfield boiler explosion injuring 16 men, two of whom died. The brickfield was abandoned in 1897 and sold to Southwark vestry to be used as a ***rubbish dump***. To the west of Otford Road was another brickyard, the Bat and Ball Brickworks run by Durtnell the builders from the 1870s until 1938 when it was levelled. Sevenoaks Brickworks, also known as Greatness Brickworks, located on the eastern side of the railway line, was set up by Basil Jones in 1928. By 1936, 65,000 sand lime bricks were being produced daily by 60 men. Sevenoaks Brickworks had another works half a mile down Greatness Lane producing burnt clay bricks and tiles. The Brickworks,

owned by Ibstock Brick, closed in 1991 due to the lack of demand, and in partnership with Cory Environmental the site was used for landfill with the intent of being returned to fields.

William Thompson of Kippington set up what became the Dunton Green Brick, Tile & Pottery works at Pounsley in 1862, to make fine quality bricks and tiles. Ebenezer Breething became his manager in the 1880, and his son Owen the owner of the brickfields in 1904. Bricks for the local parish church and primary school came from the brickworks. Most of the workers lived in ***Dunton Green***. Some of the workers took over the huts formerly used by the miners digging the ***railway tunnel***, whilst others lived in cottages built for them in Pounsley Road. By 1956 the vein of clay was exhausted and the brickfield closed. The site was later developed by ***West Kent Storage Company***, demolished in 2011. There were also brickworks on Sevenoaks Common behind the White Hart, where Garth Road is now situated. The Dowager Countess ***Amherst*** made an agreement with the South Eastern Railway Company to have brickworks on her land at White Hart Wood from 1863 to 1868. There was also a brickworks between Solefields Road and Weald Road, known as Upper and Lower Brickfields. Owned by Chittenden and Simmons between 1899 and 1913 it lasted for about 50 years. Brickmaking employed large numbers of men many of whom lived in the ***Greatness*** and lower ***St Johns*** areas. Until the mid-19th century women and children were also employed in brickworks. Local signs of brickworking remain: the Brickmakers Arms in Chipstead, but the Bricklayers Arms in Sevenoaks High Street has now gone.
Newman (2008); Cufley (1998)

Brittains Common
This area of grassland and woodland was purchased by ***Sevenoaks Town Council*** from Kent County Council in 2008 and has been registered as a common since 2009. It extends from Braeside to Upland's Way/Brittains Lane and along Brittains Lane to Montreal Park estate. An oak tree has been planted on the common each year by the Mayor, and will continue until there are seven.

Brittains Farm
Brittains Farm (Britton's) and the Oast House were rebuilt on the instructions of Sir Thomas ***Farnaby*** between 1750 and 1751 of ragstone and brick with roof and hanging tiles made near ***Longford Mill***. Parts of its barn date back to the 15th century. A house has stood on this site since before the Norman Conquest, alongside the ***Brad*** stream. The farm is recorded in Domesday Book and there is an early connection with Henri de Bruton from which comes Breton, Bryton, and finally Brittains in the records. In the mid-15th century the land was acquired by ***Knole*** and then leased back to the farmer for £6 10s per annum for five years. Beer was brewed at the Oast House for the household at Knole. Sir Frances ***Austen*** bought the ***Kippington Estate*** of which the farm formed part from ***Farnaby*** at the end of the 18th century. The last estate owner was ***Julius Runge*** on whose death in 1935 it was split up, leaving Brittains Farm with four and a half acres. From 1937 it has been a private house, now a Grade II listed building.

Brooks Place, Riverhead
A Tudor house known to have been the home of the Scott family from *c.*1580 through to the 17th century. It was sold to the ***Ambersts***, and inherited by Jeffrey Lord Amherst (1717-97) after his return from North America in 1764. He demolished the house and had built a new stone mansion for himself on what he now called ***Montreal Park.***

Arthur Carnarvon Brown (1876-1961)
Medical practitioner, practised in a large house 'Egdean' in the Dartford Road. He formed a partnership with Dr ***Gordon Ward*** in 1915, and worked with him for 30 years. Brown was one of the founders of the Babies Welfare Clinic in 1914 and the first radiologist at Sevenoaks Hospital. After his death the house was demolished and a cul-de-sac of new houses built, named Egdean Walk.

BT Building
The large three-storeyed glass-fronted building at 160 London Road was purpose built for British Telecom in 2000-01 on the site of the former cattle market. Designed by Auckett Associates, the building greatly changed the landscape of the railway station area.

Buckhurst Avenue
The road to the east of the High Street was laid out in the late 19th century. It was named after Buckhurst in Sussex, the birth place of Thomas Sackville, the first of the family to live at Knole; he was created Lord Buckhurst in 1567.

Buckwell's grocery and cheese shop
A small grocery store in Dorset Street, at the entrance to the ***Shambles***, occupying a late 18th-century building with an arch on the first floor to the next building, was run by the Buckwell family from 1861 to 1988. The last in the line to run the shop was John Buckwell who was also town mayor 1991-92, and 1996-97.

Bulimba
Bulimba was a very large, grand, neo-Jacobean mansion built of ragstone in 22 acres next to ***St Mary's Church***, Kippington, in 1890. It was built for ***William Hemmant*** who made his money in the Australian wool trade and railways. After his death one of his daughters continued to live in the house. Between 1926 and 1929 'Bulimba' was a girls' school, and then St Margaret's Welfare College which trained children's nannies. The college closed in 1932 and was demolished the next year, the land being subdivided into nine plots fronting Kippington Road and 11 fronting Oakhill Road.

James McGibbon Burn-Murdoch (1828-1904)
Educated at Edinburgh and Cambridge Universities, Burn-Murdoch graduated in 1859. Earlier he had been an army officer and served in India and the Crimea. He left the army in 1856, married, and was ordained in 1861. Burn-Murdoch came as a curate to ***Riverhead,*** becoming vicar in 1864, a post he held for the next 40 years. The net value of the benefice was

nil but he was a wealthy man and a great benefactor of the church. In 1898 he was made an Honorary Canon of Canterbury.

bus services
A horse-drawn omnibus service left the Dorset Arms for London at 9 o'clock each morning ('Sundays excepted') in the 1840s. The journey took three hours; 'fares, 3s. outside; 6s. inside'. There were also 'bus' services of sorts within the town. One account, from 1871, of getting from Tubs Hill station to Knole states 'a "bus" in the form of a superannuated carriage, conveys us to the park gate for an almost nominal sum'. The first motor buses came in 1911 when George Humphrey ran a service from Sevenoaks to Oxted. By 1913 'an omnibus' ran from the town to Tubs Hill station 'meeting most trains'. More motor buses, and increased competition, came after the First World War. Fred Pearce, who lived in the Quaker's Hall area, established his West Kent Omnibus Service in the early 1920s, his blue vehicles, with white roofs and gold insignia on the side, serving various parts of the town. Most early buses had driver-conductors who issued tickets to passengers. In the late 1920s fierce competition existed between local rival bus operators. The result was local mergers and then take-over by one of the 'giants', the Maidstone and District, Southdown, and London Transport Country Services, which continued to compete with each other to control local services. A bus garage was built at ***Dunton Green*** in 1921; the bus station in ***Blighs Meadow*** opened in 1936. When Sevenoaks District Council wanted the land to build a new shopping centre at Blighs, the bus station was demolished and moved to its new location at Buckhurst Lane in 1992.
McCall (1980)

Butter Market
Name of a small square on the north-west corner of the Market Place, where men and maids waited to be chosen by their future employers on market days.

C

Cade's rebellion
In 1450, near the end of the Wars of the Roses, a rebellion broke out in Kent, and large forces gathered on Blackheath, under a leader who called himself Jack Cade. The rebels complained of mis-government by Henry VI, the loss of lands in France, and several specifically Kentish issues. As the King's men gathered to put down the rebellion, Cade and his followers retreated past Sevenoaks and were attacked at ***Solefields*** just south of Sevenoaks, by a force led by Sir Humphrey Stafford. Stafford and his brother were killed, and Cade was able to advance on London. In the ensuing fighting, ***James Fiennes***, Lord Saye and Sele, who then owned ***Knole***, was captured and beheaded, but the revolt eventually collapsed and Cade himself was soon killed. A hundred years later, William ***Lambarde*** complained sourly that this was the only occasion when Sevenoaks became famous.

Camden
The Earls and Marquises Camden (family name ***Pratt***) owned land in Sevenoaks, bordering the ***Wildernesse estate*** in Seal which they acquired in 1705. They were lawyers and politicians; the first Earl Camden became Lord Chancellor, and his son the first Marquis was a leading minister in Pitt's cabinet. They are remembered in local street names (Camden Road, Bayham Road) and in signs (the elephant's head was their family crest; it appears on the lodge at the end of Hillingdon Avenue, and was used to adorn the former Elephant's Head pub nearby). One of the elephant head crests is on display in Sevenoaks Library. The family also owned much land in Camden Town, in Chislehurst and at Bayham Abbey. They sold Wildernesse to ***Charles Mills*** in 1881.

Carrick Grange
A double-fronted brick house that stood between ***Mount Harry Road*** and ***Hitchen Hatch Lane*** in six acres of grounds, built in the late 19th century. During the ***First World War*** it was lived in by Sir George Croydon Marks, the engineer and Liberal politician. In the early inter-war years it was bought by ***Edward Meyerstein***. In 1937 he had it converted into a nursing and maternity home to accommodate 17 patients; weekly fees ranged from five to ten guineas, and for maternity cases seven guineas. The house was demolished in 1956 and Carrick Drive now occupies the site.

carriers
Farmers with their carts often provided a commercial service carrying local goods. A system of longer-distance carriers using horse-drawn carts delivering packages and parcels across the country existed by the early 17th century. Local Sevenoaks carriers in the 1830s operated a twice-weekly service to London and to Dartford, and also to Maidstone, with others serving the surrounding villages. Carriers from Tonbridge also came to Sevenoaks each day. The coming of the railways increased the volume and variety of goods and also the number of carriers, many in villages, who provided a service carrying people and goods from stations to local villages, farms and houses. In the 1890s Mrs Fanny ***Quinnell*** was among the last to run a carrier service in the town, which operated three days a week to London, also delivering to towns and villages en route. During the next two decades motor vehicles steadily replaced the horse-drawn carrying trade, including the daily service to London run by Quinnell & Sons, as the firm had become by 1912. The removal of household effects was undertaken by local carriers. Larger houses required specialist removers, the most expensive having steel-sprung wagons.
Alan Everitt (1985)

census returns
The first official national census of ***population*** was taken in 1801, and thereafter conducted every ten years, except in 1941. An earlier attempt had been made to calculate Sevenoaks's ***population*** by Gregory King in 1695. The 1801-31 census schedules were destroyed and all that remains in central archives are the statistical tables. The census was collected by local officials who from 1841 onwards recorded in 'enumerators' returns' the names and age bands of people living in each household. From 1851 more

detail was added: relationships within the household, reported age, place of birth, and visitors. The records are closed for 100 years.

Chamber of Trade/Commerce
The Sevenoaks & District Chamber of Trade was founded in 1910 in order to promote and assist businesses in the community, following a special meeting to consider ***electric lighting*** in the town. Although this was thought desirable, the Chamber wanted the ***Sevenoaks Urban District Council*** to defer any decision until the following year to allow time for a full consideration of the scheme and find out the views of the town. At the same meeting they agreed to urge the Council to stop fairs being held in Bligh's Meadow as they were a great nuisance to the town. The first president was E.J. Payne followed in 1913 by Walter Horncastle. Membership expanded beyond local traders to include small to medium entrepreneurial enterprises and larger national and international organisations.

Chantry
The Chantry to the south of ***St Nicholas church*** is one of the grander and more significant buildings on the Upper High Street. A chantry was a chapel attached to a church endowed for the singing of Masses for the soul of the founder or others designated by him. In 1257 Boniface, Archbishop of Canterbury, issued a grant of chantry for Henry De Grand, the Rector 'on behalf of the souls of his father and mother and all Christian souls for ever'. The Chantry was abolished in 1548 during the Reformation. In the late 17th century the site was occupied by a farmhouse with one acre of adjoining land. It is likely that the house was built on earlier footings as

9 ***The Chantry***, in a modern watercolour by Roger Fitz-Gerald. A late 17th-century red-brick house, with early 20th-century additions facing and very close to the upper High Street. This area of the upper High Street is wide, possibly indicating the site of the town's earliest market place.

the cellars contain an apsidal space, which may have had an ecclesiastical purpose. Early outbuildings to the south of the main bloc, including what appears to be a two-storey barn extending to the road, were presumably survivals from the farm. These were demolished in 1905 when the house was greatly extended by additions to Chantry House and Chantry Cottage, skilfully imitating the materials and details of the earlier building.

chapel

Chapel has several meanings: a place of prayer or worship attached to a large house, for example at ***Knole***; from the 17th to early 19th centuries Roman Catholic places of worship were often referred to as chapels; so also were nonconformist buildings which developed after 1662, for example the two chapels at Bessels Green. Chapels-of-ease were created 'for the ease of parishioners' who lived in parts of the parish distant from the parish church, thus ***St George's Weald, St Mary's Riverhead,*** and ***St John's Sevenoaks.***

charcoal burning

Charcoal was used for a variety of industrial purposes and also by blacksmiths. In the Sevenoaks area charcoal was usually obtained from the underwood of coppices, which was charred in an airtight chamber. Alan Everitt describes charcoal burning at Maggoty Hole, Godden Green, in the 1930s: 'a big circular mound of turf-covered wood, quietly smouldering, and the burners strange tent, like a great sail draped over a branch'.

Chartism

The Chartist movement took its name from the six points on the radical charter for political reform published in 1838 by the London Working Men's Association. At the time a few reform-minded people formed a Political Union in Sevenoaks. Robert Gammage, the Chartist lecturer, passed through the town in 1840. Although the movement was weak in southern English towns, a few Sevenoaks people subscribed to the Chartist Land Plan.

Chatham Hill Road

The road leading to the ***Bat and Ball station,*** the original terminus of the Sevenoaks ***railway*** from Swanley, opened in 1862. The line was later absorbed into the London Chatham and Dover Railway, often called the Chatham line, from which the road takes its name.

Chequers Inn

The Chequers Inn is probably a 16th- or early 17th-century timber framed structure on the site of an ancient inn. In a prime site with access to both the High Street and London Road, it was at the heart of Sevenoaks ***market.*** Outside the Chequers was the regular spot for sheep pens. On market days the money changer would set up his bench covered with a chequered cloth, hence the name.

Cyril Stapley Chettoe (1946-1963)

A founder member and chairman of the ***Sevenoaks Society,*** Chettoe lived in Blackhall Lane, and devoted his energies and talents to the preservation of the Kentish countryside. A keen supporter of the National Trust, he was also a member of the Council for the Preservation of Rural England and of the Society for the Protection of Ancient Buildings. He was responsible for the revival of the Committee for the Preservation of Rural Kent, of which he was a very active chairman. On his death, seven trees were planted on high ground alongside the recently completed ***Sevenoaks by-pass*** and adjacent to ***Hubbard's Hill*** bridge, overlooking the Weald. A modest metal plaque holds the inscription, 'These trees were planted by the Committee for the Preservation of Rural Kent in memory of their late Chairman Cyril Stapley Chettoe who did so much for the preservation of the countryside'.

Chevening House
The present Chevening House was built between 1616 and 1630 by Richard Lennard, 13th Lord Dacre, on the site of a previous rambling three-gabled building. House and estate passed down the generations until inherited by Thomas Lennard, Lord Dacre, who died at Chevening in 1715. The estate was inherited by his two daughters who sold the house, the Manor of Chevening and all the lands, some 3,500 acres, in 1717 to James ***Stanhope***. The house and estate remained in the ownership of the Stanhope family until the death of the 7th Earl Stanhope in 1967. He had no heir and for some years was concerned over the continuity and well-being of the house and estate after his death. This was secured by the passing of the Chevening Estate Act of 1959, where, upon his death, house and estate were to be administered by a Trust as a country residence for a nominee of the Prime Minister. In practice, in recent years Chevening has been used as the country residence of the Foreign Secretary.

Henry Chichele (c.1362-1443)
Archbishop of Canterbury 1413-1443, Chichele took a prominent part in national and international politics, helping to end the schism which had seen two, and sometimes three, rival popes. He appears in Shakespeare's Henry V, diverting attention from the King's attempts to seize church property by encouraging the invasion of France. There is little record of his time in Kent; he is known to have lived in his palace at ***Otford***, but, like previous archbishops, certainly used ***Knole*** and owned much land around Sevenoaks. He died at 80, and was buried in Canterbury Cathedral.

children's homes and orphanages
There were several such homes in Sevenoaks, one official, the others created by Christian and humanitarian benefactors. Rock House was a large house constructed of ragstone in Chipstead Lane, formerly a beer house known as the Rock Inn, which had been closed by Lord Stanhope following an incident when 'rowdies overturned a carriage on the way to Chevening'. The house was purchased by the Guardians of the Poor in 1911 and opened as the workhouse's children's home the following year. It initially accommodated 30 girls, but later also took boys under ten. The home closed and was sold in 1916 by the trustees of Chipstead Place Estate. The Mount Hermon Girls' Orphan Home, 2 and 4 Park Lane, founded in London by Mary Ann Cole, moved to Sevenoaks to the premises of the former Hip ***Hospital*** in Park Lane in 1905. According to the brochure of the time: 'The Home shall be for the benefit of orphan girls under the age

10 St Augustine's. Many years later Fred Snow recalled his time in the orphanage in St John's Road from 1921-25: 'When I imagine St Augustine's Home for Boys, I see only grey. I see the sun shining overhead – but not on this building. Inside, I see spirits frozen in the thin air. They are images of children with hurt but tearless eyes. They wear numbers. I see cold stone walls saturated with their muffled cries. . . . a children's prison.' *Snow (2000), p.24.* The orphanage closed in 1937, later was developed as flats, and then demolished in the 1980s and replaced with a red-brick apartment block.

of 13 years who have lost one or both parents, such children having been born in lawful wedlock. Each child shall be well and suitably educated, and trained in all domestic and general needlework.' On average there were 25 girls living at Mount Hermon. The Home relied on donations and every year a 'Pound Day' was held when gifts of all kinds were also received. Girls wore a uniform which then consisted of dark plaid dresses and red coats. They all attended the Vine Hall Sunday school. Some were pupils at ***St John's*** School, some at ***Cobden Road School***, and others at ***Lady Boswell's School***. At fifteen or sixteen years of age the girls were provided with an outfit, and placed in suitable situations as domestic servants.

Mount Hermon closed in the late 1940s. Two orphanages in Sevenoaks were run by the Church of England 'Society for Waifs and Strays'. St Michael's Orphanage for Girls, at 4 Vine Court Road, in 1891 had 10 girls aged two to 13 years. The orphanage closed in 1921 and the premises were taken over by Sevenoaks Preparatory School. St Augustine's Home for Boys, from 1921-37, occupied a tall gaunt building at the top of St John's Road previously used as a school. It was a cheerless place housing 48 boys subjected to an insensitive regime, who were destined mainly for the army or as emigrant labourers to Canada. From 1933 until it closed St Augustine's served as an Approved School.

Very different was the home and care provided for the children of missionaries at Hazelholme Missionary Children's Home, 37 Dartford Road, founded in 1936 by Dr and Mrs Watney who lived at neighbouring

'Beechcroft'. They gave the house to the Unevangelized Fields Mission to be used for missionaries' children, in memory of their daughter Hazel who died aged eight.

Chipstead
The name means 'market place'. Fish brought from Rye were traded at Chipstead which was on the ***Rye road***.
Draper (1999)

Chipstead 'Caves'
The 'caves' were tunnels driven downwards and horizontally into silver sand deposits on the hillside south of Chipstead High Street from the mid-19th century to the 1930s. The land was owned by the Martin family. The silica sand was relatively easy to extract, using pick and shovel, but considerable skill was needed to shape the arched roof required to spread the weight of the overlying strata upon the soft sand beneath. The sand was used in the production of whitening in the on-site factory, for adding to plaster, putty, distemper and silver polish. The works employed six men in the 1920s. At the start of the ***Second World War*** part of the system was used as an air-raid shelter. Electricity was installed along with a first-aid post and canteen, and bunks for more than one hundred local people, mainly women and children.

Chipstead Lake
The excavation of the lake began in the 1920s by the company of ***Walter Smith***, involving the removal of the overlying gravel and then the valuable underlying sand; the gravel was washed and also sold. After exhausting their original pit, leaving behind a large round pond, which is now the property of Holmesdale Angling Club, Smith moved to excavate the meadows to the north, east and west of the river ***Darent***, part of Windmill Farm and Froghole Farm in Chipstead. A small lake was soon formed, at first extending almost to ***Riverhead*** and greatly extended to the west and north later. In 1939 Walter Smith produced 88,000 cubic yards of sand rising to 244,000 in 1949. The firm, conscious of the welfare of its employees, established tennis courts and a cricket ground on land it owned to the east of Chevening Road. The cricket club, called the Amblers, had to move when their cricket pitch was excavated for sand, and they merged with Chevening cricket club. Redland who had many quarrying interests in the South East became part owner of Walter Smith, and Marley Tiles leased land at the eastern end of the lake at Riverhead in 1934, and setup a factory to make tiles, using sand supplied by Walter Smith. In 1981 planning permission was sought to dig up another 60 acres to the north of the present lake, but after strong local objection this was not proceeded with. Dredging finally finished in 1984 leaving the present lake of 61 acres with a maximum depth of 80 feet.

Chipstead Place
There was a large house at Chipstead for several centuries but the date of the original house is unknown. It was bought, together with the surrounding estate, in the late 17th century by William Emerton, a London lawyer, who pulled down the old house and built a Palladian-style mansion which stood for over 200 years. The house was owned by the ***Polhill*** family

11 ***Chipstead Place*** in 1930. A decade before this photograph was taken Chipstead Place was bought by the recently knighted Rowland Frederick Hodge, a Newcastle shipbuilder, who had been found guilty of hoarding food in wartime. Despite this, he had received one of Lloyd George's dodgy 'honours'. Hodge and his wife lived at Chipstead until 1925.

from 1711 to 1829. It was then bought by Frederick Perkins, a partner in the London brewers Barclay Perkins, whose family lived there until the 1860s when it was let to a succession of tenants. During the ***First World War*** the house was a hospital for wounded soldiers. Dr Albert Thurston bought the house and estate, but unable to find tenants he auctioned the panelling, carved chimney pieces and staircases prior to demolition. He sold off parts of the estate starting with ***Packhorse Road***, a site of 23 acres, and then before his death in 1964 the remaining holdings of land, formerly the grounds of Chipstead Place, on which Nursery Place, The Old Garden, Woodfields, the Old Carriageway and more have been built.

choirs

The first known mention of a choir in Sevenoaks dates from November 1778 when 'a select party of the Sevenoaks choir sang to the King and Queene' who were visiting Montreal Park. From the 1840s onwards local Anglican churches had choirs composed of lay singers, men and boys, who sang from choir stalls placed in the chancel. The revival of church music was associated with the High Church revival. Choir stalls were part of the refurbishing of ***St Nicholas*** parish church in the 1870s. Local choral groups are reported in the local press for the later 19th century. The St John's Choral Society was formed in 1897; it later became the Sevenoaks Choral Society, before becoming part of Sevenoaks Philharmonic Society in 1956. At the centenary concert in 1997 Verdi's 'Requiem' was performed.

Christian Science church

The first Christian Science Society gathering of followers of Mary Baker Eddy (1821-1910) in Sevenoaks was held in a private house in 1904. Later

members met in the ***Oddfellows Hall***, moving to the back of a shop in the High Street and then to rooms in the Market Place. In 1912 a plot of land in South Park was given and a building fund started. The first services in the new church, which could seat a congregation of 200, were held in 1936. Next to the church a reading room was built to serve as a bookshop and reading room for Christian Science publications. In 2011 a planning application was lodged to demolish the church and use the land for housing.
Killingray (2004)

cinemas
The first purpose-built building to show films, the Elite Palace, opened in Station Parade, ***Tubs Hill*** in 1912. However, moving films were first shown in Sevenoaks in the converted Smiths Brewery in the High Street, named the Cinema Electric Theatre in 1911. Fifteen years later a purpose-built 'Cinema' opened on the same site and lasted to 1935. A third, much grander Plaza cinema opened on the same site in 1937, complete with restaurant and uniformed commissioner. At the height of cinema-going in the late 1940s the town had four cinemas: the Majestic in the London Road (later named Odeon, the present Stag Theatre); the Palace on Tubs Hill; the Granada (formerly Plaza) in the High Street; and the New Theatre on St John's Hill, later renamed the New Picture Theatre and then the Carlton in 1935, which had seating for 250. The development of television undermined the appeal of the cinema and by the early 1960s all but the Odeon had closed.
Hornsey (2011)

Citizens Advice Bureau
In September 1940 Sevenoaks Citizens Advice Bureau opened for the first time in the ***library*** at the top of the Drive. It was part of a national organisation giving information on wartime regulations and changes. The man responsible for setting up this new service in Sevenoaks was ***George***

12 St Nicholas church choir, at the west door of the building, on 30 October 1907. This was probably a final photograph for the retiring white bearded Rev. Thomas Samuel Curteis who had been Rector of Sevenoaks for 33 years. He, and his curate, the Rev. Philip Dalby, wear birettas on their heads, an indication of their High churchmanship. Most of the men sport moustaches while several of the boys are wearing sturdy lace-up boots. The chap not wearing a surplice is probably Harry Southby, the clerk and sexton.

Bennett, the librarian. Most enquiries at that time were about rationing, billeting and evacuation. The Bureau also provided a link to the Red Cross postal message scheme which enabled people to send messages to relatives in prisoner-of-war camps and in occupied countries. In 1965, when Bennett retired, the Bureau closed. Within a few months it had re-opened, thanks to the efforts of Sir ***John Dunlop***, and has continued since to help people with a variety of problems. In 1976 the Bureau was moved to bigger premises in Pembroke Road; in 1986 it moved to purpose-built offices adjoining the new library in Buckhurst Lane.

Civil Wars 1640s
In a county that predominantly supported Parliament, Sevenoaks, dominated by the owners of a few large estates, stood out as a Royalist stronghold. At ***Knole***, the Countess of Dorset had been governess to Charles I's children and, at ***Bradbourne***, Sir William ***Boswell*** had been Charles's ambassador at The Hague. Thomas ***Farnaby*** at ***Kippington*** and William ***Lone*** at ***Sevenoaks Park*** were also supporters of the king. Violence broke out first at ***Knole*** in August 1642, when Parliamentary forces sacked and took possession of the house following the discovery of a plot organised by Lord John Sackville. Then in 1643, following a disturbance at Ightham in which a villager was killed, local people began to gather on the ***Vine***, led by Farnaby and Lone and supported by nearly all the surrounding gentry. Parliament sent a regiment to the town under Colonel Browne and most of the 'rebels' slipped away but about 500 were chased south, the two sides fighting for three and a half hours at the Hilden Brook, north of Tonbridge. After Browne's victory, the Parliamentary forces made Knole the headquarters of the County Committee. Money was raised from the town's inhabitants, and goods and horses were confiscated. Sackville's steward later reported that the Roundheads had cut down much of the wood on Seal Chart while camped in the area. Some townspeople made money by supplying goods and services to the new occupants of Knole, but the general atmosphere in the town was probably hostile: the Parliamentarian account books show large sums paid for bodyguards to protect their officials when attending ***St Nicholas church*** or the town market house. The pro-Royalist rector of St Nicholas, ***Nicholas Gibbon***, was ejected from his church in 1643 and replaced by Thomas Kentish, a 'preaching minister'.
Everitt (1966); Eales (2001a); Eales (2001b); Melling (1960)

Claridge House
A double-fronted house in the Upper High Street dating from the late 18th century, named after the Claridge family who occupied it from 1800 to 1857. In the 20th century it was used by various government ministries, the Women's Voluntary Service and the Forestry Commission; it is now part of ***Sevenoaks School***.

Clenches Farm
When Francis ***Austen*** purchased the ***Kippington*** estate in 1795 there was no home farm, as the previous one, ***Brittains Farm***, had been sold to meet the ***Farnaby*** family's growing debts. However, there was an isolated field barn and plantation at what is now Clenches, and Austen

developed this into a new home farm, erecting further buildings and cottages. The name of the new farm was taken from the field between the plantation and Cross Keys, where the houses in Grange Road now stand. After ***William Thompson*** purchased Kippington in 1865, farming activities were scaled down, the cottages being sub-divided and used to accommodate a variety of estate workers. Later, the opportunity for development created by the new ***railway*** led Thompson to sell off parts of his land and, in the early 1890s, he sold Clenches farm to the Home Counties ***Dairy***.

The existing farm buildings were converted, and a bottling plant and manager's house built across the road. Milk came from local farms and, until the late 1940s, much of the necessary transport was provided by horses. One former resident of the road recalls having rides on the dairy carts during her war-time childhood. The bottling plant closed in the late 1960s, after which the milk arrived, ready-bottled, on large lorries. However, the site continued to operate as the centre for milk deliveries to Sevenoaks and the surrounding villages until 2004.

Anne Clifford (1590-1676)
Lady Anne Clifford was the well-educated daughter of a wealthy northern English family. In 1609 she married Richard Sackville, soon to be 3rd Earl of Dorset. Anne kept a diary from 1603 to 1619 which provides an account of her rather miserable life at ***Knole*** where she endured the infidelities of her feckless husband. Her sadness was increased by the death of three of her five children and by disputes with her husband over the welfare of the surviving girls. No wonder that in portraits Anne appears rather tight-lipped. She dressed badly and increasingly looked frumpy. The Sackvilles separated in 1616, Richard dying in 1624. Anne remarried a few years later but that also proved to be an unhappy relationship.
Clifford (1990); Sackville-West (2010)

> *In 1616 the Sackville's separated and Richard demanded that one of his daughters come to live with him. Anne wrote: 'Knole 12 May 1616. All this time my Lord was in London where he had all and infinite great resort coming to him. He went much abroad to Cocking, to Bowling Alleys, to Plays and Horse Races, & [was] commended by all the World. I stayed in the Countrey having many times a sorrowful & heavy Heart & being condemned by most folks because I would not consent to the Agreement, so as I may truly say, I am like an Owl in the Desert.'*

coaching inns
Before the coming of the ***railway*** in 1862 the usual way to get to London from Sevenoaks was by a stage coach, a journey lasting three to four hours. Wherever there was a steep hill, an inn appeared near the summit. For coaches travelling to London from the coast, the White Hart on Sevenoaks Common was a good place to stop after the long haul up Riverhill. The coachman could water his horses whilst his passengers found refreshment at the inn. In the town itself, the ***Royal Oak, Rose and Crown***, and the ***Royal Crown*** provided rooms and meals for travellers on the coach route. An

13 Children at Cobden Road school *c.*1900. Lined up at the main door of the school in Hartsland, the children of class 4 concentrate their gaze so as not to spoil this specially posed photograph with their teachers and Miss Roberts, the headmistress (right). Many of the boys and girls are wearing lace-up black boots, the standard footwear for working-class children for the next three decades. The headmistress's dog is a gentle addition.

official survey in 1686 showed that inns in the towns could accommodate 80 people and more than 100 horses.

coal supply
A basic fuel throughout most of Sevenoaks's history was locally grown wood. It was used to cook food and heat houses, and if free was much sought after by the poor. Before the coming of the ***railway*** to Sevenoaks in 1862, coal was used in the town for domestic purposes and also in the first ***gasworks*** established at ***Hartsland***. Some coal came from Gravesend. Another source was Tonbridge after 1740 when navigation of the river Medway was improved. Once the railway reached Tonbridge in 1842 further supplies of coal came by waggon to Sevenoaks. By the mid-19th century coal was widely used in the town and coal yards were established at both railway stations. This continued until the 1980s when the use of coal rapidly declined as houses increasingly used gas and electric central heating.

Cobden Road School
A school built in 1877, administered by the recently created local School Board, for the children living in the ***Hartsland*** area. It was typical of such schools built after the 1870 Education Act, single-storey

red brick, with large high windows, lofty ceilings, pointed cowls on chimneys, picturesque detailing in its brickwork, and with a marching yard. Originally for the education of boys and girls from five to seven years, this was extended in 1884 to include schooling for girls up to the age of 14. In 1899 the register shows an attendance of 324 pupils, 193 girls and 131 infants. In the 1934 edition of the *Cobnut*, the School magazine, news of old girls showed that most were employed as clerks in shops, or as domestics. The school closed in 1975. The building, owned by the Sevenoaks District Council, was for many years leased to Age Concern.

Codsheath

The name of the meeting place for the military, judicial, and administrative Hundred of Codsheath from Anglo-Saxon times to the 17th century. The name may derive from 'God's heath', and indicates a sandy piece of land, probably to the west of Riverhead parish church and on the present site of the sandpit recreation ground by Pontoise Close.

Map 2 Map of ***Codsheath***. Sevenoaks was part of what was known as the Hundred of Codsheath until the early 19th century. This map was drawn for ***Hasted***'s famous history of Kent, and shows the main road, including the turnpikes, woodland, and two ranges of hills, the 'white' chalk hills of the North Downs, and the 'red' hills of the sandstone ridge to the south. Also shown are the houses of the wealthy landowners, the kind of people who were most likely to buy Hasted's volumes.

Map 3 and 4 The heart of Sevenoaks in 1867 and 1936. On these two maps, one from 1867, the other dated 1936, the closely packed terraced houses in the alleys and courtyards in the centre of the town are shown. By 1936 sanitary conditions had improved but houses, such as those in Redman Place, were slums. Major changes had occurred: the site of the *Royal Crown Hotel* by 1936 was occupied by a 'Picture theatre'; the 'County Court and Corn Market' of 1867 had become public lavatories; and the *Rose and Crown Inn*, with its stabling behind, had been replaced with Young's department store.

14 Coffee House Yard. One of the many 'close' yards and alleys in the centre of Sevenoaks. For those who lived and worked in such over-populated and insanitary places it was not 'a pleasant town'. Many of the houses and workshops survived well into the 20th century, some being demolished only after 1945. The artist Vincent New sometimes drew sketches of places that were unlikely to appear on picture postcards.

Combe Bank
Built in Tudor times, Combe Bank was one of the great local houses in Sundridge. In the 16th century it belonged to Sir William Isley, executed for his part in ***Wyatt***'s rebellion. The house passed to the Crown. In the 18th century it was bought by John Campbell and rebuilt. Later owners included William Manning, father of the future Cardinal, and Dr William Spottiswood, President of the Royal Society who bought Combe Bank in 1864 and invited members of the Royal Society, including Charles Darwin, to the house. Robert Mond of Imperial Chemicals bought Combe Bank in 1907 and during the ***First World War*** used the farm as a convalescent home for troops. He sold it to a Roman Catholic order in 1924 and since then it has been a girls' school.
Raybould (1986)

Community Centre
By the initiative of the Sevenoaks Community Association, formed in 1968, funds were raised and the Centre on the Otford Road opened in October 1983 to serve Sevenoaks and the neighbouring villages. Much credit is owed to the efforts of the first two Association chairmen, Reg Quinnell and Gwenneth Mehew. The Centre was on a site owned by the District Council and leased to the Association at a 'peppercorn' rent. Due to increasing costs the ***Sevenoaks Town Council*** agreed to take over the operation of the Centre and the lease. The Community Association was dissolved in 2001.

Congregational Church
The first United Congregational Chapel in Sevenoaks was the disused former ***Baptist*** chapel in ***Hartsland***, bought in 1863. This proved too small, and a new site was purchased at the top of St John's Hill. The

new building, completed in 1866, was built of Kentish rag in Gothic style. The seating capacity was over-ambitious and not realised, and due to financial problems the building had to close. Additional costs were incurred when the original spire was deemed unsafe and had to be removed in 1880. A mission hall was also built in the mid-1880s in Greatness Road to provide local services. The Hartsland chapel proved inadequate for the growing Sunday school and in 1888 a new red brick church hall was built in Hollybush Lane. This could accommodate up to 350 adults, and was also used for public meetings. During the ***First World War*** it became a VAD hospital for British and Belgian soldiers. In 1991-92 St John's church was remodelled with a floor inserted in the nave providing rooms below for meetings and associated activities. The Hollybush Lane hall was redundant and sold, being sympathetically converted into two houses. In 1972 the Congregational Church and the English ***Presbyterians*** combined to form the United Reformed Church.
Killingray (2004)

Conservation Areas
These first came into being as a result of the Civic Amenities Act of 1967. They were intended to identify any valuable visual or historic characteristics in a locality that warranted special measures in order to protect and conserve them. In Sevenoaks town, ***Brittains Farm,*** Granville and Eardley Road, ***Kippington*** Road, Sevenoaks High Street, the ***Vine, Vine Court,*** and ***Wildernesse*** were all designated as conservation areas, with ***Hartsland*** in 2011.

Conservation Council
The Council was formed in 1976, a result of a joint initiative by the ***Chamber of Trade*** and the ***Sevenoaks Society*** following the local government re-organisation of 1974, to conduct a survey of the town with a view to preserving its historic character and establishing design guidelines to assist in planning decisions. The Council consisted of representatives of the ***District*** and ***Town Councils,*** the Chamber of Commerce and the Sevenoaks Society and met quarterly with the local Conservation Officer. Its task was to disseminate information, and to make representations about planning applications, particularly those in ***Conservation Areas.*** In 2011 it secured some changes to conservation issues in the Core Strategy of the Local Development Framework as a result of its representations at a public inquiry.

Conservative Party
The Conservative, or Tory, Party has been the dominant political presence in the Sevenoaks district for most of the past 150 years. Only once have the Tories lost the parliamentary constituency, briefly in 1923, and control of both the County Council and the town council in 1995. In the mid-19th and early 20th centuries, Conservatives could rely on the support of many local landowners and prominent people in the town, while the ***Primrose League*** helped promote the party to new voters. In 1931 Stanley Baldwin launched the Tory election campaign in ***Knole Park.*** There were several local Conservative politicians who devoted much energy to the welfare of

15 The Constitutional Club south of The Vine. This was the local Tory club. Conservatives in the town rarely had to plan how to win elections; but they did have to encourage voters to support the party even if their majority could be guaranteed at most local and national elections.

the town, including Dorothy Parrott (d.1978), an indomitable lady who had wide interests and concerns.

Constitutional Club

Built in 1889 on a site between Dartford and Seal Hollow Roads, the red-brick building was intended for ***Conservative*** social and political meetings and contained billiards, smoking and committee rooms, a refreshment bar and cloakrooms. The Club Hall on the north side had seating for 500 people for concerts, meetings and entertainments. Between the two World Wars, the Club Hall was the largest available in the town. The building was destroyed by a bomb in 1940. The Constitutional Club, also known as the Conservative Club, closed in 1957 due to declining membership. The building was turned into apartments in the late 1990s.

Co-operative housing

The architect Raymond Unwin, a pioneer of co-operative housing, designed houses for the Sevenoaks Co-operative Society, who set up the Sevenoaks Tenants Estate at St Botolph's Road and Holyoake Terrace. There was also Co-operative housing at Sevenoaks Farm where four houses were built in 1910, and at Sevenoaks Weald where the ***Rogers*** family gave land for 11 houses to be built on the village green, named 'Prudence', 'Felicity' and 'Patience' cottages. In 1903-06, 28 cottages were built on a two and three quarter acre strip of land immediately west of Tubs Hill station. ***Frank Swanzy*** donated £7,000 to build the cottages which he said were ideal for 'small city men', i.e. clerks, as they were rented for 6s. 6d. and 7s. 6d. a week. The terrace was named after G.J. Holyoake (1817-1906), the 'father' of co-partnership. The Tenants Association also built 25 houses on two acres of land donated by Mrs Laura Thompson, wife of the vicar of ***St Mary's church***, Kippington, on the north side of ***St Botolph's Road***, which formed St Botolph's Avenue, completed in 1907.

Reid (2001)

16 The junction of the London and Dartford Roads looking north, 1905. Although more than one hundred years old, Charles Essenhigh Corke's painting of central Sevenoaks is easily recognisable. On the left there is E. J. Payne, the grocer, advertising Suchard chocolates across his window (a shop which remained until 1966); the tile-hung Bishop's house is beyond Rockdale Road; further along the London Road is the red-brick branch of the London and County Banking Company, built in 1874 (now NatWest); and yet further the Royal Crown Hotel, the plushest place in the town. Centre of the picture is the West End Dairy, and the drinking fountain. Corke's picture shows a town on the cusp of change: the rural, with sheep being driven along the London Road towards a stationary hay cart, and the 'modern' noisy open motor car that breathes smoky fumes and stirs up the dusty road.

Charles Essenhigh Corke (1852-1922)
Artist and photographer, who was born in Sevenoaks, where he established a studio in the late 1870s. By 1881 his photographic shop was at 39 London Road. Many of his paintings of local scenes were published as postcards by J. ***Salmon*** & Co, and they also appeared in Elizabeth Reid Hope, *English Homes and Villages (Kent & Sussex)* (Sevenoaks, 1909). He moved to the ***Pump House*** in 1910 and built a studio in the garden. Corke provided sketches of local scenes for Frank Richard's book *Old Sevenoaks* (Sevenoaks, 1909). Charles's son, Henry (1883-1919), a pioneer of colour photography and a keen botanist, had his own studio next door. He died in the post-war 'flu epidemic.
Thompson (1994)

Cornwall Hall
The Hall stands behind the ***Methodist*** church in The Drive and consists of a large hall surrounded by a smaller hall and a range of rooms, plus a kitchen. Opened in 1906, it was paid for and equipped by ***Henry Swaffield*** who intended it for the use of members of the Church and the people of Sevenoaks. During the ***First World War*** the building was used as a hospital as commemorated on a plaque inside the entrance. In the ***Second World War*** it was used as a British Restaurant.

courts
In medieval times there were two main courts in the Sevenoaks area. The Hundred Court met regularly and was responsible for administering the law and maintaining the peace. Fines and other ***punishments*** could be delivered, and matters of taxation decided. Disputes over titles to land were recorded in the 'Feet of Fines' (Latin *finis* meaning 'end'), each record being

in triplicate. In early medieval times each lord of a manor had a court for his tenants. The Manorial Court was usually presided over by the lord's steward. Both these court system were in decline by the 17th century. By then Magistrates' Courts, conducted by Justices of the Peace, became the mainstay of the local legal system dealing with petty crime. The magistrate's court was in the police station from 1864-1973 and then moved to new buildings in Morewood Close on the London Road.

Covell's Farm
This covered the area of present-day Eardley, Granville, Gordon and Argyle Roads. Knott's ***windmill*** stood in one of the fields.
Richards (1901)

Thomas Crampton (1816-88)
The great Victorian engineer and contractor was born in Broadstairs. He trained on Brunel's Great Western Railway, improving locomotive design and performance. Crampton was responsible for constructing the Swanley to Bat and Ball ***railway*** in 1861-62; he supplied two-thirds of the capital, subscribers in the district the other third. Crampton bought 81 acres of the ***Greatness*** estate which became a small industrial area with ***brick fields***, a second ***gasworks***, and much later working-class housing. He also had financial interests in a chalk and lime works at Otford. In 1904 the ***Sevenoaks Artisans' Dwellings Company*** built a terrace of 20 houses in Cramptons Road, the start of a scheme to provide more working-class housing in the town.
ODNB (2004)

17 Thomas Crampton. Crampton was the epitome of the successful Victorian entrepreneur, a technical man who was not afraid to get his hands dirty but who could also operate in the world of finance capital. It was an age when the old landed squirearchy continued to look down on those who had made their way in 'trade' and many of the new commercial professions. Inevitably money helped undermine such rigid social class ideas.

Thomas Cranmer (1489-1556)
The last Archbishop of Canterbury to own ***Knole*** and ***Otford Palace***. He was appointed by Henry VIII in 1533 to succeed ***Warham***. In 1538 Cranmer was forced to hand over Knole 'voluntarily' to the King. By then the Church of England had broken away from the Roman church, and Cranmer played a leading part in these moves and in the King's divorce from Catherine of Aragon. When the Catholic Queen Mary succeeded her father, Cranmer was declared a heretic and burnt at the stake.
ODNB (2004)

Francis Crawshay (1811-1878)
Coal mine owner and iron master of Cyfarthfa, South Wales, who bought and retired to live on the ***Bradbourne estate*** in 1867. He was an eccentric man with interests in Druids, and also stone monuments, several of which he erected in the grounds of his estate; one can be seen in Bradbourne Park. Crawshay also delighted in bells, installing two great bells on tripods outside the Hall. Being an early riser, rumour says, he would ring the bells

at six every morning 'to wake the lazy people of Riverhead'. Crawshay's other passion was sailing his steam yacht; the monument to him in St Martin's church, Brasted, is decorated with maritime motifs. His widow continued to live at Bradbourne Hall, where she died in 1896.

cricket

Cricket clubs did not exist in the early 18th century. Games were played, often for a wager, between different parishes, and the teams made up from those employed by the gentry. The Sevenoaks Vine Club was formed late in the 18th century, and score sheets exist for matches with East Malling in 1800 and Homerton in 1802. The Napoleonic Wars led to a decline in cricket and the Club probably became dormant before being revived in 1848 by Captain ***Northey*** of ***Vine Lodge***. Later in the century it appears that matches were played on Lord Hillingdon's ground at ***Wildernesse***. In the summer of 1934, a Bicentenary Cricket Match was held on the ***Vine*** to celebrate the 200th anniversary of the first cricket match to be widely reported in the press. The Vine Cricket Club is obliged to pay ***Sevenoaks Town Council*** a rent of two peppercorns per year – one for the ground and one for the pavilion. In return the Club must pay Lord Sackville one cricket ball, the ceremony taking place annually on 21 July. The Holmesdale Cricket Club was formed in June 1840, when Vine Cricket Club was going through a period of inactivity. Lord ***Amherst*** was the first president and his eldest son, Lord Holmesdale, the vice-president. The Amhersts donated the ground which was part of ***Montreal Park***. Unlike the Vine Cricket Club, the Holmesdale Club seems to have enjoyed a continuous existence since the Amherst's generous gift. During the ***Second World War***, many of those who were too old, too young or in reserved occupations served the country in the Civil Defence. As the war progressed a Civil Defence Club was formed and used to meet on the present ***Sevenoaks Town***

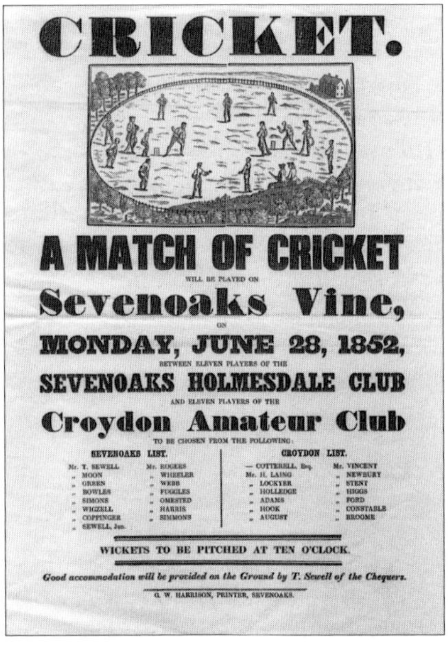

18 The Sevenoaks Vine Cricket Club marked it origins in 1734. The *London Evening Post* 23 August 1734, reported: 'The Match at Cricket between the eleven Gentlemen of Sevenoaks in Kent, and the Gentlemen of London, on Tuesday last, on Sevenoaks-Vine, was not determined that Day, there being four Wickets to go down, and twenty-three Notches to fetch to win when the Time was out; but the Match was ended Yesterday, in favour of London, by six Notches only.'

Council offices site. In 1942 some of the members started playing cricket matches and in 1948 Lord Sackville allowed them to play on the ***Knole*** ground. After the war the cricketers decided to continue, taking the name *Sennocke Cricket Club* in 1951.
Richard (1901); Smart (1983); Underdown (2000)

Cronk family
The Cronk family lived in Seal in the late 18th century. By 1845 William Cronk had moved to Sevenoaks and was partner in a firm of 'surveyors, auctioneers and appraisers'. Several sons continued the business as Messrs Cronks, with offices in the High Street. Another son, Edwyn Evans Cronk (b. 1846), became an architect and surveyor.
Journal of the Auctioneers' and Estate Agents' Institute (1932)

Curteis family
Six generations of the Curteis family provided Rectors of ***St Nicholas*** Sevenoaks from 1716-1907, made possible because they owned the patronage which gave them the right to appoint the clergy. Thomas Samuel Curteis (1849-1913) was the last of the line, reluctantly taking office in 1874. He held High Church ideas and introduced such rituals and practices to St Nicholas, annoying many parishioners. In the 1870s he remodelled the interior of the building at the cost of £32,000. When he retired in 1907 Curteis sold the right of patronage to the highest bidder, which happened to be an evangelical trust. However, he kept the right to appoint the clergy at ***St John's*** which in his will he left to the Anglo-Catholic Guild of All Souls. For some time Curteis was chairman of the local ***Conservative Party***.
Yates (1990, 1997); Killingray (2004)

D

dairies
Dairy products such as milk, cream, eggs, and butter were produced by local farms, such as ***Brittains Farm, Clenches Farm, Else's Farm*** in Weald, for direct sale to customers. In the later 19th century many people in the town bought dairy products from local shops, some set up by dairy farmers. For example, Else's Farm from 1867 had a shop in the London Road, a business taken over by French's Dairy in 1931, while in 1908 the Vine Dairy on the Dartford Road offered 'pure rich milk' from 'selected cows' on Sevenoaks Common and Hollanden Farm, also 'new laid eggs, fresh butter and cream'. Many farms and dairies delivered milk from door to door, initially in cans, later in sealed bottles. In the late 20th century milk delivery to houses was increasingly hit by supermarkets selling milk in cardboard and plastic containers, so that by 2000 fewer than one in ten households had milk delivered to the doorstep.
Terry (2000), 29-31

Darent
The Elizabethan poet Edmund Spenser, in 'The Faerie Queene' written in 1596, hailed 'The still Darent, in whose waters cleane, Ten thousand fishes

play and decke his pleasant streame'. The river Darent rises from springs in Westerham and flows approximately 21 miles, from its source, eastward to Dunton Green, and then meanders north to enter the Thames beyond Dartford. The river flows through ***Chipstead Lake*** and the Sevenoaks ***Wildlife Reserve*** formed from old gravel pits. In the past every few miles there was a ***water mill***. The river also served ***swimming*** pools or lidos at Brasted and Longford Mill in ***Dunton Green***.
Wood (1983)

Davis garage/coaches
A family business founded in 1919 by William Davis. He started using his home at Oak Cottage, Buckhurst Avenue as his office and garaged his one vehicle in the yard of the Blackboy pub. By 1926 he moved the business to ***St John's*** Hill and called it the Blue Star Garage which provided cars for hire, 'horseless charabanc' outings, a repair shop, and accessories for motorists. During the ***Second World War*** his coaches and one of his petrol pumps were requisitioned. The coach business was sold in 1972 and the firm specialised in selling new cars under franchise. In 1994, the Company sold the garage and workshop in Golding Road and moved to new premises in the Otford Road.
Davis (1996)

deer parks
Sevenoaks had two deer parks: ***Panthurst***, first recorded in 1348, deparked by the 1560s, probably for economic reasons, and ***Knole***. Knole is one of the few deer parks in England to have survived the past 500 years and the only one in Kent. First enclosed in 1456 by ***Thomas Bourchier***, the fence kept in deer and served as a barrier to poachers. The northern boundary wall of the Park runs from Seal Hollow Road to Bowpits cottages, and was built in the early 19th century of coursed ragstone blocks. In places a ditch runs parallel to the wall, the traditional method of preventing deer jumping over. In 1867 Knole Park had 400 fallow deer; in 1892 it was reported as having more than 700; and by 2000 a herd of 800 head. Knole and Panthurst also had cony warrens to supply meat for the estate and also for the local market, one field at Panthurst in 1630 being called 'Conybearye Meade'.
Pittman (2011)

Kate (1839-1929) and Mamie Dickens (1838-96)
Both of Dickens' adult daughters are buried in ***St Nicholas*** churchyard, though the reasons behind this are currently unknown. Catherine, or Kate, studied at Bedford College. Her first husband died and she married Carlo Perugini (1839-1918), an Italian-born painter. By then Kate was developing her own career as a painter. Their only child died and was the first of the family to be recorded in the Perugini family grave at St Nicholas. Dickens is thought to have stayed on some occasion at 2 High Street, so it is plausible that the Peruginis may have been living or lodging there when the baby died. Mary Dickens, known as Mamie, never married and was of all his ten children the closest to him. Her grave is adjacent to the Perugini family grave. Carlo Perugini was buried there in 1918 and finally Kate.

Dibden

Dibden Lane was once part of the ***Rye road*** from the south coast to London. The route through Sevenoaks ran from the top of ***Riverhill*** across ***Sevenoaks Common*** to Dibden and ***Bessels Green***, crossing the river ***Darent*** at ***Chipstead***. ***Salters' Heath***, where fish were salted, was just north of Dibden. The current line of Dibden Lane, down through the marshy Dibden Bottom, is relatively recent. From the south, the road originally kept to the higher ground and ran past Dibden Farmhouse. The remains of the old hollow way can still be seen at the north end of the Bottom. In the 19th century, increasing exploitation of the adjoining ***Whitley Forest*** lands under ***Amherst*** ownership led to the building of two pairs of cottages along the western side of the re-aligned lane through Dibden Bottom, one pair at the north end, where the stream passes under the road, the other at the south end, by the track leading to Whitley mill. The former pair were demolished after the ***Second World War***. The latter pair remained, derelict, until the building of the Sevenoaks ***bypass*** in 1968-71.

Dibden farmhouse

The first recorded settlement at Dibden dates from 1270. Dibden is again mentioned on a map titled Sub-Manors and Farms of the Great Manor of Otford dated 1400. The house was probably built in the early 16th century and was either divided into three small cottages or it could have been a small hall house. Dibden House is situated on a hill beside the original ***Rye road***. The course of the road can still be seen in front of the house which was probably a hostelry servicing passing traffic. In 1630 the property was sold to Thomas ***Farnaby***. The Farnaby family appear to have owned Dibden and the surrounding area until the late 18th century when it was sold to Francis Motley ***Austen***. The property was inhabited by the Cogger family from before 1666 until 1740. A will dated 1666 mentions property left to John Cogger's wife when the farm consisted of a hall, a chamber over the hall and a chamber over the buttery. Another Cogger will, of 1707, indicates that the house had been enlarged. In 1740 a Thomas Cogger released Dibden house by way of a mortgage to Ralph ***Bosville***. From 1851-91 the house was occupied by agricultural labourers and gardeners.

disease

Regular outbreaks of epidemic and pandemic disease were a common cause of death until the late 19th century. Probably over half Sevenoaks' population died during the ***Black Death*** of 1348-49. In 1640 a Sevenoaks petition to the House of Commons stated 'That ... many poore inhabitants ... make use of well water whereby your petitioners are become more infirm and subject to infections and sickness'. The ***water supply*** was poor, and the failure to remove human and animal waste was a constant threat to health. Many houses in Sevenoaks were poorly built, damp, cramped, smelly, and overcrowded. Rats and other vermin were common, encouraged by food openly displayed in shops. The cause of disease was often unknown and there were no cures for influenza, the ague (malaria), measles, cholera, smallpox (vaccination was introduced in the late 18th century), and the plague. Plague hit Sevenoaks in 1665-66, indicated by the increase in burials in those years. When cholera visited in 1854, one of the few actions available was to isolate people in the

pest house. Typhus and diarrhoea were also killers in the town in 1857. ***Railway*** building brought navvies housed in insanitary camps where disease was prevalent. Outbreaks of diphtheria caused many local deaths in 1900-03. The worst demographic disaster of the 20th century was the influenza pandemic of 1918-19; the first Sevenoaks victim was a schoolgirl, and thereafter several dozen people died from the virus.

> The Chairman of the Nuisances Removal Committee of Sevenoaks, September 1864, quoted by Karl Marx, *Das Kapital* (1867): '... an isolated house, called the Pest-house, which is set aside for parishioners who might be suffering from infectious diseases, has been continually occupied for many months past ... in one family five children died from small-pox and fever; that from the 1st April to 1st September this year ... there have been no fewer than 10 deaths from small-pox in the parish, four of them in the [navvies'] huts ....'

Domesday Survey
Sevenoaks barely existed when the Domesday Survey was conducted in the 1080s, so it is not mentioned in that great record of land ownership. Otford and Sundridge were more significant and both villages are recorded.

domestic servants
Many women and girls went into domestic service, the number increasing through the 19th century. Pay was low, conditions varied greatly, young women were particularly vulnerable to abuse and the law gave them little protection. Before 1914 the major form of paid employment for women was domestic service. The Great War provided new opportunities for women and the number of domestic servants declined.

John Donne (1572-1631)
Poet, essayist and cleric, Donne was the largely absentee Rector of ***St Nicholas church*** from 1616-31 through the gift of his patron Richard Sackville, 3rd Earl of Dorset. He held the posts of Dean of St Paul's Cathedral and Rector of Sevenoaks simultaneously until his death. He is recorded, in the diary of Lady ***Anne Clifford***, as having preached only once in St Nicholas, on 20 July 1617.

drama
Touring, or portable, theatres regularly visited Sevenoaks. Richardson's Theatre is shown in ***Corke***'s painting of the ***Sevenoaks Fair*** in the 1860s, and Wildman's Mammoth Theatre, with its five wagons, was in the town in the 1870s. Amateur drama groups performed in the Club House and in the ***Drill Hall***, and schools regularly put on plays. The Sevenoaks Players gave their first performance in February 1923 and since then, other than the War years, have regularly performed light opera, musicals and dramas in the town. The venue from the 1950s until 1980 for musicals was the ***Drill Hall*** in Argyle Road. When that became unavailable in 1981 the Sevenoaks Players used the Focus Cinema building a stage with

scaffolding, known as the 'boxing-ring', in front of the main screen and using the two small cinemas as dressing rooms. A long campaign by a pro-theatre group resulted in the creation of the ***Stag Community Theatre*** in 1983.

Drill Hall

In 1897 ***W.J. Thompson*** gave a plot of land in Argyle Road for the erection of a Drill Hall in honour of Queen Victoria's Diamond Jubilee. An appeal for funds was held and the Hall opened the following year for the 1st Volunteer Battalion of the Royal West Kent Regiment who were billeted in Sevenoaks. An adjoining residence was for the Sergeant Instructor.

droveways

For centuries cattle and pigs were annually driven by farmers from the ***North Downs*** up the sandstone ridge and down into the woods and pastures of the weald to graze or root around for food. The two main roads that converge in Sevenoaks and continue to ***Riverhill*** probably started as droveways. There are others, such as the old road down ***Hubbard's Hill*** into ***Weald*** village, but also tracks deep cut by long use that descend into the weald, for example at Carter's Hill.

Du Boulay (1961); Everitt (1986)

19 An ancient droveway: Carter's Hill to Kettleshill Farm. Long use, probably from early medieval times, of animals being driven to pannage in the 'dens' or clearances in the weald, helped cut these droveways. It is not known when the Carter's Hill droveway was first used.

Dry Hill

Formerly a ***ragstone*** quarry to the west of Sevenoaks. Ragstone was quarried there before the 1840s. It became a publicly owned quarry in the 1920s and a narrow gauge railway helped increase production of what was mainly road gravel. After the quarry closed it became a public park and picnic area.

John Dunlop (1892-1974)

Soldier, military historian and author of *The Pleasant Town of Sevenoaks: a history* (1964). Dunlop studied at Cambridge and London Universities. He served in the Great War, where he was wounded and received the Military Cross. In the 1920s Dunlop was with the army in India. From 1932 he 'devoted energies to work on behalf of the Territorial Army', gaining a War Office appointment and rising to the rank of Brigadier during the ***Second World War***. From 1945-49 he was a member of the Control Commission in Germany, and then Consul-General in Hamburg. Besides military history he also wrote a short history of Germany. Dunlop moved to Sevenoaks in 1922, was elected to the ***Sevenoaks Urban District Council*** which he chaired in 1964. He was knighted in 1956.

Dunton Green
Dunton Green, a small village, straggles along the London road two miles north of Sevenoaks. Originally part of Otford, it became a separate ecclesiastical parish in 1890. The main road from London crossed the river ***Darent*** by ***Longford Bridge***, built in 1636. Nearby stood a mill, known since the 1870s as Hamlin's Mill. ***Bricks*** had been produced in the area since the 17th century, an industry greatly expanded by the building of the ***railway*** in the 1860s. Navvies building the tunnel and railway also temporarily expanded Dunton Green's population and gave the local pub its name, the Miners Arms. A branch line linked the village to Westerham in 1881; it was closed in 1964 but the road bridge remains. Traffic in Dunton Green has long been a problem. In 1909, the Parish Council wrote to the Home Secretary drawing his attention to the danger to life, limb and property by the reckless and illegal driving of motor cars, often over 25 miles an hour. The Council requested that an Army patrol be stationed in the village to enforce the law. The bus garage, opened in 1921 on the London Road, was closed in 1998, demolished, and houses were built on the site. A major housing development began in 2012 on the former site of the ***West Kent Storage Company*** in Rye Lane.
Newman (2008)

E

'eastern way'
This inner by-pass road was first proposed in 1965. The plan was to divert traffic from the High Street by a road skirting round the east of Sevenoaks from the junction of Tonbridge and Solefields Road, through ***Sevenoaks School*** land and part of ***Knole Park*** to meet with the present Suffolk Way. After huge local protests, the plan was finally scrapped in 1995.

education
Formal schooling was available to few children before the mid-19th century, Sunday schools providing some with a basic knowledge of reading and writing. Literacy and numeracy were fundamental to primary schooling in the 19th century, while the ten subjects of the National Curriculum of 1988 replicated those of the Secondary School Regulations of 1904. In contrast, the nature and purpose of individual institutions of education have frequently changed over time. Thus ***Sevenoaks School***, founded in 1432 whose master was required to teach 'all poor boys whatsoever coming there for the sake of learning' without fee, is now a private fee-paying institution for boys and girls. Other schools, both charitable and private, have simply disappeared. Part-time weekday education for factory children was secured under a series of Acts of Parliament begun in 1802, one local example being the school provided by the ***Nouaille*** family at the ***Greatness*** silk mill. From 1833 central government made grants to elementary schools under the aegis of major school societies such as the National Society, established in 1811 with Anglican and Conservative party support, and the British and Foreign School Society of 1808, more closely associated with nonconformists and Liberals. From 1862 grants for performance in reading, writing and arithmetic were paid on the contentious principle of

'Payment by Results'. In 1870, Gladstone's Liberal government established locally-elected school boards empowered to raise ***rates*** to build and support new schools to 'fill up the gaps' in elementary school provision. The seven-member Sevenoaks School Board was formed in 1875 and built schools in ***Cobden Road*** and ***Weald***. By 1880 compulsory attendance of all children was required to the age of ten, raised to 11 in 1893 and 12 in 1899. Subsequent changes were to 14 in 1918, 15 in 1947 and 16 in 1972. The right to free elementary education dates from 1891.

In 1902, Balfour's Conservative government sought to rectify perceived deficiencies in the 1870 Act. The Education Act of that year was warmly welcomed by Roman Catholics and most Anglicans but bitterly opposed by the majority of nonconformists who had handed over many of their schools to the school boards. Voluntary schools were now to receive rate aid, and nonconformists inveighed against what they saw as a plot to bolster the position of the Established Church and to subsidise 'Rome on the rates'. In Sevenoaks opposition to the Act was such that in a parliamentary by-election of 1902 the sitting Conservative member, ***Henry Forster***, saw his majority of 4,812, the largest in England, reduced to 891 with his Liberal opponent claiming a 'moral victory'. The *ad hoc* school boards were abolished and responsibility for elementary and secondary education passed to Kent County Council. The most immediate need was for secondary schools for girls, but none was supplied in Sevenoaks although a grammar school for girls opened in Tonbridge in 1905.

The 1944 Education Act saw the categories of 'elementary' and 'higher' replaced by 'primary', 'secondary' and 'further', but Sevenoaks still lacked a maintained grammar school. 'Voluntary' primary schools were run by Anglicans (***Lady Boswell's***) and Roman Catholics (***St Thomas***), who continued to control the governing body, the appointment of staff and provision of religious instruction, receiving grants for teachers' salaries and other running costs, but having to pay a proportion (initially 50 per cent) of building costs.

In 1965 the Labour government introduced Circular 10/65 inviting LEAs to submit plans to end the 11-plus examination and to reorganise their schools along comprehensive lines. Although in 1970 the incoming Conservative government removed this requirement, by 1995 over 90 per cent of secondary-age pupils in state schools were being educated in comprehensive schools. In Kent, however, selection was retained. Secondary school organisation remained a key issue in national and local ***politics***. Despite opposition, the town's two secondary schools, Bradbourne for girls and ***Wildernesse*** for boys, merged as ***Knole Academy*** in September 2010, sponsored by a local financier, Sevenoaks School and Kent County Council.

Yates, Hume, and Hastings (1994)

Jane Edwards (1792-1868)

In the mid-19th century Jane Edwards wrote her 'Recollections of old Sevenoaks', an account of some of the people who lived in the town. Daughter of a linen draper, she was a member of the local Baptist church. 'Recollections' was written as if to her aunt; she did not intend it for publication. Edward's account started with the ***'top of the town'*** and described, in quaint language, people and the houses in which they

lived. Although not always accurate, the 'Recollections' provides a view of Sevenoaks in the early 19th century which is useful to the cautious reader. Parts of the manuscript were first published in the *Kent Messenger* in 1929, and in the local press in 1949 and 1980; a full copy was published by the Sevenoaks Society in 1985.
Edwards (1985)

electricity supply
Several big houses, including ***Knole*** and ***Combe Bank***, installed their own private generating plants in the early years of the 20th century. There was an abortive attempt to set up a public supply in 1900, when the London-based Electricity Power Distribution Company obtained powers to construct a generator and distribution system in the town. The ***Sevenoaks Urban District Council*** then obtained powers to light the streets with electricity, but did nothing about it for 50 years. In 1913 the newly-established Sevenoaks Electricity Company (affiliated to the London company, Cromptons) took over the powers of public supply; a temporary plant in the town was, within a few months, replaced by a permanent power station at Sundridge. It had monopoly rights in the Urban District and in surrounding towns and villages between Oxted and Seal. Supply from the new station rapidly extended to all these areas, especially after the end of the war in 1918.
Dunlop (1964); Fox, Williams and Mountfield (2007)

Else's Farm
Else's Farm now comprises about five acres. It stands due east of the centre of Sevenoaks Weald, on Morley's Road. The first resident for whom definite documentary evidence exists is John Everest, a farmer, whose will dates from August 1672. It reveals that the then farmhouse contained a large hall on the ground floor with several much smaller rooms off the sides and upstairs. That medieval layout is very different from the present substantial farmhouse, which was erected in the 18th century. In the 19th century the farm had various owners and milk and hops were produced. The poet Edward Thomas lived at the farmhouse in 1904, and he was a great friend of the tramp poet W.H. Davies, who in 1908 wrote his best remembered book, *The Autobiography of a Super Tramp*, at a nearby cottage. Else's Farm ceased to be a working farm in 1994 and the land was sold off. In 2003 it was sympathetically redeveloped into seven residential units which retain much of the period charm and feel of the original.
Lansberry (1988,) 111-14

enclosure
The enclosure and protection of land by fences, hedges, walls, and ditches was the gradual work of people clearing and delineating land for arable and pasture use. Kent was a county of ancient enclosure, most fields and woods being enclosed by 1600. This is indicated by scattered farm sites, small areas of woodland, and narrow twisting lanes on the chalk Downland and in the clay Wealden area. Many fields today retain the same shape as 400 years ago, while post-1850 buildings and road patterns in the town often follow the lines of old field systems. ***Knole*** and ***Panthurst*** parks, both hunting preserves in the 16th century, were emparked or enclosed to

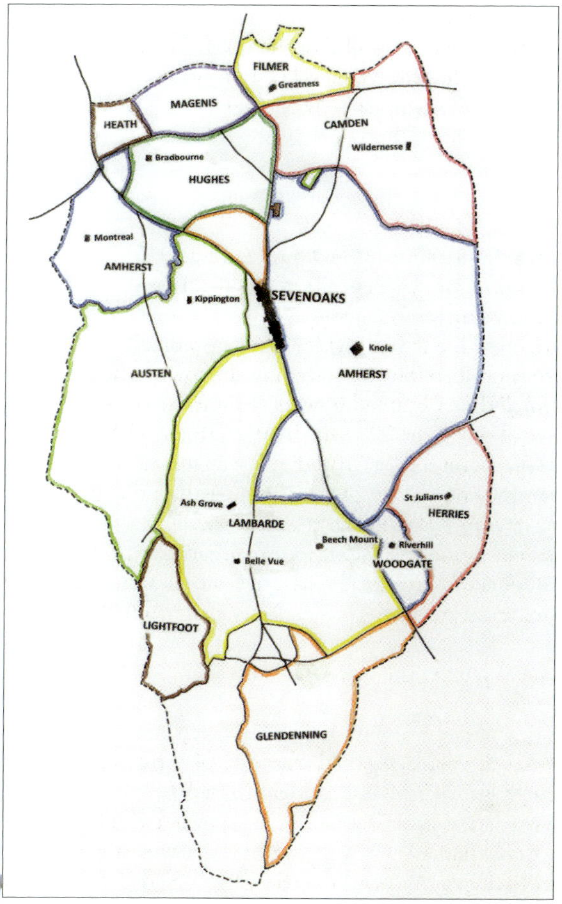

Map 5 Major landowners in the 1840s. In the mid 19th century a handful of wealthy families owned most of the land in Sevenoaks, as can be seen from the Tithe Award map of 1841. Carefully arranged marriages helped to strengthen family fortunes and to strengthen the power and influence of the propertied classes both locally and nationally.

keep in the deer. In the 18th and 19th centuries the few remaining areas of common land or waste in the Sevenoaks district were enclosed either by local agreement or by landowners nibbling at land adjoining their estates. For example, Chipstead Common was enclosed in the early 18th century; the area between Hillingdon Avenue and the modern A25 was enclosed by Lord ***Camden*** in 1803; ***Gallows Common***, part of St John's between Bradbourne Road and St John's Hill, in 1800; also enclosed was ***Sevenoaks Common***, Bowzell Common, and small areas in the Sevenoaks ***Weald***. Other acts of enclosure in the 18th century to protect aristocratic and gentry privilege involved the redirecting or closure of roads close to ***Montreal Park*** and ***Chevening Park***.
Tate (1943)

estates
The landscape and development of Sevenoaks was greatly influenced by the large estates of wealthy families. The most significant was ***Knole*** with land on the eastern side of the town. Housing development in the 20th century has largely been determined by the sale of large estates such as ***Greatness***, ***Bradbourne***, ***Kippington***, ***Wildernesse***, and ***Montreal***.

Alan Everitt (1926-2008)
Everitt was a leading historian of Kent. He was born in ***St John's***, Sevenoaks where his family attended the local closed ***Brethren*** meeting. His book on *The Community of Kent and the Great Rebellion* (Leicester, 1966) was a socio-political study which focused on the provincial strategies and rivalries within the County. He was Professor of English Local History at Leicester University from 1968-82. Following his retirement he published his major work, a detailed topographical study of Kent, *Continuity and Colonisation: the evolution of Kentish settlement* (1986). Later he wrote an acutely observed and nostalgic memoir of his childhood in St John's, 'The Harvest is past' which remains unpublished.

F

fairs
Before the Reformation two fairs were held annually in Sevenoaks, one in early December, the other in late June. Later the Sevenoaks fair was held annually, on three days in early October in the old ***market*** square. Cattle and other animals were bought and sold, stallholders traded goods, local labour was hired, patent medicines promoted, and a variety of entertainers performed. ***Charles Essenhigh Corke***'s drawing of 1900 depicts the fair

fifty years before, with its many stalls and booths. Shopkeepers, who paid ***rates***, increasingly resented the commercial rivalry of the fair, and a growing number of middle-class people objected to its intrusion, smell, noise, and the resulting mess. It was often argued that undesirables such as pedlars, gypsies, and thieves accompanied the fair, although it seems that people of all social classes enjoyed the spectacle and the range of goods on offer. By the mid-19th century pressure had grown in many small towns for fairs to be ended or moved outside the town. The Fairs Act 1871 empowered the Home Department, on petition from local people, to abolish a fair. The Sevenoaks petitions were predictable: working people demanded that the fair remain, while shopkeepers and 'respectable' people that it be closed. Those with power and influence won the day and in 1874 the fair was abolished.
Parkin (2009)

> *George Richmond, the painter, often stayed near the White Hart. He described the Sevenoaks fair in the mid-19th century: '... all classes of people attend the Sevenoaks fair – the parson, the doctor and the schoolmaster. It is a local people's fiesta.'*
> *Stirling (1926), pp. 111-16.*

farms
In the 14th century there was a ring of farms about a mile and a half distant from the parish church of ***St Nicholas***, comprising of ***Brittains, Kippington,*** Wickhurst, ***Panthurst,*** Rumstead, ***Knole, Blackhall*** and ***Greatness*** farms. Closer in were Park Farm (the home farm of ***Sevenoaks Park***), the ***glebe*** land farmed near the Rectory, ***Covell's Farm, Locks Bottom*** by the 'Hole in the Wall' on ***Seal Hollow Road,*** Hillborough (later known as ***Quaker's Hall*** farm) and ***Bligh's*** farm. ***Agriculture*** was the main industry in the area until the 1940s.

Farnaby
The Farnaby family owned and lived at ***Kippington*** from 1636 to 1794. Thomas Farnaby (1575-1647), was a scholar, a soldier and then a teacher running a school for the sons of the nobility and gentry. He published several books and made so much money from his teaching that he moved his school from London to Sevenoaks and bought ***Kippington***. During the ***Civil Wars*** Farnaby was a Royalist, suspected of involvement in the rising near Tonbridge in 1643, and imprisoned by the Parliamentarians. His house and land were sequestrated and he died in 1647 some time after release from Newgate Gaol. The family regained the estate and Farnaby's grandson, Charles, was sheriff of Kent and knighted in 1726. The third baronet, Sir Charles Farnaby-Radcliffe (*c*.1738-98) was elected MP for Hythe (a seat controlled by the Sackvilles), but there is no record of him speaking in Parliament during his 33 years there.

female suffrage
The Reform Act of 1832 confirmed women's exclusion from the right to vote. Before 1868 most men were also not allowed to vote, although there were always loopholes to the system. After 1870 women who were

property owners and paid ***rates*** could vote and stand in local elections for school boards and to become poor law guardians; after 1894 this included election to the new urban and parish councils. Jane Escombe, the painter (d.1905), was a parish councillor in Penshurst and she battled the Sevenoaks Rural District Council to provide municipal housing for rural workers. In national elections women were denied the vote until 1918. In Sevenoaks there were branches of the two suffrage movements: the constitutional-minded National Union of Women's Suffrage Societies, and the militant Women's Social and Political Union, formed in 1903. Campaigning by both groups was suspended when war broke out in 1914. The Representation of the People Act 1918 gave votes to women aged over 30 (as well as to many working-class men); in 1928 this was extended to all women aged 21 and over.
Hollis (1987); Crawford (2006)

Elijah Fenton (1683-1730)
Fenton was a teacher and poet. The youngest child of a wealthy attorney from Staffordshire, he studied at Cambridge but, being a staunch Jacobite, refused to swear the oath of allegiance and could not be ordained. Instead he became a schoolmaster, briefly as headmaster of ***Sevenoaks School***, 1708-1711. As a teacher he was outstanding and enhanced the reputation of the School, engaging Elizabeth ***Austen***, great-grandmother of Jane, to act as housekeeper.

Henry Fermor (1667-1734)
Fermor was born in Crowborough, made his fortune in London, and came to live at ***Suffolk House*** with its 70 acres, situated 'between the horseway and the footway from Sevenoake to Seale', in 1722. In his will he provided money to be given each year to 'forty industrious poor people' in the parish of St Nicholas. The Fermor trust continues today.

festivals and competitions
In the 19th century festivals were mainly religious occasions or concerned with music. The Sevenoaks Three Arts Festival, first held in 1951, was an annual competitive performing arts festival which focused on speech and drama and music, providing valuable performance experience for its competitors, particularly for young people. Since 1995 the Sevenoaks Young Musician of the Year Competition has been a regular feature of the Three Arts Festival. The Sevenoaks Summer Festival was established by ***Sevenoaks School*** in 1970 and became a town event in 2000 run by a small Organising Committee of volunteers. It soon became established as a community festival representing a diversity of local arts activities, typically featuring 100 performances by 60 groups. The Sevenoaks Literary Celebration, an offshoot of the Summer Festival, became an independent literary festival in 2004. In late September and early October it has offered a two-week programme of varied literary events which feature novelists, biographers, historians, poets and writers with local associations.

fields
Until the late 19th century much of Sevenoaks parish consisted of fields and woodlands, most of which had names, some recorded on old maps and plans. Fields varied in size with well established hedges, some with mature

Map 6 Town growth 1870-1970. House building was encouraged by the coming of the railway to Sevenoaks, although not always with the results that speculators in land and housing hoped for. The area in red shows the built-up area in 1870; the shaded area shows housing and industrial development by 1970, most of which occurred in the 20th century.

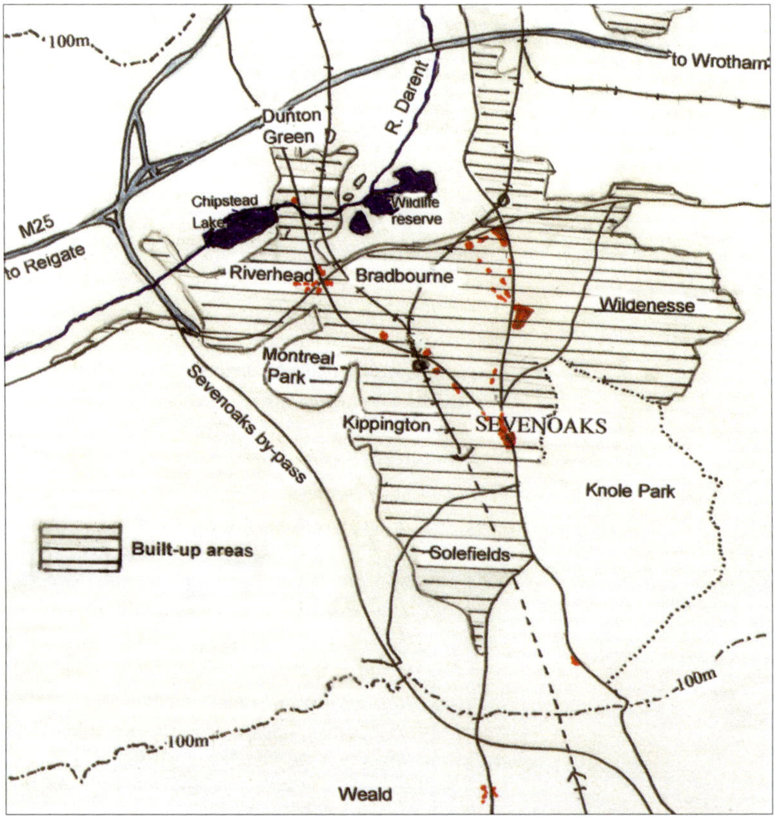

trees, but new chestnut paling fencing and barbed wire were increasingly being used by farmers. Many modern fields remain unchanged in shape and name from those shown on the large scale OS map of 1869. From the same maps it is also possible to see how housing development and new roads have followed old field patterns.

James Fiennes (c.1395-1450)
Fiennes, Lord Say and Sele, was Lord Lieutenant of Kent and owner of ***Knole*** in the 15th century. He was killed in 1450 by the rebels during the ***Cade Rebellion***. His son William sold Knole to ***Bourchier*** in 1456.

Filmer family
The Filmers were an old Kentish gentry family. Sir Edward Filmer (1809-57), Tory MP for West Kent from 1838 to his death, bought ***Greatness House*** from Peter ***Nouaille*** in 1827. On the death of Sir Edward Filmer the estate was administered for the family by a number of trustees. Filmer Road is named after the family.

films
Sevenoaks has appeared in a number of films. An early amateur film was 'Garden Fete at Broughton House' (1926). The Sevenoaks Ciné Club

was founded in the 1930s and a number of films made by members have survived, recorded on 'Sevenoaks Scrapbook' (1937-1945). In the early 1960s, the Sevenoaks Preservation Society, concerned about proposed redevelopment of the town, commissioned the film 'Look, Love and Preserve' (1964). A recent amateur film was of 'Sevenoaks cattle market' (1999). ***Knole House*** and ***Park*** have been used by professional film makers on a number of occasions, for a 'Beatles' commercial (1967), 'The Other Boleyn Girl' (2008), and 'Burke and Hare' (2010).

fire services

The Sevenoaks Fire Engine Association, with a horse-drawn fire engine, was formed in 1830 to protect property in the area. It was paid for by local residents, manned by volunteers, and administered by the ***vestry***. In 1871 the Local Board took over the administration of the fire services, but the existing equipment remained in the ownership of the Association. In 1883 the Association bought a new horse-drawn engine called 'The Ready' and the brigade was called 'The Ready Volunteer Fire Brigade'. In 1894 the new ***Sevenoaks Urban District Council*** took over the administration of the fire service, and in 1902 bought 'The Ready' from the Association. After the ***First World War*** horse-drawn engines were replaced by motorised ones. During the ***Second World War*** the Auxiliary Fire Service was formed. The Sevenoaks service was expanded into four centres, each with vehicles and crews. During air raids the centres dealt with many fires at bombed buildings. After 1945 local service became part of the Kent County Council Fire Service. The fire station was in Eardley Road from the 1870s to 1972, when a new station was built at Morewood north of the railway station.

First World War

The echoes of the Flanders bombardment carried by an east wind and the regular soundings of 'Reveille' and 'The Last Post' by the buglers of the many units stationed in the town area were a constant reminder to Sevenoaks's people of the Great War. Many local men, Territorials and Kitchener volunteers, had departed before conscription in 1916. As the war effort became total under the Lloyd George coalition from December 1916, austerity, with rationing, grew and the means of transport diminished as many thousands of horses were commandeered by the military. Quite suddenly varied work opportunities were available for women, not least middle-class women, few of whom pre-war had been expected to work. Hospital and convalescent home service, in particular, seemed to attract such patriotic women. A regular stream of wounded and convalescent soldiers, British and Belgian, arrived at the ***Cornwall Hall***, ***St John's Hall*** in Hollybush Lane, the stables at ***Wildernesse***, and the converted farm on the ***Combe Bank*** estate.

The Cornwall Hall ***Voluntary Aid Detachment*** hospital was managed by Mrs K. Mansfield, wife of Dr Mansfield. Appointed Commandant in March 1915, she was awarded the Royal Red Cross by the King in March 1918. Soldiers taken to the Hollybush Lane Hall would have, in turn, come under a team of nurses directed by Vita ***Sackville-West***, Aurea ***Lambarde*** of ***Bradbourne*** Hall and, finally, Lady Angela Campbell of Everlands. Violet

Mills, the unmarried youngest daughter of Lord ***Hillingdon***, took charge at ***Wildernesse***, won the MBE and continued nursing after the War.

Troop training for the War drew many men to the Sevenoaks area, including the 5th Battalion, Royal West Kents and, in 1914-1915, the 5th Battalion King's Own Royal Lancashire Regiment who were almost wiped out at Ypres. By 1917 the ***Wildernesse estate*** housed a complete military camp with four main tented encampments, each with 120 tents with associated facilities. The Yeomanry encamped at ***Solefields***. Army tents were to be seen on ***Bligh's Meadow***. The ***Vine***, with its cricket square fenced off, was used for drilling and football. There were many soldiers encamped in ***Knole Park*** – where they were reviewed by Sir John French in 1917. Trainee officers were brought to Sevenoaks, billeted in the ***Royal Crown Hotel*** and taken to Knole to prepare for their future responsibilities; they included the author, Henry Williamson, who recalled the sergeant's throat 'tore terrible howled sounds of command, echoing back from the grey stonework of Lord Sackville's historic mansion'.

More than 220 combatants, drawn from all those who had served, died on active service. The decisive Allied victory left many lives shattered, physically and psychologically. Prominent and ordinary families alike paid a heavy price, and this served to mute the town's peace celebrations. The ***war memorial*** on the Vine became a sight of sad memory, while a German field gun prominently sited in front of the Argyle Road council offices proclaimed victory.

The wartime demand for men reduced the local labour force, which was further affected as some Sevenoaks people were attracted to better

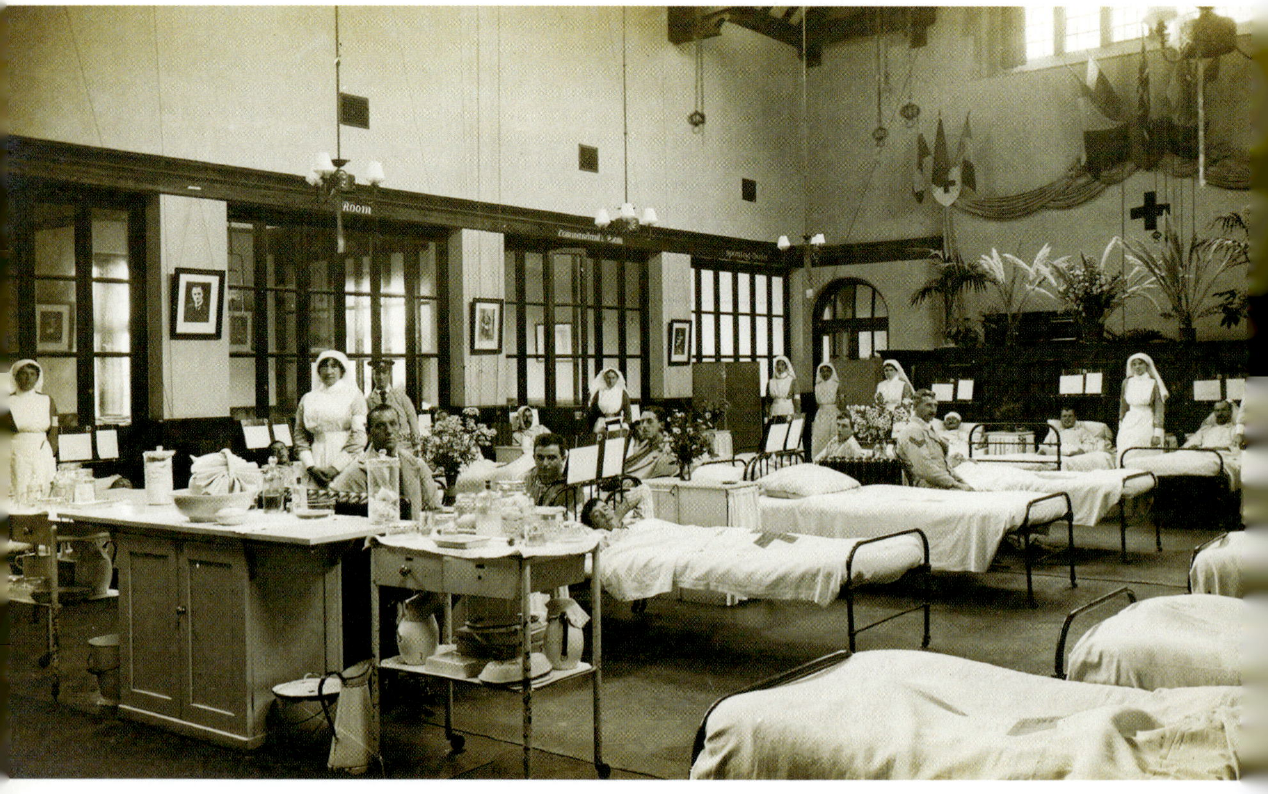

20 Wounded soldiers in the ***Cornwall Hall***. Millions of British and Imperial soldiers were wounded during the First World War; many died of their wounds. Houses and halls, particularly in southern England, became emergency hospitals and wards for men from the Western Front, who were nursed by women of the Voluntary Aid Detachment. The Sevenoaks VAD nursed 3,000 wounded soldiers in the Cornwall Hall on The Drive. The men in this photograph are NCOs and other ranks; officers were in separate wards.

paid war work in north Kent factories. Older children and the Women's Land Army took on agricultural work, a task made vital as the German submarine blockade threatened imported food supplies. By 1917 a County War Agricultural Committee directed ploughing-up grassland on the North Downs and in the weald to increase home corn production. A few American tractors appeared on local farms. Official restrictions on beer consumption resulted in a decline in hop acreage. The labour shortage pushed up farm labourers' wages and also local membership of agricultural trade unions. Farmers, both owners and tenants, saw farm profits rise through the war years, but falling land rents further reduced the wealth and influence of the old landowning class. The war deaths of heirs to great estates had lasting consequences on local landowning: at ***Chevening,*** Lord ***Stanhope*** lost his brother Richard Philip on the Somme; at ***Wildernesse*** Lord ***Hillingdon***'s heir, Charles Thomas Mills, was killed at Loos and his young nephews Michael and Oliver also perished; at ***Montreal,*** the heir, Jeffrey John, who became the last Earl ***Amherst,*** was twice wounded. And the Rev. John Rooker of ***St Nicholas*** and George Heslop, headmaster of ***Sevenoaks School,*** both lost sons.
Williamson (1955), 150; Ogley and Perkins (1999); Armstrong (2001)

fishmongers
Fish was a central part of the diet for people in pre-Reformation England; people were not supposed to eat meat on Fridays. The ***Shambles*** in Sevenoaks sold locally caught fish and sea fish that came along the ***Rye road*** en route to London. Ice, vital for keeping fish cold, was manufactured and delivered by cart to the five fishmongers in Sevenoaks in 1895 (there were

21 Fred Pearce & Son, fishmongers and poulterers, High Street, Sevenoaks, photographed in the early 1920s Fred Pearce was a fishmonger, the son of Charles who had moved to Sevenoaks in the 1860s to work on the ***railways.*** The family moved into a cottage in Quaker's Hall Lane. Family legend is that in the 1860s Fred's mother gave him half a crown and told him to buy a box of fish at the station and hawk it. He appears on the 1871 census as a hawker, but soon after he opened a shop in Cobden Road and then in larger premises in Dorset Street. By the early 20th century he had another fish shop in Riverhead and a shop in the London Road which sold china and toys. Before 1913 he had moved into 94 High Street. By that time, he and his four sons were well known in the town and after the War the business was run by his two elder sons, Charlie and Fred (d. 1936). Charlie kept the business going until the late 1940s, but after he died the next generation, who had other professions, sold the business to MacFisheries. The Pearces were the last to use the ***Shambles*** in its traditional role as ***slaughterhouse*** and commercial yard. Many shopkeepers had a delivery boy who rode a heavy bike without gears. The deliveries were carried in a box in a metal frame at the front, and often a panel beneath the crossbar advertised the name of the shopkeeper.

six in 1913). The gradual introduction of refrigeration in the 20th century revolutionised the fish, poultry and meat businesses.

folly
There are several local follies, for example Knole Bird House, and the ***Bradbourne Clock House*** which looked like a distant chapel on the hillside when viewed from ***Bradbourne Hall***.

football clubs
For centuries football was a popular game requiring little equipment other than a suitable ball. Football as a spectator sport developed in the 19th century. It was encouraged in schools, by some churches and in certain work places. Sevenoaks Town Football Club was founded in 1883. The Club played Royal Arsenal on 26 April 1893 and more than 1,000 spectators watched the game at Knole Paddock. At the time the Club, one of the founder members of the present Kent League, was the only professional team in the South of England. In 1906 the Club became one of the founder members of the present Sevenoaks League. The Club amalgamated with another local team, St John's United, in 1951 and became a member of the Kent Amateur League, which later became the Kent County Football League. In 2003-04 the Club ground and pavilion at Greatness Park, owned and managed by ***Sevenoaks Town Council***, was improved with floodlights.

forges
Blacksmiths had vital skills much in demand in any town or village. They could work metals, shoe horses, and repair most basic machinery. The forge relied initially on charcoal and increasingly on coke by the 19th century. In 1839 the town's blacksmiths included Thomas Guest who had a forge in the Upper High Street on the site of the old Royal Oak Tap. Then there were George Humphrey next door to the Holmesdale Tavern in the High Street, and James Simmonds in ***Post Office Yard***. This latter forge later became Terry's Forge and did not close until 1981. There were also forges at the foot of Tubs Hill, in London Road where Hoads Shoe Shop is situated, at Locks Yard, and at the cross roads at the ***Bat and Ball***. ***Knole*** had its own forge. Sevenoaks ***Weald*** also had a blacksmith. Many blacksmiths became adept at transferring their skills to repairing new mechanical devices such as bicycles and motor vehicles. After 1920 forges steadily declined in number; blacksmiths turned to making gates and domestic implements, although with the increase in leisure horse riding their skills were still in demand.
Terry (2000), 152

Henry William Forster (1866-1936)
Forster was born in Catford, then part of Kent. He became Conservative ***Member of Parliament*** for the Sevenoaks constituency from 1892 to 1918, and then briefly for Bromley. He was appointed a Conservative whip in 1902-11; in the wartime Coalition Government he served as financial secretary to the War Office 1915-19. Raised to the peerage in 1919, he became Governor-General of Australia in 1920.

22 Fort Halstead 1920s. The Boltons, who lived in the Bradbourne area of Sevenoaks, out for a walk on the North Downs, had their photograph taken outside the gate to Fort Halstead. By then the Fort was no longer in use as part of the defence system of London, although the railings were intended to keep out intruders.

Fort Halstead

Three miles north of Sevenoaks on the North Downs and surrounded by a fence over five miles long the Fort (as referred to locally) has an aura of invisibility. As a military installation it was not shown on Ordnance Survey maps. Originally erected in 1892 as part of the southern outer defence ring for London, it served as a Mobilisation Centre and stores for the Territorial Army. That original purpose was abandoned in 1906 but the site was used for ammunition storage again in the ***First World War***. It then lay derelict until 1937 when used during the ***Second World War*** for filling anti-aircraft rockets and as an armament research facility. Later many of the departments of Woolwich Arsenal were transferred to Fort Halstead and it eventually became the Royal Armament Research and Development Centre involved in work on Britain's first nuclear bomb and also rocket development. By 2000 the Fort employed 1,300 people; the next year it was sold to a private defence technology company. A planning application to build a new community of 2,500 people on the site was refused in early 2011. By June of that year, the 840 staff still employed in the Government's Defence Science and Technology Laboratory learned that the Laboratory was to close.

Draper (1999), 202-05

fountains and water troughs

Clean and pure drinking water was not common in 19th-century Sevenoaks. To meet this need the drinking fountain at the junction of the London Road and the High Street was given by an anonymous benefactor in 1882. Another fountain in Riverhead marked Queen Victoria's diamond jubilee. Until the 1930s horses were a common means of haulage. During the 1880s granite water troughs for horses and cattle, provided by the Metropolitan Drinking Fountain and Cattle Trough Association (founded 1859), were placed at the northern end of ***St Botolph's Road***, St John's and ***Bradbourne Road***, and opposite the Police Station. After the ***Second World***

23 Public charity for animals and humans. The horse trough and drinking fountain, placed at the top of St John's Hill in 1886, can still be seen there although it has a new use. Horses and cattle drank from the trough; most thirsty people used a cup attached by a chain to the steel eye which can be seen on the lip of the fountain.

War these fell out of use and became large flower pots maintained by ***Sevenoaks Town Council.***

John Frith (1503-1533)
John Frith was born in Westerham and attended Sevenoaks grammar school. He became an outstanding academic and a close friend of William Tyndale, helping him translate the Bible into English. At the age of 30 he was burnt at the stake, the first English martyr to be executed for publishing Reformation doctrines.
Raynor (2000)

fruit growing
Fruit picking was seasonal work which drew on itinerant labourers including gypsies and people from London. The ***railways*** made it easier for working-class Londoners to get to rural sites. Fruit pickers at ***Blackhall Farm*** had bread, tea and sugar given to them by the London City Mission who raised the money through jumble sales. The Mission held open-air meetings for the pickers and their children every Sunday in the picking season. Modern fruit picking relies on machinery and, as with much seasonal agricultural work, labour mainly from Europe.

Thomas Fuller (1654-1734)
A pharmacist and medical practitioner, Dr Fuller owned the ***Red House*** from 1688 until 1734. He wrote a book of prescriptions and left on record his views about the excellence of beers and the risks of tobacco smoking. Before giving medicines to patients he tried them himself.

fulling
In the mid-17th century the Jeffery brothers, who were cloth workers, owned the mills at ***Greatness***, one of which was a fulling mill. Fullers earth, which came from Surrey, was used for cleansing and thickening woollen cloth. Water-driven hammers beat the earth into the woven cloth in order to scour and cleanse it.

G

galleting
Also known as 'snecking': placing small pieces of stone in the mortar of ***ragstone*** walls as a decorative feature and also, supposedly, as a means of protecting the wall. It came from France (Fr: *un galet* = a pebble) into south-east England in the 15th century.

Gallows Corner or Common
The name given to a triangle of land on the west side of ***St John's*** Hill which may date from 1554 when some of the leaders of ***Wyatt's rebellion*** were hanged there. It does not seem to have been used for that purpose again. Public hanging was usually carried out at Penenden Heath near Maidstone until the early 19th century, and thereafter outside Maidstone gaol until 1868.

gardens and gardening
Until recent times most people, if they had gardens, used them for growing foodstuffs. The wealthy could afford to own gardens for their own leisure and to employ gardeners, for example at ***Knole*** and ***Montreal Park***. Gardening as a leisure activity grew as personal incomes increased from the mid-19th century onwards. Many houses built in that period had gardens, and local nurseries supplied seeds, plants and implements. The Sevenoaks local authorities also bought and maintained ***public gardens***.

Samuel Rawson Gardiner (1829-1902)
Gardiner was the great historian of 17th-century Britain. In later life he came to live in South Park, so that he could be near the ***railway*** station to get to London to work in the Public Record Office and the British Museum Library. Gardiner's 20 volumes, some still in print, covering the years 1603-56 rested heavily on primary sources, setting a standard of scholarship for all later historians. Gardiner was buried in ***St Nicholas*** new graveyard. Since 2002 the ***Sevenoaks Historical Society*** has organised an annual Gardiner lecture to bring a distinguished historian to the town to give a free public lecture.
ODNB (2004)

gas
The original Sevenoaks Gas Company, founded 1838, was an unregistered and unlimited private company. It established its gasworks at the Gas House in the then empty fields at ***Hartsland***, at the junction of Hartslands Road and Hollybush Lane, now a small office development called The Mews. Many of the gas workers lived in the small terraced houses and cottages which were being built for the labouring classes in the Hartslands area. By 1840 the two main streets in the town were lit by gas lamps. The reaction of local residents was mixed. Some thought the expense too high and the quality of gas too low. Once the first ***railway*** arrived at Bat and Ball in 1862, the rival Sevenoaks, Riverhead and Seal Gas Light and Coke Consumers Company was set

24 Women sorting coke at the Sevenoaks gas works, Otford Road *c*.1900. One of the most poignant photographs of Sevenoaks's past. Picking over coke – a dispiriting and back-breaking job, which probably meant that these women were among the lowest paid in Sevenoaks, doing dirty work that only the very poorest would take on. Yet the women, all wearing hats, try to retain some dignity, as they pose for this photograph.

up, and local capital was sought. It may have been connected to the Sevenoaks Railway Company, as its prospectus implied, and it boasted that 'with the advantages of cheaper carriage for coal and all the latest improvements in the manufacture of gas', it would soon undercut its competitor – indeed, it seems to have absorbed it within a few years. It soon built the new gas works and three storage tanks at ***Bat and Ball***, linked to the railway by a horse tramway along Cramptons Road. During the ***Second World War*** the gas works was hit in August 1940 by several high explosive bombs and the gas holders set alight, resulting in some casualties. In 1911 the conversion of street gas-lighting to electricity in the town was discussed and rejected; it was not until 1959 that electric lamp standards were erected despite strong opposition. Gas production ceased in Sevenoaks in 1960.

geology
The variety of rocks in the Sevenoaks area has influenced the landscape, land use and transport patterns of the area. The town stands on a ridge of the Lower Greensand south of the chalk escarpment of the ***North Downs***. Greensand is a sandstone. When fresh it has a greenish colour due to the presence of glauconite, but on exposure to the atmosphere this oxidises to limonite giving a yellow/brown staining. The prominent physical features are the chalk and greensand escarpments. The chalk forms part of the North Downs and has a fairly constant height of about 220m. rising to 268m. at the western limit. The greensand is a more uniform feature due to bands of ***ragstone*** and chert which provide the upper horizon to the Hythe Beds in the Lower Greensand. The highest point in the area is at Toy's Hill which stands at 244m. The main drainage in the area comes from the river ***Darent*** that flows easterly from Westerham to Sevenoaks and then north through the gap in the Downs. The soil of the Lower Greensand varies from fertile to fairly sterile. On the fertile soils grow chestnut, hazel and oak, but on the poorer soils Scots pine and birch predominate. The major local building stone since ***Roman*** times has been ragstone, a coarse sandy limestone found in the Hythe beds, the lower of the four beds of the Lower Greensand. Considerable sand and gravel extraction has taken place over the years. Exhausted pits now form the recreational areas of ***Bradbourne*** and ***Chipstead Lakes***. Extraction continues at the Sevenoaks Quarry at ***Bat and Ball***. A section of the Greensand in West Kent, from Limpsfield Chart near Westerham to Sevenoaks and Plaxtol, forms part of the Kent Downs 'Area of Outstanding Natural Beauty', known as the Sevenoaks greensand ridge. The first geological map of the area was compiled in 1819. More detailed coloured maps were published between 1862 and 1893.
Dines (1969)

Betty Germaine (1680-1769)
Lady Elizabeth Germaine was a friend of the 1st Duke and Duchess of Dorset and spent many years of her widowhood at ***Knole***. Records show her gratuities to the servants between 1719-1765. When she died she left her house at Drayton, Northamptonshire, to Lord George Sackville who then assumed the name Sackville-Germaine.

25 *James German.* A magistrate and highly respectable member of the community, German nevertheless took an active role in opposing Lord Mortimer ***Sackville*** who obstructed entry to ***Knole Park*** in 1884.

James German (1820-1901)
German was born in Preston of a textile family. He became mayor of Preston in 1849 and sought to improve the health of the town. A successful businessman, and several times an unsuccessful Liberal candidate for parliament, he moved first to London and then to Sevenoaks. He lived as a tenant of the ***Lambardes*** at ***Vine Court*** before he had ***Maywood*** built in Bradbourne Road in 1874. He was a member of the Sevenoaks Local Board and supported schemes to improve the town's sanitation. With ***William Thompson,*** he bought 64 acres of land lying between the railway and Hitchen Hatch Lane for housing. He died in 1901 at Belmont, on the Vine.

Nicholas Gibbon (1605-1697)
The scholarly Nicholas Gibbon became rector of ***St Nicholas*** in 1631. He was a Royalist and had little sympathy for Puritan ideas. During the ***Civil Wars*** he was ejected from office in 1643. With his 11 children Gibbon 'was forced to take sanctuary in a poor cottage, which with some small parcel of Land, he rented at Four Pounds a Year. There he was obliged to throw aside his Canonical Habit and to drive the Plow himself'. Gibbon was restored to the Sevenoaks living in 1660.
ODNB (2004)

glass and bottle making
Sevenoaks provided ideal condition for glassmaking with sandy soils and abundant woodland for furnaces. A 'glashowse' is mentioned in records of 1586 but the exact site has not been established, although possibly in the area of ***Hubbard's Hill.*** Probably the glass needed for the many windows of ***Knole*** was made locally. Early workers in the industry may have been French. Another 'Glass House', at ***Panthurst Park,*** is mentioned in the conveyance of 1736 when the park was sold to the ***Lambarde*** family. The fields called the Glasses, shown on the tithe map of 1841, may be those mentioned in the conveyance documents. By the 18th century many more houses were using glass in windows, small pieces for leaded windows being produced locally. Glass bottles and jars were also produced in Sevenoaks in the 19th century, for example by Horsley & Co whose business was taken over by John William Woods in 1891. In the late 19th century the ***railways*** enabled glass manufactured elsewhere, including plate glass which fell in price, to be brought to Sevenoaks, and local bottle making ceased.
Ward (1931) 17-19.

glebe land
Traditionally the glebe land was the land farmed (or leased out) by a parish priest. Land might also be added to the glebe as a gift to the clergyman which increased his income. An ecclesiastical visitation usually produced a glebe terrier which provided an account of the parsonage and the land belonging to the priest. Glebe land was rarely sold until the 20th century by which time all Anglican clergy received a regular salary. The ***St Nicholas*** glebe in 1905 was 15 acres and produced an annual income of £600. ***St Mary's Riverhead*** possessed 3½ acres of glebe which brought in £108 a year, while the eight acres of glebe at ***St George's***, Sevenoaks ***Weald,*** produced £160 annually.

Alexander John Peace Glendining (1789-1870)
In 1847 Alexander Glendining's house, ***Ashgrove***, was listed among the nine 'seats of the nobility and gentry' in Sevenoaks. A wealthy and colourful character, he was a substantial landowner owning over 300 acres in Sevenoaks (almost half at ***Else's Farm***) along with 63 acres at Ashgrove. Glendining sat as a Sevenoaks magistrate 1843-50, and was also High Sheriff of Kent. Married with three children, he appears to have designed the family vault in ***St George's Weald*** while the church was being built; he is interred there with his two daughters. Glendining's marriage to Sarah (1802-93) appears to have failed and, according to a family story, he died in Penshurst 'whilst living with his nurse and constant companion'.

Godden Green
Godden Green is a hamlet within Seal parish on the eastern side of ***Knole Park***. In the 18th century the green was dominated by Gouldings Farm with a cluster of cottages around the pond, and the parish workhouse was at Bow Petts at the end of Back Lane. The first pub was probably The Hen and Chickens on the north side of the green. There was also one, The Stock Tavern, near Blackhall Farm at one of the gates to Knole Park. The Bucks Head, the present pub, is a 16th-century building with an 18th-century façade. Most of the later cottages were built by the Knole Estates for its workers. In the second half of the 19th century the gentry started to move in. Thomas Blackhall, vicar of ***Seal*** 1846-1874, built 'Fairholme' above the green, and other large houses were 'Stormont Court', later occupied by the architect C.R. Ashbee, 'Medlars Mead' (now a clinic) and 'Fawke Cottage',

26 Godden Green. The small hamlet to the east of Knole Park appeared on a postcard produced at the beginning of the 20th century. The Buck's Head is shown, and also the pond which for some local people was their local water supply.

which became part of ***Sevenoaks Preparatory School***. By 1900 the hamlet had a post office, shop and national school as well as the clubhouse for the Wildernesse ***Golf*** Club. Now, apart from the pub, the clinic and Sevenoaks 'Prep', all have been converted to housing.

Goffe Foundation
Hugh Goffe was a pupil at ***Sevenoaks School*** who died in 1964 aged 16. In his memory his parents set up the Hugh Goffe Foundation, a charity which paid for the sixth-form education of promising students from abroad whose parents could not afford to send them to England. Students were selected by the committee and Sevenoaks School, the boys attending that school, the girls going to ***Walthamstow School***. The Foundation closed early in the 21st century.

golf
The first local golf course was laid out on the ***Wildernesse Estate*** in the late 1880s by Lord ***Hillingdon*** for his house guests, a nine-hole course around the mansion house. In 1890 a more formal nine-hole course was laid out around Chance Wood, to the east of Park Lane, and extended to a full 18 holes in 1892. Although initial membership was only nine, this grew rapidly; a clubhouse was built at Godden Green and by 1914 membership had reached 170. After the ***First World War***, the estate was put up for sale and a country club, incorporating the golf course, was based at Wildernesse House. However, conditions for the continuation of golf were considered too onerous by the membership, the majority of whom moved to establish Knole Park Golf Club nearby in 1924. Nevertheless, golf continued to be played intermittently until, in 1927, the syndicate running the country club was bought out by George Fawcett, a local resident, and the golf club was re-established and flourished. After the ***Second World War***, the country club became economically unviable and Fawcett's son Bernard sold the mansion to the Royal London Society for the Blind in 1954. A group of members raised finance to build the present clubhouse on Park Lane and in 1955 The Wildernesse Club was formed. Knole Park Golf Club was funded with the help of Lord Sackville who agreed to the construction of a course in ***Knole Park***, paid for by members of the new club. The inaugural match was played in November 1924. ***Sam King***, later to play in the Ryder Cup and British Open competitions, caddied that day. Sackville had the clubhouse built and many of the original Wildernesse trophies continued to be played for at Knole Park. During the Second World War golf was played, despite obstructions placed on the fairways to prevent enemy gliders landing. In the 1960s the course was lengthened to create a Par 70, and the clubhouse and course have been modernised and squash courts built. In 1927 The Artisans Golfers Association approached the newly formed Knole Golf Club to establish a section for artisans. Lord Sackville agreed and The Sevenoaks Town Golf Club was formed. Membership was limited to 20 with an annual subscription of £2 12s. 6d. The clubhouse came later. This club was deliberately named the 'Town' and not the 'Artisans' to reflect the wish expressed by Sackville in 1924 'that the townspeople of Sevenoaks should be able to use the course'.
Boe (1989)

27 Granville Road – a long line of houses that descends north towards the railway station at Tub's Hill. The substantial houses were sold or let to middle-class owners and tenants, some of whom commuted to London. Most of the houses were built with accommodation for servants, usually in attic rooms. The names, ages, gender, occupations, and places of origin of both householders and domestic servants can be found in the census enumerator's returns for each decade.

Granville area

This area to the north-east of the town centre was laid out as residential streets shortly after the coming of the ***railway*** to ***Tubs Hill*** in 1868. It consists of Granville Road (named after the Foreign Secretary in Gladstone's government), Gordon Road (Lt Colonel Charles Gordon, who recently had made a name for himself in China; later killed at Khartoum in 1885), Eardley Road (probably after the prominent evangelical Christian Sir Culling Eardley, 1805-63), and Argyle Road, which provisionally was named Amherst. Most of the houses were built in the 1870s-80s. By 1896 Clarendon Road was marked out for development (presumably named after Lord Clarendon, foreign secretary 1865-70).

Granville School

The School was founded on VE Day in 1945 by Ena Makin (d. 2001), starting at 84 Granville Road with just six pupils aged three to eight. As the number of pupils expanded, Greystone Lodge, a large house opposite, was purchased. In 1957 the primary school moved to its current location in Bradbourne Park Road.

Greatness House and park

The house is believed to have been built in the 1760s by Peter ***Nouaille*** III after his marriage to Elizabeth Delamare, heiress to Peter Delamare of Greatness in February 1760. On Andrews and Drury's map of 1769, it appears as a substantial building the size of Bradbourne, with formal

28 ***Greatness House.*** Many large houses in Britain became a burden to their owners and were also difficult to let. Greatness lay derelict for many years. It was eventually acquired by a film company and in 1919 blown up in spectacular fashion to provide a dramatic scene for a film about the ***First World War.***

gardens and a lake between it and the mill. Peter III invested heavily in the mill and the workers' cottages but went bankrupt in 1778. He rallied and was able to retire in 1800, dying at Greatness House in 1809 aged 86. With the business much in decline as industrial processes advanced, his son Peter IV closed the silk mill in about 1827 and sold the house to the ***Filmer*** family, moving into St John's Lodge – later incorporated into what became Sevenoaks Hospital. The Filmers do not appear to have lived in the house but rented it out, for example, in 1864 to ***Thomas Crampton*** who, enriched by his railway business, was able to purchase the house and 81 acres of Greatness Farm and St John's Farm from the Filmers. When Crampton died the estate was split up. ***Sevenoaks Urban District Council*** purchased some of the land from the Filmer estate in 1914 to build the first council houses in Sevenoaks. The Council also purchased land for playing fields and a recreation ground at Greatness, ownership being transferred to ***Sevenoaks Town Council*** in 2007. A skateboard park was opened in 2008.

29 Public mourning – the Kraftmeier mausoleum. In 1908 Esme Kraftmeier died aged 12 and was buried at Greatness Park Cemetery. To inter and also commemorate their daughter, ***Edward Kraftmeier*** and his wife Emmie commissioned an art nouveau-style mausoleum built of granite with a barrel vaulted copper roof. In 2003 it was listed as a grade 2 monument.

Greatness Park Cemetery

The Cemetery lies to the north of the Seal Road, the modern A25. It was opened as a public burial place in 1906 by ***Sevenoaks Urban District Council*** who passed it to ***Sevenoaks Town Council*** in 1974. The cemetery was extended in 2003 to provide expected burial space for the next 45 years. Within the approximately 10 acres there are a chapel, workshop, and lodge.

Samuel Green (1869-1853)

Builder, surveyor, and papermaker. Green lived in Sevenoaks for much of his life, in the 1830s at ***Vine Lodge***. He was a Unitarian and a member of Bessel's Green chapel. In 1838 he took over Hayle Mill, Maidstone, from his brother John who was facing bankruptcy. By careful and prudent management Samuel resumed papermaking, concentrating on handmade papers for a specialist market. He weathered the economic storms of the

30 Gypsies at Polhill *c.*1950s. Travelling families were a common sight in the Sevenoaks area, many gypsy families living in areas where there was seasonal farm work and money to be earned from re-cycling scrap metal. In this photograph caravans are descending down ***Polhill*** on the A21. There were several 'illegal' gypsy encampments in the district, including one at Dry Hill in the early 1960s. A widely held official and public view was that gypsies should be 'settled' and 'rehabilitated'. By the Caravan Sites Act, 1968, local authorities were obliged to provide sites for gypsies 'residing in or resorting to their area', one being at the foot of Polhill.

1840s and the firm slowly prospered. The family firm passed to his son John Barcham Green (b.1823).
Green (2011)

Green Belt
The Green Belt, an area of open country surrounding Sevenoaks, has served to prevent urban sprawl from the London conurbation. This was, and remains, the purpose behind Green Belts first created in 1938 and encouraged by the Town and Country Planning Act of 1947. The ***Sevenoaks Society*** has been vigilant in maintaining the character of the Green Belt, as has the London Green Belt Council (founded 1955) of which the Society is a member, constantly monitoring developments in the Green Belt and proving to be a very effective pressure group. In 2011, a renewed threat to Green Belt land appeared in the form of the draft National Planning Policy Framework, which for the first time stated that the default position in planning applications is that there should be a presumption in favour of development. Both national and local organisations objected to this as being a serious threat to Green Belt land and other open countryside

Daniel Grover (1794-1880)
Born in Sussex, Grover moved to Sevenoaks with his brother who was also a builder. In the late 1830s Grover bought the 14-acre site to the east of St John's Hill which was developed as ***Hartsland*** in the 1840s. Grover lived on St John's Hill.

Guzzle Brook
For a large part of its route, the approximately 3½-mile-long Guzzle Brook forms the boundary between ***Seal*** and Kemsing parishes. The stream rises east of Seal and runs west along the ***Vale of Homlesdale*** to join the river ***Darent*** near where the Otford Road crosses the M26. In the past it carried

more water; sheep dips were built on its course, and in living memory the shallow valley in which it runs has flooded several times, for example in the floods of September 1968. At one time there was a water mill at Gunhilder Bridge on Childsbridge Lane; part of the mill pond embankment can still be seen.

Gypsies
Gypsies were first recorded in England in 1505. Their Romany language, which has similarities with Sanskrit, suggests an Indian origin. Gypsies were travellers and lived in close-knit family groups, working as tinkers, drovers, and seasonal agriculture labourers as hop and fruit pickers. As itinerants they were often viewed by communities with suspicion and regarded as outsiders. Without a fixed abode, gypsies did not qualify for parish poor relief before 1834, and rarely did they seek it. After the ***Second World War*** their itinerant life became more difficult. Agriculture was increasingly mechanised, and required fewer seasonal workers, while the modern welfare state more closely monitored children's school attendance, their health, and tried to settle travellers on fixed sites.
Evans (1999)

H

William Haldimand (1784-1862)
Banker and politician. In the early 1820s Haldimand, then the MP for Ipswich (1820-26), moved to the mansion house at ***Ashgrove*** where he lived until 1828. A wealthy man, he became a governor of the Bank of England at the age of 25, and his abilities were praised by the renowned political economist David Ricardo. Haldimand supported the Greek struggle for independence, and presented anti-slavery petitions to the Commons in 1823 and 1824. While living at Ashgrove he employed the architect George Basevi to remodel the house. In addition he financed much of the building of Belgrave Square in London, also designed by Basevi. In 1828 Haldimand retired to Lausanne.

Henry Hardinge (1785-1856)
Hardinge was a ***Sevenoaks School*** boy who joined the Army, rising through the ranks to become Wellington's Divisional Commander in the Peninsular War. By 1828 he became Secretary of State for War and, in 1848, Governor General of India. His portrait is in the ***Sevenoaks Museum***.

Harrison family
The Harrison Institute was founded by Dr James Harrison in 1930 in Bowerwood House, **St *Botolph's Road***, as a zoological museum specialising in mammals and birds. He was supported in this work by his elder son Dr Jeffery Harrison. Together they instigated the ***Wildlife Reserve***; the visitor's centre is named after Jeffery. Under Dr David Harrison (James's younger son) the Institute has focused on research on the taxonomy of mammals; there is a specialist library, and books, papers and articles are published.

31 Cobden Rd, ***Hartsland***. Until the 1950s Hartslands (as it is often called) remained largely a working-class community, older inhabitants often calling it the 'village'. Thereafter houses were sold off, some being demolished and replaced. By the end of the 20th century terraced houses in Hartslands became desirable residences, although roads were filled with parked cars.

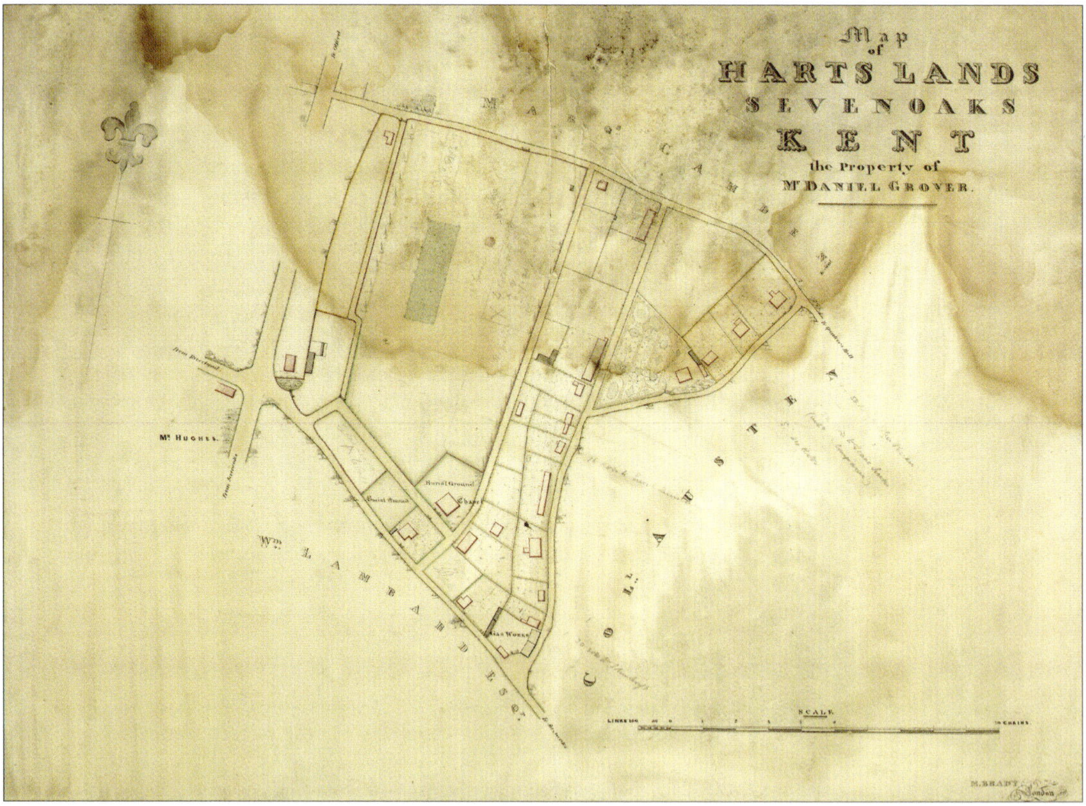

Map 7 Hartsland 1844. In the Tithe Award map of 1841, Hartsland is shown as grazing land. Within a decade nearly 300 people were living in what had become a working-class 'village', near the town gas works, and separated by open country from Sevenoaks. This is the earliest known map of Hartsland and was produced for Daniel Grover the builder and developer in 1844.

Hartsland (Hartslands)
In 1841 the area was a 14-acre arable field owned by ***Daniel Grover***, a local builder, who probably bought it from Multon ***Lambarde***. On the southern edge stood the town's ***gas*** works. In the next decade the area was transformed into a working-class 'village' with several roads of terraced houses, a ***Baptist*** chapel, a beer shop, a public house, several builder's yards, and with a population of over 400; it was 'the poorest and most thickly populated part' of Sevenoaks. Most of the inhabitants were described as 'journeymen and day-labourers'. The first houses were built in Bushes Road (by 1905 listed as Prospect Place, later Road), Cedar Terrace Road, Sandy Lane, and Hartsland Road. In 1850, open country and the occasional large house and estate separated Hartsland from Sevenoaks town. During the next decade north Sevenoaks grew: new and larger houses were built on the west side of St John's Hill; in 1858 ***St John's Church*** opened; and by 1862 the ***railway*** had arrived at ***Bat and Ball***. The closely packed houses of Cobden Road were built in the early 1870s. Educational needs were catered for by the ***St John's*** National Mixed School, opened in 1873 opposite the parish church, and the local authority school for boys and girls in ***Cobden Road***, opened in 1877. Several ***laundries*** opened in Hartsland in the early 20th century.

Edward Hasted (1732-1812)
Author of *The History and Topographical Survey of the County of Kent*, originally published in four volumes between 1778 and 1799. It was reprinted in 12 volumes in 1798-1801, which was then reprinted, with an introduction by ***Alan Everitt***, in 1972. Volume three deals with the Sevenoaks area.
Thirsk (1993); Black (2001); ODNB (2004)

Hatton School
Hatton was the former name for Sevenoaks School for Girls. It opened as a secondary modern in September 1951 on the site now occupied by Sevenoaks County Primary School, and was described by Mary Soames, youngest daughter of Winston Churchill, as 'an absolute palace'. The School included ***Maywood***, the present Adult Education Centre. The majority of girls in the area attended and for much of the 1950s left at the age of 15. The School was named after Lady Fanny Finch-Hatton (1820-1909). The School moved to a new site north of the A25 in 1974 which cost £587,000, and was renamed Bradbourne School for Girls. In 2010 the School merged with ***Wildernesse School*** for Boys to become ***Knole Academy***.

Hearth Tax Return 1664
Following the Restoration in 1660, King Charles II's government was desperate to raise taxes and was constantly on the look-out for new sources of revenue. Between Michaelmas 1662 and 1689 a tax on hearths was levied twice a year at one shilling per hearth in each dwelling house. Householders too poor to contribute to Church ***rates*** were exempt but, nevertheless, their names and number of hearths were recorded. The returns provide an idea of house size and population, based on an accepted multiple of 4.25 head count per hearth. The records for Lady Day 1664 indicate that Sevenoaks town had a ***population*** of some 800 with 4,000 in

the ancient ***Codsheath Hundred***. In Sevenoaks town the largest houses were ***Knole*** (85 hearths), ***Kippington*** (18), the ***Lambardes'*** residence (14), and ***Bradbourne*** (18).
Harrington, Pearson, and Rose (2000)

William Hemmant (1837-1916)
Draper and politician, Hemmant emigrated from Yorkshire to Australia in the late 1850s. He worked as a miner, then grew wealthy in the wool trade and railways, and was prominent in Queensland politics. Hemmant with his family returned to England in 1877. He had ambitions to enter high society in England building his grand house ***'Bulimba'*** in ***Kippington***, near to the large homes of wealthy owners. He partly realised his ambitions when one of his daughters married a peer, although his son was killed in the ***First World War***.

Herb farm
Established by Dorothy Hewer in 1926 on a two-acre plot (where Ash Platt Road now runs), who also took pupils and employed local staff. She specialised in medical herbs and developed a new sub-species of 'Seal Lavender'. Much of the produce was sold at her shop in London. She and her successor Margaret Brownlow kept the farm running through the ***Second World War*** (when a V-2 rocket landed there, killing Mr Johnson who worked there). They both published books about herbs and designed herb gardens elsewhere including one at Knole. The farm closed after Miss Brownlow's death in 1968 and the site was sold for housing.

Herries
The Herries family owned the ***St Julian's*** estate south of Sevenoaks. John Charles Herries (1778-1855) leased the property in 1819, and with his cousin Robert (1773-1845) had a large house built. The estate was gradually extended to the south and by 1910 exceeded 2,000 acres. Both Herries were High Tories opposed to parliamentary reform; Charles had made his money as a civil servant specialising in financial affairs and as Commissary-in-Chief to the British Army during the latter stages of the Napoleonic wars. He became an MP in 1823 and very briefly served as Chancellor of the Exchequer in 1827-8. Thereafter he held several cabinet posts and was a protectionist Tory in the 1840s. Members of the Herries family lived at St Julian's until the late 1940s.
Bates and Killlingray (2003)

James Arthur Higgs-Walker (1892-1979)
Higgs-Walker, or 'Jimmy' as he was affectionately known by the pupils, was headmaster of ***Sevenoaks School*** from 1925 to 1954. When he came to the school there were just over 100 boys and when he left there were 360. He truly laid the foundations of the school as it is now. After steady growth and new building during the 1930s there was the setback of the ***Second World War*** and the immediate post-war period. Following the 1944 Education Act the decision was made to become an independent school. Under Higgs-Walker's leadership the number of students increased and new buildings were erected. Higgs-Walker studied at Oxford, and served in the ***First World War***. He taught history before coming to Sevenoaks,

32 Upper High Street: a watercolour by Roger FitzGerald. The High Street extends south from The Drive (Lower) to just beyond ***Sevenoaks School*** (Upper).

a school which then had no sixth form and was in a building, so he said, that a lady visitor thought was a barracks, prison or workhouse. It was his inspiration (he had played first-class cricket) that started the sporting and cultural traditions the School.
Scragg (1993)

Rowland Hilder (1905-93)
Landscape painter and President of the Royal Institute of Painters in Watercolours from 1964-1974. Hilder, a descendant of the Hilder family from ***Quaker's Hall***, was renowned for his paintings of the Kent

countryside. After the ***Second World War*** he had a studio at ***St Julian's.*** With his wife, Edith, he illustrated the Shell 'Guides to the Countryside'; Rowland would paint the landscapes and Edith the flowers.

Hillborough estate and farm
A farm of this name is shown in Domesday Book as one of the farms of the manor of Otford. By the 16th century, the farm was owned by the ***Petts*** of ***Riverhill.*** William Pett gave a part of the land, later known as ***School Lands,*** as an endowment for ***Sevenoaks School*** in 1510. Thomas Pett sold the remaining land to John Beckett in 1630. By 1654 ***Nathaniel Owen*** the ***Quaker*** owned it. After his son Benjamin's death in 1719, the estate was sold and the estate split in two parts. The larger southern portion was renamed Stoneville but known as ***Quaker's Hall Farm;*** the northern area was bought by Thomas Hilder in 1748, and his son Thomas who built Hillborough House, known as ***Quaker's Hall.*** In the early 19th century the southern section, Stoneville, was owned by Francis Motley ***Austen,*** and by the mid-1830s, by Colonel Thomas Austen. It was sold for housing development in 1876. By the 1880s houses were being built speculatively by ***Henry Owen*** in Bayham Road and Serpentine or Circular Road, Holmesdale and Knole Roads for people attracted to the town by the ***railway.*** The Hilder family retained ownership of the estate, in 1896 selling part of the land to build Bayham Road School, and, in 1898, the northern fields to William Davys for housing development. Elizabeth Daw, grand-daughter of Elizabeth Hilder, built the row of terraced houses, Hildercrest, on the site of the barns and oast houses. The Daws left Quaker's Hall in 1900 and the house was let to a succession of tenants. Alice Florence Daw inherited the property by marriage in 1907, and in 1923 sold the last remaining field to Kent County Council for playing fields for Bayham Road School.
Hollybush Residents Association (1999)

Hillingdon Avenue
John Pratt, 1st Earl of ***Camden,*** laid out a continuous avenue to his house at ***Wildernesse.*** It ran from Hillingdon Lodge at the western end of the estate, and followed a course to avoid the flooding of the dip in the Seal road at Chapmans Ford near the end of Mill Lane. This is the line followed by the modern Hillingdon Avenue, which continues into Wildernesse Avenue.

Hillingdon estate
Sevenoaks Urban District Council borrowed £600 in 1924 to purchase 48 acres of land from the ***Wildernesse estate*** for ***social housing.*** In 1926 the programme of building council houses to form the Hillingdon Estate began. The 131 houses in Hillingdon Rise built between 1945 and 1946 all had hot water, bathrooms, gas, good cupboards and gardens.

historians of Sevenoaks
The first historical writing about Sevenoaks was by ***William Lambarde,*** whose *Perambulation of the County of Kent,* the first real county history in England, was published in 1576. Lambarde knew Sevenoaks, where his family later settled, but his description and history is brief. He was

33 Hillingdon lodge *c.*1905. This photograph shows the children of the Bolton family standing at the door of their home, the lodge to the long drive up to Hillingdon House. James Bolton was a signwriter and grainer. A few years later the family moved to a house in Bradbourne Road. The lodge, facing onto the Seal Road, has recently been enlarged but the lower façade remains.

followed in the late 18th century by the antiquarian ***Edward Hasted***. Typical of his age, he documented the property and marriages of the landed elites. In 1901 Frank Richards (b.1868) had published *Old Sevenoaks*, many of the chapters having first appeared in the *Sevenoaks Chronicle* for which he worked as company secretary. He described his book as 'not a history of the town' but dealing with 'phases' in the past which offered 'the most interesting contrasts to the life and customs' with his own time. ***John Rooker***, the Rector of ***St Nicholas***, wrote articles on the town's history that were published in the *Chronicle*, some of which appeared as a history of St Nicholas in 1910. The solicitor ***Herbert W. Knocker***, a keen antiquarian and collector of documents, wrote articles on the area. He collaborated with his close friend ***Gordon Ward***, whose book *Sevenoaks Essays* appeared in 1931. However, Ward's major contribution is the data collected and recorded in his many note books which have proved a useful source for subsequent researchers on Sevenoaks. The only attempt to write a history of the town was by ***Sir John Dunlop***, *The Pleasant Town of Sevenoaks* (1964), which has been widely read. Hugh Wyatt Standen wrote a useful history of ***Kippington*** (1958), and other lesser studies have also been written on parts of the town. Two academic historians who wrote on the area were the distinguished medievalist F.R.H. Du Boulay (1920-88) and ***Alan Everitt***.

Hitchen Hatch Lane

This is one of the older roads in Sevenoaks. A map of 1740 identifies 'Hutchen Hatch Fields' in the London Road near Tubs Hill. A 'hatch' was a gateway and this suggests that there was a gate off the road into the long meadow and path leading to Kippington. In 1769 Hitchen Hatch Lane ran from the Vine down to a ***pond*** on the London road. The fields and woodland to the south formed the ***St Botolph's*** estate; to the north lay the fields of the ***Bradbourne*** estate. By 1896 the landscape had greatly changed. The two ***railway*** lines opened in the 1860s created a demand for middle-class commuter housing, and a few suburban villas were built along Hitchen Hatch Lane. In 1895 the only property on the northern side of Hitchen Hatch Lane was the Lodge to ***Carrick Grange*** (a second lodge was in Mount Harry Road). During the ***First World War*** the house now known as 'Lynton' was used as a convalescent home for the military. Medicine bottles from that era are still to be dug out of the adjoining gardens in Hitchen Hatch Lane. The influence of the railway is still evident in the continued redevelopment of the large houses and gardens for more commuter housing. The disappearance of Winchester House School, White Lodge and other large Edwardian properties in recent years is part of a continuing process.

hockey
The Sevenoaks Hockey Club started with 15 members early in 1912, comprising men and women, thus forming a mixed team. There continued to be mostly mixed matches with the occasional men's match for the next two seasons. The outbreak of the ***First World War*** called a halt to matches in Sevenoaks; however, it is recorded that several players who had joined the 4th Battalion Queens Own Royal West Kent Regiment enjoyed the benefits of playing hockey in India during this time. Once they returned, the Club started playing matches again in 1919 with a membership of 30 players, allowing men's, ladies' and mixed matches to be played. For many years the Club was basically nomadic, playing wherever they could find a ground in the Sevenoaks area with help from ***Sevenoaks District Council***; the use of Hollybush Recreation Ground goes back to 1925. This changed in 1963 when the Club, by agreement with Sevenoaks *Vine Cricket Club*, used the Vine pavilion during the winter months. The Vine Club bought land in Otford in 1983 to create two more hockey pitches plus those at Hollybush Recreation Ground and Vine cricket ground, though in later years only the ladies were allowed on the hallowed turf as they were not so heavy footed! By this time there were ten teams playing every Saturday – seven men's and three ladies' with some mixed matches on Sundays. The Club secured control of its own Astroturf pitch at Hollybush Recreation Ground in 1989.

Hodder & Stoughton
The well established publishing company of Hodder & Stoughton, founded in 1868, moved its production arm from London to ***Dunton Green*** in 1972. It built new offices and a warehouse on Mill Road, near ***Longford bridge***. The company employed a large staff and specialised in publishing religious and secular books. In 1992 Hodder & Stoughton was acquired by Headline, leading to the closure four years later of the Dunton Green plant. The site has now been developed for housing.
Attenborough (1975)

Hollybush Court Sheltered Housing
The sheltered housing was built in 1989 on land formerly owned by ***Sevenoaks District Council***. The complex of 52 one- and two-bedroom flats is managed by West Kent Housing Association, while a day care centre is run by Sevenoaks Age U.K. in Hollybush Court.

Hollybush Lane
When ***Vine Court*** was demolished in 1897, and its grounds divided into plots for development, the large detached Edwardian houses built on the east side of Vine Court Road acquired plots behind their houses to build small coach houses, stables or other out-buildings which could be accessed from Hollybush Lane.

Holmesdale Road
The eight pairs of semi-detached Victorian houses in Holmesdale Road, four on each side of the road, were built in 1877 as properties for rent by the new commuters attracted to the town by the coming of the ***railway***. The road was named after the ***Vale of Holmesdale***. The road terminates at Hollybush Recreation Ground. The Hollybush Cottages adjacent to the Recreation Ground were built in 1962 for employees of the Parks Department.
Hollybush Residents Association (2000)

hops
Hops were introduced into Kent in the mid-16th century. The flowers, a vital part in making beer, were picked and then dried in oast houses, most of which by the 19th century were rectangular buildings of brick and/or ragstone. Two oast houses stood at the top of Pembroke Road until the early 20th century. By the mid-19th century Londoners, and also ***Gypsies***, came annually into Kent to help with the hop harvest. In 1823 Sevenoaks had 148 acres of hops. In the late 19th century changes in brewing technology and the import of foreign hops drove down hop prices and

34 Hop picking was only a short season, but it provided an opportunity for Londoners to come to the countryside for a working holiday. Special trains brought whole families into Kent. Accommodation for hop-pickers invariably was a basic shed with a standpipe and rudimentary lavatories provided by farmers. This photograph, produced as a postcard, was taken early in the 20th century, and indicates that hop-pickers were seen as part of Kent's exotic scenery which could be turned to commercial use.

reduced local acreage. The ***First World War*** continued this process. Hops ceased to be grown in the Sevenoaks area after the 1970s although wild hop bines remain common in many hedges.

hospitals

Before the late 19th century institutional care for the sick was largely provided by Christian and charitable organisations or individuals. The earliest recorded hospital in Sevenoaks, in 1292, was the St John the Baptist Hospital/chantry for the poor, aged and sick, run by Canon Regulars of St Augustine of Hippo, which probably stood on the site of the future ***Bat and Ball*** inn. Dissolved during the Reformation along with other ***chapels*** and chantries, the former Master, John Claiton (by then vicar of ***St Nicholas*** church), was given a pension of £8 in 1538. The lands of the former hospital retained the name of St John's Farm until much later. The parish ***workhouse*** also had a hospital.

An example of private charity was the Hip Hospital established by ***Emily Jackson***. In 1871 she nursed children in a small cottage on the site of the present Baptist Church on the Vine. When the cottage was sold along with the ***Vine Court*** estate in 1876, the hospital was moved to 2 Park Lane, a house bought by Emily's father, which became the Vine Hip Hospital. Between 1880 and 1892, additions were made to the hospital, including a new wing built on the west side (now 4 Park Lane), to accommodate a dispensary, dining room, a small new ward, and three bedrooms on the second storey. By 1897, Emily had 25 patients, and it was decided that a new larger hospital was needed. In 1900 she raised more than £10,000 to buy two acres of land off Eardley Road and to build a hospital with 45 beds. The hospital was designed by her brother, ***Thomas Jackson***. With the help of a colleague, she gathered together a nursing team to look after children inflicted with tubercular hips, then a scourge among many young people. The Hospital merged with the Cheyne Hospital for children in Chelsea in 1948, forming the Cheyne and Sevenoaks Hip Hospital. In 1958 the Hip Hospital closed and the building was taken over by Sevenoaks Hospital as the Emily Jackson Wing, used for geriatric nursing; it closed in 1988. The house lay derelict until taken over and refurbished by Westminster Health Care and later Barchester Health Care, as a private nursing and care home for the elderly frail, known as Emily Jackson House.

A succession to the ***pest*** house, for people suffering from infectious ***diseases***, was the new Isolation Hospital built on a plot of land near the junction of Fig Street and Oak Lane in 1902. Dr ***Gordon Ward*** complained in 1930 of patients getting inadequate attention due to an influx of 16 cases of scarlet fever and lack of equipment to deal with such a large number. In 1948 the Isolation Hospital was taken over by the National Health Service and became known as the Oak Lane Hospital. By 1956 it had changed from being a hospital for children to a hospital for geriatric patients. In 1972 the hospital was sold to Kent County Council who converted it into a home for children with disabilities, named The Croft, which has now closed.

In 1870 a voluntary fund was set up for the purchase of land and the building of a hospital in Sevenoaks. Three years later the small Sevenoaks and Holmesdale Cottage Hospital was opened on the site

35 Sevenoaks hospital, St John's Hill. In its first year, 1873, the hospital had one nurse and eight beds and dealt with 38 patients. The next year there were 53 patients, some of whom had successful operations. The medical staff soon expanded but not the accommodation. In 1904 two new wards were built by voluntary contributions. X-ray equipment was added in 1909. The aim of the hospital was to give medical treatment and good nursing to persons of the industrial classes (including domestic servants). Weekly charges per person were between 3s. 6d. and 10s. 6d., according to means, or by insurance contributions of 2d. per week. Other funding was from gifts by charitable local people.

of the present hospital at the bottom of St Johns Hill, supported by 'voluntary subscriptions'. Lord Lister, father of antiseptic surgery, was Honorary Consultant Surgeon between 1892 and 1905. During the ***First World War*** the local ***Voluntary Aid Detachment*** helped with the nursing and the ***Cornwall Hall*** was used for a ward. In 1928 the hospital was extended with a children's ward. Extensions in 1935 increased patient accommodation to 64 beds, which grew to 100 in 1939. After the National Health Service reorganisation in 1948, the Holmesdale was removed from local authority responsibility and became the Sevenoaks Hospital. The hospital expanded and a pathological department was added in 1958. In 1965 a 26-bed maternity unit and an out-patients department were opened. Nurse training was part of the programme from 1953 to 1978. Regional management structures and services changed over the years with many services, for example the maternity unit in 1987, moving to the better facilities of another hospital in the group. A G.P. unit was created at Sevenoaks for minor surgery and post-operative care. Between 1995 and 2011 a new hydrotherapy pool was built at the hospital after a public appeal by the Sevenoaks League of Friends. Out-patient clinics were expanded but several times it was feared that the hospital would close. The hospital has, however, recently undergone major refurbishment with an upgraded minor injuries unit being opened in March 2011.
Page (1926)

hotels and inns

Until the coming of the railway the ***coaching inns*** of Sevenoaks, on the route from the coast to London, provided a convenient overnight stopping place. Salmons *Guide to Sevenoaks* for 1901 lists several hotels: the ***Royal***

Crown Hotel in the centre of the town, the ***Royal Oak Hotel*** in the Upper High Street, and the White Hart Hotel, a country inn about a mile from the town on the Tonbridge Road which was there in the late 18th century; all served a higher class of clientele. Cheaper accommodation, suitable to the increasing number of commercial travellers, could be had at Blighs in the High Street, the Dorset Arms in London Road, the Rose and Crown Hotel in the High Street, the ***Lime Tree Temperance Hotel***, the Sennocke Arms, and the Railway and Bicycle at Tubs Hill Station. The number of hotels steadily declined with the growth of motor car ownership after the 1950s. By 2010 Sevenoaks had only two hotels, the ***Royal Oak*** and the Moorings in Hitchen Hatch Lane.
Ward (1931)

house numbers
As can be seen from the early census enumerators' returns and street directories, houses in most streets were not numbered until the development of the modern postal service in the mid-19th century. Smaller houses might be identified by a terrace name, such as Cedar Terrace in ***Hartsland***. Also in Hartsland there was Hortus Place, four dwellings on the west side of Prospect Road, which after the 1940s became simply numbers 1, 3, 5 and 7 Prospect Road. At the same time, the individually listed Prospect Place (12 houses), Prospect Villas (4), East View (6) and Cleveland Place (3) were renumbered 9 to 53 Prospect Road. Similarly, the first eight houses on the east side of the road, at the southern end, lost their 'Limes Cottages' nomenclature, and became simply numbers 2 to 16 Prospect Road. In the 19th century larger houses were named by owners, and when sold the name could change. Many of the large houses built on the new estates of Kippington and Greatness were not numbered but only had names.

Hubbards Hill
A steep hill descending the sandstone ridge from Sevenoaks Common to ***Weald*** village, and a place of frequent accidents. In 1840 a 'new line of Road from the Common to the Chapel in the Weald, to wind round the Hill, to avoid Hubbard Hill', was cut at the cost of £800. Hubbards Hill was slightly realigned and carried by a bridge over the ***Sevenoaks bypass*** in 1968.

Henry Hughes (1779-1865)
Hughes bought the ***Bradbourne*** estate from Thomas Lane in the 1830s. Hughes willed Bradbourne to his nephew Admiral George William Hughes-D'Aeth (1786-1873), who did not live in Sevenoaks but soon sold the estate to ***Francis Crawshay***.

Baron Hunsdon
Henry Carey, cousin to Queen Elizabeth, was created the 1st Baron Hunsden (sometimes spelt Hunsdon) in 1559. She granted him various properties in Kent, including the ***manor*** of Sevenoaks. Carey insisted locally that he receive all the ***market*** rights in Sevenoaks previously owned by the Archbishops. Hunsdon Drive in Sevenoaks is named after him.

hunting
Hunting animals, usually with dogs, was a popular activity of the wealthy in medieval times. ***Deer parks*** provided privileged space and captive game for hunters mounted on horses. 'Field sports', as it was called, developed in the 18th century. Gentry and farmers on horseback with hounds chased to corner and kill foxes, and sometimes deer. The West Kent Hunt hunted over a large area in the 19th century. The West Kent Harriers hunted hares, a practice usually known as coursing. Hunts developed their own local costumes and rituals, encouraged the special breeding of horses and dogs, and employed an army of keepers and dog handlers. Horse racing also took place in the 1870s at Halls Green, Weald. The Game Laws, which became more draconian in the early 19th century, preserved game animals, such as deer, rabbits, and pheasants, as the property of landowners. Poaching was widespread and often dealt with harshly by landowning magistrates. Until 1881 it was illegal for even tenant farmers to shoot game on land they rented. Hunting of all kinds declined in the second half of the 20th century, although shooting for game continued as a rural activity and a source of income for landowners.
Page (1908)

I

ice houses
Many large houses had in their grounds dome-shaped icehouses which acted as 'refrigerators'. That at ***Knole*** dates from the late 17th or early 18th century. Ice cut from lakes and ponds in winter and stored in the icehouse provided a place of cool storage, a source of ice-creams and other cold delights, and ice for medicinal purposes to treat fever and inflammation. By

36 The ice house at Knole. In a bill dated 24 December 1726 is an item: 'Getting 80 load of ice and putting it in ye Ice House and £1.15s 3d.' Until the mid-20th century most households in Sevenoaks did not have a refrigerator. Perishable food was bought daily and home produce stored in sealed glass bottles. Ironically, in the post-1960 age of prosperity and refrigeration more food was wasted than in earlier years.

the mid-19th century ice was being imported from Norway and Canada to keep up with growing demand.

industries
Sevenoaks's major industry until the late 19th century was ***agriculture***. Most other manufacturing industries were small-scale and related to local agricultural production, for example milling corn and animal feeds, brewing, tanning, shoe making, tailoring, and woollen cloth working. There were also people engaged in the building trades, wood and iron work, the quarrying of stone and building materials. Smiths, who worked in iron and also dealt with horses, survived in Sevenoaks until the mid-20th century. ***Brick*** making expanded from the late 16th century. Until *c*.1850 the main source of power for industrial processes was supplied by manual labour and animals, or from wind and water. The original machinery in ***windmills*** and ***watermills*** was constructed from timber, increasingly replaced in the later 18th century by iron which was used for water wheels. Water mills were used for a variety of industrial purposes – grinding corn and animal feed, fulling as at Greatness in the 17th century, paper making (at Sundridge, Shoreham, and Eynsford), and sawing timber. In the late 18th century one of the two mills at ***Greatness*** was converted by Peter ***Nouaille*** for the production of silk, and by 1816 it employed more than 100 people, mainly women and children. Cricket ball making was a cottage industry. The coming of the ***railway*** to Sevenoaks in the 1860s stimulated industry, particularly brick making and quarrying. As the town grew, bricks and tiles for new housing came from existing brickfields on the Otford Road and new ones opened at Dunton Green, while roofing slates were imported from Wales and elsewhere. The ***gas*** works employed more men, and also women. The growth of electricity supply in the early 20th century enabled new industries to be sited in Sevenoaks, for example light engineering, plastic piping made by Marley, printing, and publishing by the Geographer Map Co. (1962-92) and by ***Hodder & Stoughton***. Motor repair and sales also grew after 1960 as more people bought and owned cars which were more technically complex and required specialist attention.

iron churches
In 1878 a temporary iron church to seat 250 people was erected in Granville Road to be used for services pending the building of ***St Mary's***

37 ***St Luke's*** iron church. Iron churches, with a cast-iron frame and galvanised corrugated iron walls and roof, were manufactured in increasing number after 1850. They were 'prefabs' that could be ordered and then easily put up on a prepared site. Relatively cheap to buy and build, these 'tin tabernacles' were intended to be temporary, although a good number have survived.

Kippington. Subsequently it was used by St Luke's, and also as a parish centre; a flying bomb destroyed the building in 1944. The ***Roman Catholic*** community also built an iron church in Granville Road as a temporary church, the first mass being held there in October 1880. When a replacement small brick church was built in 1884, the iron church was transported to the ***Bat and Ball*** where it was re-erected for the St John Ambulance.

J

John Jackson (1837-1911)
Born in Suffolk, and trained at Spurgeon's College in London, Jackson was the Baptist minister in Sevenoaks 1864-74. He then moved to Surrey for ten years. Jackson returned to Sevenoaks and with his wife founded and ran the Boys' School at Scottiswoode House, for the next 20 years. Jackson played a major role in building the new Baptist church on the Vine. In the 1880s he was elected to the Local Board, and then the ***Sevenoaks Urban District Council*** which he chaired in 1901 and again in 1908. Jackson was an active voice for nonconformist causes in Sevenoaks.

38 Emily Jackson. Although Emily Jackson died nearly a century ago, her name is still remembered in Sevenoaks. She was typical of many middle-class Victorian women who carved out for themselves careers in social service. Emily helped to nurse a girl suffering from tuberculosis and that led her to establish the hip hospital in Sevenoaks. Her name lives on in the work of caring for others that she pioneered.

Emily Jackson (1840-1916)
Younger daughter of Hugh and Elizabeth Jackson, and sister of ***Thomas Jackson***. In 1872 she founded and served as Superintendent of the Children's ***Hospital*** for the Treatment of Hip Disease.

Thomas Graham Jackson (1835-1924)
A nationally known architect whose works included a number of buildings in Sevenoaks. He was born in Hampstead but the family moved to Sevenoaks in 1867 and lived in Vine Cottage. Jackson studied at Oxford and served his articles under George Gilbert Scott; he set up his own practice in London in 1862. Some of his early and major work was for Oxford colleges: 'No other architect has altered the appearance of Oxford so greatly as Jackson'. In 1880 Jackson married the daughter of William ***Lambarde*** of Sevenoaks; they had two sons. Jackson's buildings in Sevenoaks included the chancel of ***St George's, Weald*** in 1872, two years later ***Maywood*** for his friend ***James German***, and the ***Emily Jackson*** Hospital in 1901. In the late 1870s, Jackson and his father, both ***Liberals***, bought land in the centre of the town earmarked for middle-class development. There they had built ***Lime Tree Walk*** in 1878-79, a small working-class community of 24 cottages and a coffee shop/temperance hotel (dated 1882), a public declaration of where their sympathies lay. Jackson received a baronetcy in 1913.
Jackson (1950); ODNB (2004)

jail
The site of the old town jail, now a furniture store, is at numbers 14-18 London Road. The cellars underneath are said to have been used for keeping prisoners and believed to be where local rebels were held after ***Wyatt's rebellion*** in 1553. Sevenoaks had a lock-up where law breakers and

suspects were lodged; by 1857 it was reported as defective. New cells were provided in the ***police*** station built in 1864.

John Jay (1805-72)
A building and civil engineering contractor, Jay was responsible for extensive work on the Great Northern line and the Metropolitan underground railway. In the 1860s he contracted to build the Hither Green to Tonbridge section of the ***railway*** through Sevenoaks which included two long tunnels. He leased ***Kippington House*** from the ***Austen*** family and moved in with his two daughters. Responsible for hundreds of navvies, he built huts for them to live in at White Hart Wood, retained the services of a doctor and paid for an iron church to be erected for them on Tubs Hill, also used as a school for the navvies' children. When the Sevenoaks tunnel hit underground water and flooded he was forced to retire from the contract.
ODNB (2004)

Charles Plumtre Johnson (1853-1938)
Benefactor and chairman of the Governors of ***Sevenoaks School.*** Johnson, the son of a royal physician, trained as a solicitor but by 1895 he was also involved in insurance work, becoming vice-chairman (1910-32) of the Legal and General Life Assurance Society. He came to live at Park Grange in 1911. In 1913 Johnson became a governor of Sevenoaks School, serving as chairman from 1926-38. He, and his brother Edward, gave generously to the School: 'Thornhill' (now 'Johnsons'), in Oak Lane with its four acres, given as a boarding house in 1927; the Johnson Hall in 1932, now the School library; and after Johnson's death £75,000 held by trustees for the benefit of the School which resulted in the acquisition of ***Park Grange*** in 1948. Johnson was a keen yachtsman, book and art collector.

Judds Piece
Walter and Rosaline Judd, owners of ***Vine Lodge***, sold the estate to Kent County Council in 1948, apart from a triangle of land opposite the ***Vine***, bounded by Seal Hollow Road to the east, and Hollybush Lane to the west. This triangle of land, known as Judds Piece, was given to ***Sevenoaks Town Council*** to manage as woodland.

K

Sam King (1911-2003)
Samuel Leonard 'Sam' King was an English professional golfer for over 40 years, best known for playing in three Ryder Cup teams. He was born in a cottage 200 yards from the boundary fence of Knole Park and his father and grandfather were tenant farmers on the Knole Estate. Sam started playing ***golf*** using balls he had picked up on his way to school in Seal. He was a boy caddy at the Knole Park Club; in 1929 he became the assistant Club professional and began playing in local and national tournaments. Sam first qualified for the Open in 1932 and his final appearance was in 1962. He had nine top-10 finishes between 1939 and 1959. He was a member of Great Britain's 1937, 1947, and 1949 Ryder Cup teams,

including scoring his team's only point in 1947. Additionally he qualified for the 1939 team, which was cancelled after the outbreak of the ***Second World War***. He returned to professional golf in 1946. Sam King became the head professional at Knole Park Golf Club in 1955, and later won the PGA Seniors Championship in both 1961 and 1962. He retired in 1976 and moved to Lincolnshire, before returning to Sevenoaks later in his life where he spent many happy days in the clubhouse regaling members with stories of his glory days.

Kippington house and estate
The 268-acre Kippington estate was formerly the house and parkland called Kippington House and covered the area between Oak Lane in the south, Brittains Lane in the west and London Road in the east and north. The first known owner was Reginald de Cobham, a clothier who died there in 1362 but, by 1636, it had been divided into Great Kippington, centred on Kippington House, and ***Little Kippington***. The owners in the 16th and early 17th centuries were rich clothiers who had made their money in the Kentish wool trade. In 1636 Thomas ***Farnaby*** bought the estate. Sir Charles Farnaby, a descendant of Thomas, rebuilt and enlarged Kippington House in the 1780s. In 1796 Kippington was sold to Francis Motley ***Austen***, the son of Francis Austen, the Sevenoaks solicitor. Colonel Thomas Austen inherited Kippington from his father in 1817. The Austen family at first lived in Kippington House; in 1862 they lived elsewhere on the estate. They sold a strip of land to the South Eastern Railway Company in order to build the ***railway*** line from London to Tonbridge. They also let Kippington House to the contractor ***John Jay***. When he withdrew from the Sevenoaks tunnel contract, the Austens in 1865 sold the house and the estate to the tea merchant, ***William Thompson***. The completion of the railway in 1868 divided the estate in two parts. Thompson sold land east of the railway line for building development and kept the western part of the estate for larger houses.

In the 1860s a new road was built from north to south, called Oakhill Road. Kippington Lodge was built about 1860, on the London Road end of Oak Hill Road, intended as a gatehouse to control traffic entering the estate. Parts of the estate were sold off for large houses, some built by Thompson. The Thompson family owned Kippington House for 81 years, but let it for much of the time, living in other houses that they had built on the estate, for example ***Kippington Grange***, in which W.J. Thompson lived, and later ***Kippington Court***, and ***Bulimba*** built on a large plot between Kippington and Oakhill Roads. In 1889 the house was leased, between 1907 and 1919 to the Ecclesiastical Commissioners when it became the residence of the Bishop of Rochester, known as 'Bishop's Court'. Between 1919 and 1938 it was a girls' boarding and day school. In 1946 it was sold to Kent County Council who used it as a home for the elderly. In the 1980s the building was sold to a developer and converted into nine flats. In the late 19th century and in the 1920s and 1930s, more houses were built, several being designed by well known architects such as ***Baillie Scott***. Some, such as 'Farnaby', 'Garvock' and 'Rosefield', would later be demolished and replaced by side roads carrying on the names. Others were sold off in plots; '***Bulimba***', for example, was

39 *Kippington House,* early 19th-century print. Kippington house survives although now divided into apartments. Although the present house is smaller than in the time of Sir Charles Farnaby, basically it is his house and the façade and shape is largely as he left it in the late 18th century.

subdivided into nine plots fronting Kippington Road and 11 fronting Oakhill Road. Development of the estate since 1950 has been steady.
Standen (1958)

Kippington Court
Originally called 'Craigmore', Kippington Court, built in 1900, was designed by Thomas Potter as a Victorian country mansion. When ***William J. Thompson*** leased the house in 1903 he changed its name to Kippington Court, and built the stables and accommodation for the coachman. ***Julius Runge*** took a short lease on the house in 1926 before buying it. Runge completely remodelled and extended the house, making it resemble an Elizabethan manor with formal gardens, terraces and flower beds. After Runge's death Kippington Court was put up for auction in 1937 with the rest of ***Montreal Estate,*** and bought by Charles Hopkins, a property developer. During the ***Second World War*** Kippington Court was used by the Army. After the war Hopkins gave Kippington Court to Winston Churchill, and the house was renamed Churchill Court. Churchill in turn gave the house to the Royal British Legion in 1946 to be used as a convalescent home for ex-servicemen. The British Legion sold the house in 1979 to the College of the Chartered Insurance Institute who used it as a training college until 1997 when it was sold and became a private house.
Standen (1958); Nunnerley (2000)

Kippington Grange
William James Thompson bought the ***Kippington*** estate in 1864. His brother-in-law Henry Webb built a house on the estate in 1874 and called it Kippington Grange. About 1896 William J. Thompson bought the house from his wife's brother and moved into it. Thompson died in 1904, just after he had sold the house and land around it to F.W. Amsden who sold it on to Sir Douglas Fox, the consulting engineer, for £10,500 three years later. He and his wife lived there for 14 years and then sold the house to Lord Hawke for £14,500. In 1939 Lord Hawke died and the house was requisitioned by ***Sevenoaks Urban District Council***. During the ***Second World War*** it was used for boys evacuated from Shooters Hill Secondary School, and in 1944 the requisition was transferred to the Ministry of Works to be used as a hostel for Government workers. In 1949 Sevenoaks Urban District Council bought the house and developed some of the grounds into a housing estate. In 1952 the house was leased for use as a home for elderly people, now called Kippington Nursing Home.

John Kirk (1832-1922)
Naturalist and British political agent in East Africa. Kirk was born in Scotland and studied medicine in Edinburgh. After service in the Crimean War he accompanied David Livingstone on his second Zambezi expedition from 1858-63. Kirk returned to East Africa in 1866 as vice-consul at Zanzibar, a position he used to combat the local slave trade and which effectively made him virtual ruler of the island and coastal state. From 1886 Kirk lived at 'Wavertree' on ***Mount Harry Road***. Today his name is commemorated in Kirkhouse, the flats on that site. Kirk retired from Zanzibar in 1886 but continued to be employed by the British government on East and West African affairs. He was a Fellow of the Royal Society, and a leading member of both the Royal Geographical and the Linnean Societies. He was knighted in 1890. Several biographies of Kirk concentrate on his African years and barely mention his long years of retirement in Sevenoaks where he was active in the life of the town. He is buried in the St Nicholas new graveyard.
ODNB (2004)

Herbert Wheatley Knocker (1873-1945)
Solicitor and antiquarian. Son of the Sevenoaks solicitor William Wheatley Knocker, he succeeded his father in the family practice in the London Road. From 1929 the firm occupied the ***White House***, moving in 1935 to the ***Red House*** on the opposite side of the road. Active in the military volunteers, Knocker served in France for much of the ***First World War***, ending the war as a captain, a title he continued to use in peacetime. In the course of his work, Knocker became steward of several manors, also collecting many manorial documents about which he became a great authority. He wrote on the Vale of Holmesdale, and the Court and Manor of Sevenoaks. In 1919-20 Knocker was a member of the ***Middle Classes Union***.
Knocker (1915-)

Knole – early history
Roger of Knolle and Sybil his wife sold the manor house of Knole to Henry de Grofhurst in 1347. He in turn sold it to the Ashburnhams and they to the Grandisons and eventually it came into the hands of James **Fiennes**, Lord Say and Sele, who was executed by ***Cade***'s Rebels in 1450. His son, William Fiennes, sold Knole to Archbishop ***Bourchier*** in 1456 who rebuilt the manor house and enclosed a park round it.
Du Boulay, (1974); Sackville-West (2010)

Knole and the Sackvilles
No one is quite sure what Knole looked like in the early 15th century, 200 years before it was purchased by Thomas Sackville, Earl of Dorset, the first member of the family to live in the house. There are some remains of towers, stairs and curtain walls in the south-east corner. These scattered fragments probably formed part of a medieval manor house, and subsequently became embedded in later structures: first, a palace belonging to the Archbishops of Canterbury, and from 1536, when it was acquired by Henry VIII from Archbishop Thomas Cranmer, a royal mansion. Henry did not spend much time or money at Knole but his daughter, Queen Elizabeth, did spend the night at Knole, her property, on a royal progress in 1573.

When Thomas Sackville took possession of the house in 1604, he remodelled it entirely. He was a lawyer and landowner, with extensive estates in Sussex, but much of his life was spent at court. Years of loyal service to the Crown in national government were rewarded by a string of offices, most significantly Lord Treasurer in 1599, a post to which he was reappointed by James I in 1604. Thomas wanted Knole to proclaim his wealth and status as a senior statesman and, in five years of intensive building in the early 17th century, he created a great show house to celebrate his success. Stone leopards carrying the family coat of arms sprang from gables all over the house; and even the lead drainpipes bore his arms, his earl's coronet and his initials 'TD' for Thomas Dorset. Modern visitors follow the same ceremonial route as a grandee of the early 17th century: sweeping along the main axis of the house through two apparently symmetrical courtyards, the Green Court and the Stone Court, into the Great Hall, before processing up the Great Staircase to the door of the Great Chamber and along a parade of withdrawing rooms and long galleries, with splendid vistas, to the principal bedroom suites.

The interior decoration at Knole was, if anything, more important than the outside changes. To imagine what the rooms actually looked like then, you simply have to strip them in your mind's eye of all the existing furniture, the Old Master paintings, the 18th-century portraits, and to furnish them sparsely with a few pieces of furniture, and some wall hangings and tapestries or a brightly coloured Turkey rug for warmth and decoration. The elaborate screens, ceilings and friezes were all the decoration that Thomas Sackville needed to convey an impression of grandeur and refinement.

Thomas had very little time to enjoy for himself the transformation that he had initiated at Knole. At the time of his death in 1608, his remodelling of Knole was barely complete – and James I never came to the house in whose honour the works had been undertaken. The irony is that the house was even by then already almost out of date, and – with its alleged 365 rooms, 52 staircases and seven courtyards – far too big. Built to accommodate a household of more than 100 people, Knole's exceptional size was already an anachronism, and looked back to the late Middle Ages rather than forward to embrace modern realities. Thomas Sackville's grandson, Richard, who inherited the title and the house in 1609, spent in just 15 years what his forefathers had taken a century to acquire, leaving debts of £60,000 and Knole heavily mortgaged. He also left a wife, ***Anne Clifford***, whose diary provides an intimate account of the workings of an early 17th-century household, as well as the ups and downs of her own marriage.

Most of Knole's original furnishings have disappeared – dissipated by the spendthrift Richard, or ransacked during the ***Civil Wars***, when the house was occupied by Cromwell's troops. In 1643, the Central Committee for Kent, which administered the county for Parliament, collecting taxes and sequestering the estates of Royalists, was based at Knole. The outbuildings were used as a prison, the grounds as a magazine, and the County Committee, it is said, held their meetings in what had been the family dining room for over three hundred years. The chapel that had lain at the heart of Archbishop ***Bourchier***'s palace was adapted for Puritan worship, with the altar rails removed and the ground levelled.

With the Restoration of the monarchy in 1660 Knole's fortunes were restored. Charles Sackville, 6th Earl of Dorset, was a close friend of Charles II, who got him off two criminal charges, one for manslaughter and the other for exposing himself to the populace in 'very indecent postures', according to Samuel Pepys, from the balcony of a brothel in Covent Garden. As he grew older, however, Charles Sackville settled down. He was appointed Lord Chamberlain to William III's Household, where his job was to regulate etiquette at Court, and to supervise the domestic affairs of the monarch. One of the traditional 'perquisites' of office was to dispose of furniture from the royal palaces – particularly Whitehall, Hampton Court and Kensington Palace – when it was felt to be out of date, on the death of a sovereign or on the change of a regime. This was how Charles acquired for Knole one of the finest collections of Stuart furniture in the world: the bed in the King's Room that was made to celebrate the marriage of the future James II to Mary of Modena in 1673; the chairs of state that would have been where the monarch sat to receive important guests; and the bed in the Venetian Ambassador's Room that was made for James II towards the end of his reign.

That special feel Knole has, and has had now for over 300 years – that fading magnificence, that lustre – dates from the 1690s and early 1700s. It is the atmosphere evoked by Virginia Woolf in her description of the Venetian Ambassador's Room in the novel *Orlando*: 'The room ... shone like a shell that has lain at the bottom of the sea for centuries and has been crusted over and painted a million tints by the water; it was rose and yellow, green and sand-coloured. It was frail as a shell, as iridescent and as empty.' The silver furniture, the glowing green-and-gold tapestries that swathe the walls, the russet velvets that cover the chairs of state: it is Charles' collection that has come to define the house today.

Knole was, perhaps, at its most magnificent as a ducal residence during the 18th century. Lionel Sackville had been rewarded for his support of the

40 *Knole's* gate towers, a watercolour by Roger FitzGerald. Since 1560 visitors approaching Knole have seen the solid ragstone walls and gatehouse built by Henry VIII. Behind is the Green Court and Bourchier's mansion barely unchanged since it was built in the 1450s-80s – the west front of Knole. In 1884 angry citizens of Sevenoaks burned before the large oak doors the obstructions erected by Lionel Sackville to prevent entry to the park.

Hanoverian regime by a promotion in 1720 from 7th Earl to 1st Duke of Dorset. Knole was turned into a place for a party. Thomas Sackville's Great Chamber became a Ballroom; and some of the Jacobean state apartments on the first floor were adapted for entertainment, with fashionable elements of the classical style introduced here and there.

His grandson, John Frederick Sackville, the 3rd Duke, was the only member of the Sackville family to create a collection of his own, rather than commissioning the odd portrait, or acquiring a collection through inheritance or the perks of public office. As a young man, John Frederick, like many other young 18th-century aristocrats, embarked on a Grand Tour of Italy. Notebooks record his acquisitions. As well as the Old Master paintings from Italy, France and the Low Countries, John Frederick was a prolific patron of contemporary painters, including John Opie, Ozias Humphry, George Romney, John Hoppner and Thomas Gainsborough. His particular favourite, though, was Sir Joshua Reynolds, who became a close friend and whose funeral he attended as a pall-bearer in St Paul's Cathedral in 1792. By the time of the Duke's death in 1799, there were 20 paintings by Reynolds at Knole, of which a dozen are still there. Many of the portraits he bought from Reynolds during the 1770s now hang in the Reynolds Room. Some are of literary and theatrical acquaintances, such as Oliver Goldsmith, Dr Johnson, Samuel Foote and David Garrick. Presiding over them all is Reynolds's full-length portrait of the Duke. Here is the devastatingly handsome man, whom the Duchess of Devonshire

41 The west front of *Knole*, photographed *c.*1860s. Knole was often described as having the semblance of a small village. House and park dominated Sevenoaks, although at a discreet distance. The Sackvilles were lords of the manor, and their wealth, aristocratic power and presence demanded respect. However, by the late 19th century many townspeople expected their respect to be reciprocated by high levels of responsibility by the Duke for the community on his doorstep. The Sackville's great park, with its walls and fences, helped shape the townscape of Sevenoaks, a town that hugs but rarely penetrates the western perimeter of the Knole estate.

regarded as 'the most dangerous of men ... for with that beauty of his he is so unaffected, and has a simplicity and persuasion in his manner that makes one account very easily for the number of women he has had in love with him'.

The most celebrated of these women was the Italian ballerina, Giovanna Baccelli. La Baccelli – as she was known – had caught his eye when dancing at the King's Theatre in the Haymarket. By 1779 she was living at Knole, where she bore the Duke an illegitimate son. Twenty years later, the Duke had settled down to a respectable marriage with an heiress, and Baccelli had been pensioned off. According to an inventory of 1799, the life-size statue of the naked Baccelli that now reclines voluptuously at the foot of the Great Staircase was banished to an attic, where she spent the next century gathering dust.

There is a letter from the politician Edmund Burke that still resonates today. Declining an invitation to Knole in 1791, Burke wrote to John Frederick: 'I who am something of a lover of all antiquities must be a very great admirer of Knole. I think it is the most interesting thing in England ... I would not change Knole if I were Duke of Dorset for all the foppish structures of this enlightened age.' Burke would probably have been delighted, too, if he could see Knole today – because Knole and its collection have changed very little since the 3rd Duke's day.

Why is this? Why did building, rebuilding and collecting stop at Knole in the early years of the 19th century? One of the reasons is that the

Sackville family ran out of heirs on the death of the 3rd Duke's 21-year-old son in a hunting accident in 1815; and for the next 60 years, the family was embroiled quite regularly in succession disputes. These were followed by the agricultural depression of the 1870s and 1880s which forced down land rents and values. The Sackvilles had run out of money as well as heirs. One Duke's actions in the 1880s also led to a dispute with the people of Sevenoaks over access to the park.

The writer and gardener ***Vita Sackville-West*** grew up at Knole at the turn of the 20th century, later immortalising the house and the period in her novel *The Edwardians*. Electric light and central heating were installed, and there were house parties most weekends. As her mother Victoria later boasted: 'Everyone says that I made Knole the most comfortable large house in England, uniting the beauties of Windsor Castle with the comforts of the Ritz and I never spoilt the old character of Knole.'

And yet, although Knole in 1900 may have appeared as grand as it had been in the 18th century, the show of wealth was a façade. Between 1890 and 1940 a trickle of possessions from Knole were sold, and in 1935 worries about the future of Knole encouraged Charles, 4th Lord Sackville, to enter into discussions with the National Trust. These negotiations continued throughout the war until, in 1946, the Sackville family finally handed the house over to the National Trust with an endowment towards its maintenance. The family retained possession of the park and many of the contents of the house, and were granted a 200-year lease on various private apartments within the house. The handover of Knole to the National Trust more than two generations ago guaranteed the survival of the house, at a time when country houses were being demolished at the rate of up to one a week.
V. Sackville-West (1922); R. Sackville-West (2010)

Knole Academy
The name given to the merged Bradbourne Girls' and ***Wilderness Boys' Secondary Schools*** created in 2010.

Knole Farm
This name was sometimes given to ***Blackhall*** farm, to the north of ***Knole Park***, which became the Home farm for the big house, providing much of the produce needed to feed the large number of family and staff living there.

Knole gardens
Knole may have the largest walled garden in the country, at 26 acres. One of the reasons for its size is likely to be the springs which it encloses. The garden also retains many features which have disappeared in many other great country estates. The orchard has probably been in the same place since before the arrival of the archbishops in 1456, and the small walled garden within the greater one is a typically medieval garden feature.
A pair of columns on the lawn, in line with one wall of the small walled garden, mark the site of the entrance to the garden before it was extended at some point in the 16th century to enclose the area known as the 'Wilderness'. Knole's Wilderness was probably the first garden area to be so called, and contains remnants of the vast 18th-century bosquets, an area of

winding paths between high hedges. The bosquet fashion was short-lived in England, and almost all remnants have died out. The Wilderness, like the rest of the garden, contains many exotic and unusual trees, a large proportion of which are due to the work of Lionel, the 6th Lord Sackville. The garden is also on record as having the tallest cypress (or fastigiate) oak in the British Isles.
Taylor (2003)

Knole Park
The last medieval ***deer park*** in Kent, Knole Park is unusual in never having been landscaped. It consequently has dewponds, trees sited in haphazard fashion, and no large water feature. It is a Special Site of Scientific Interest on account of its unimproved acid grassland and its rare deadwood invertebrates. It covers just under 1,000 acres, of which about 50 acres belong to the National Trust and the remainder to the Knole Estate. It has varied in size over the years, and only reached its present acreage in the 19th century.

The park has valleys of varying sizes, the remains of a prehistoric glacier and river system. The largest of these valleys, which is now called the 'Gallops', was used for a form of deer-hunting in the 16th century. This valley is also called 'Riflerange Valley', the range being at the southern end, known as the 'Mast-Head' where also stood a look-out structure until the 1960s.

Many large and old trees (e.g. hawthorns) adorn the Park, some sited in (roughly) regularly-spaced lines, the meaning of which is unknown, but which may well predate the house. Around the perimeter of the park, and in places which used to be on the edge of the park, are a number of remarkable trees. The older ones, now well inside the park, are mainly pollards of a great age, notably the oak halfway along the west side of the Chestnut Walk. More recent examples are exotic specimen trees, such as cork and holm oaks near the 17th tee of the ***golf*** course, and a Corstorphine sycamore near the Hole in the Wall. Knole also boasts the tallest of many species of tree to be found in Kent, as well as the tallest sessile oak in the British Isles at 40m.

To the east of Knole's garden lies the Bird House, an 18th-century ***folly*** built by the 2nd Duke of Dorset, Charles Sackville. This, and the ruins which lie behind it, are perhaps Knole's only major concessions to 'landscaping' in the park. Recent research suggests that the ruins may indeed have a medieval origin, as there is a considerable amount of masonry below ground level. The main entrance to the Park has long been by the iron-gated lodges near ***Sevenoaks School***. There are other driveways into the park, but pedestrians have been able to enter via various gates, including the 'Hole in the Wall' on Seal Hollow Road, and also by the stone steps set in the ragstone wall reached from ***Blackhall Lane***.
Taylor (2003)

Knole Park access dispute
From 1874 to 1888, Lord Mortimer Sackville, an awkward man even to his family, closed Knole House to visitors. He also objected to people coming into the park, especially the numerous 'trippers' who came to Sevenoaks by ***railway*** at the weekends and on holidays. His distaste also extended to

42 Removing obstructions at ***Knole Park*** 1884. The Knole Park 'riots' were reported in several national newspapers. The artist who drew these illustrations for the *Penny Pictorial News*, 28 June 1884, was either a local person or had local knowledge. This is indicated by the illustration entitled 'at entrance to Knole Park', which shows the distinctive moulded wooden gate posts; the replica gate posts today are similar in shape.

the people of the town who by common use saw the park as an amenity and the bridleway from opposite ***St Nicholas church*** to Fawke Common as a right of way. In 1883 Sackville had barriers erected to block access at the Sevenoaks and Fawke Common gates. The Local Board protested, and the Commons Preservation Society demanded right of access. A large meeting of Sevenoaks people in June 1884, chaired by ***James German***, demanded action, and that evening a large crowd marched to the park, broke down the barriers, carried them up to the house, dumped them in front of the main door, and hissed the aristocratic incumbent. The next evening the crowd returned and smashed some windows at Knole, and opened the gate at Fawke Common. Sackville telegraphed for the Kent Constabulary and one third of the force, over 60 constables, was sent to Sevenoaks. Sackville sought to bring the weight of the law down on those whom, he said, had incited the crowd 'in a violent and tumultuous manner', but the Lord

Chancellor refused to act. Sackville then brought a civil case in the High Court against German and others which he won with derisory damages of five pounds. A compromise was also agreed: the defendants abandoned claims to a bridleway through the park, and pedestrians were allowed free access to footpaths. Since then the park has remained open to all at any time.
Killingray (1994); Sackville-West (2010), 164-68

Knole Road
A short road of residential houses in the Quaker's Hall area, named after the Knole estate. The houses on the west side were built by 1881, facing a sandpit; other building took place in the late 20th century.

Edward August Heinrich Kraftmeier [Kay] (1858-1915)
Kraftmeier arrived in Britain in 1874 and was involved in the manufacture of explosives. Naturalised in 1892, he married an English wife, Emmie Kay, and they lived at ***Ashgrove***. One of Kraftmeier's daughters, Esme, died aged 12 in 1908 and is interred in the Kraftmeier mausoleum, now a listed monument in the ***Greatness Cemetery***. In December 1913 Kraftmeier presented Sevenoaks with the Eardley Road ***swimming baths*** at the cost of £6,000, a mark of his appreciation of his years in Britain. When war broke out in 1914 the Kraftmeiers changed their surname to Kay. He and his wife are interred in the Kraftmeier mausoleum.

L

Labour Exchange
In response to the Labour Exchanges Act 1909, the government opened offices across the country to help the unemployed find work. These were subsequently known as Employment Exchanges, and more recently as Job Centres. The former ***Lady Boswell's School*** housed the Job Centre from 1970 to 2005. During the Depression years a Sevenoaks Unemployed and Occupation Centre for Men opened in the ***Lime Tree Hotel*** in 1932. In 1936, a new centre opened at 44 High Street with facilities for various games including shove-halfpenny, billiards, draughts and cards. ***John Dunlop*** was the Honorary Secretary and a leading figure in providing recreation for the unemployed.

Labour Party
The Labour Party was created by socialists and trade unionists between 1900-6. In 1894 Arthur Hickmott (b.1864), a Fabian and member of the Independent Labour Party was elected to the new ***Urban District Council***. When full manhood suffrage was introduced in 1918 the Labour Party increased its vote across the country. Joseph Skinner, a blacksmith, standing as an Independent Socialist in the Sevenoaks constituency in 1918, gained just under one-third of the votes cast. The local Labour Party contested general elections in 1922, 1929, and 1945. In the landslide Labour victory of 1945, John Pudney, author and journalist, was nearly 4,000 votes behind his Tory opponent. The Party office moved from Dartford Road to Hollybush Lane in the 1970s. Nearly one-

quarter of voters in the Sevenoaks constituency (which by then included Swanley) supported Labour in elections between 1997 and 2005, a figure that fell to just over 13 per cent in 2011.

Lady Boswell's School
When Lady ***Margaret Boswell*** died in 1682, she left an endowment for a school to teach poor children of the parish. The school was not built until 1818. Until that time, the schoolmaster appointed by the Trustees is believed to have had the school room in his own house. Although the Trust was established to teach 'children', until 1813 this was interpreted as boys, with preference for children of poor widows, long resident in the town. The Trust decided to build a school in 1818 and appointed the architect C.R. Cockerell to build a school large enough for 150 boys on the ground floor and 150 girls upstairs. The School was built on land in the ***Black Boy*** garden, and fronted onto the London Road. In 1972 Lady Boswell's, by then a Church of England-aided primary school, moved to a new purpose-built school in Plymouth Drive. The old London Road building was taken over by the Job Centre and Benefits Office to be followed by a Mexican restaurant on the ground floor and a dentist's surgery above.
Ogley (1976)

Lambarde/Lambard family
William Lambarde (1536-1601), who made the family name and fortune, did not live in Sevenoaks. He was a Kentish J.P. and wrote the classic primer for Justices of the Peace, and the first detailed guide to any English county, *The Perambulation of Kent* (1576), an elegantly written volume that has been greatly valued by historians ever since. He wrote of Sevenoaks 'the present estate of the towne itself is good, and it seemeth to have been (for these many yeeres together) in no woorse plight: And yet finde I not in all historie, any memorable thing concerning it, save onely, that in the time of King Henrie the sixt, Jack ***Cade***, and his mischievous meiny, discomfited there Sir Humfrey Stafford, and his Brother, the two Noble Gentleman, whom the King had sent to encounter them.' This excerpt alludes to Jack Cade's largely Kentish rebellion of 1450 and the battle of ***Solefields***.

The original memorials of the Lambarde family were placed in St Alphege's old church at Greenwich. As a result of Thomas Lambarde (1615-75), William's grandson, moving his family to Sevenoaks in 1654, via Squerryes in Westerham, these memorials were transferred to ***St Nicholas Church***, and placed in the Lambarde chapel. Thomas Lambarde bought Brick Place, possibly an early Tudor building, with its parkland, from George ***Lone***, a ***Roman Catholic*** who had suffered persecution during the Cromwellian era. Thomas later built ***Park Place*** in ragstone on the same site which offered an attractive view over ***Knole Park***. The Lambardes became the dominant gentry family in Sevenoaks.

When Multon Lambarde II married Aurea Otway in 1789, he came into possession of ***Ashgrove*** which she had inherited. He now became particularly active in the affairs of the town, developing the family's tradition. He was an 'assistant' (governor) of ***Sevenoaks School***, pressed for the rescue of the parish church, helped to organise the building of ***Lady Boswell's School*** (1818), and was associated with the 1st Earl ***Amherst*** in the building of ***St Mary's Church***, Riverhead. The Sevenoaks diarist ***Jane Edwards*** wrote in the early 1860s of the Lambarde house as having been 'a very pretty old-fashioned stone mansion with a pretty lawn with beautiful flowers and a stately peacock marching about at its pleasure'.

By 1841 Willam Lambarde III (1796-1866) was living at ***Beechmont***: the family now owned over 800 acres and had 18 tenants. Also a magistrate, William could well afford a large establishment. The 1851 census reveals that he had three sons, four daughters, one male tutor and eight servants. When William died (1866) his son Multon III inherited Beechmont. On his death in 1896 his eldest son William Gore Lambarde (1864-1939) succeeded him. He soon moved into ***Bradbourne Hall***, earlier purchased by his father from the ***Crawshays***. There Gore broke in wild horses, training them for hunting and carriage work. Master of the West Kent Foxhounds, his nephew described him as 'a typical country squire who spent the greater part of his life with hunting field, or coaching, and the remainder in dalliance, mainly in the south of France' (Scott). Separated from his wife and without sons, when his hunting days came to an end, Gore sold off the Bradbourne estate in 1927: he ended his days in an apartment at Beechmont.

Lambarde (1576; 1970 edn); Scott (1997)

Land tax

A land tax was first introduced in 1693, but replaced in 1698 by a system of quotas levied locally. Although few records survive before 1780, up to 1832 the assessments were used to determine the qualifications to vote in parliamentary elections.

43 The site of the Sevenoaks Sanitary Laundry, Hartsland. Owned by William Euston in 1904, the steam laundry in Hartsland offered a cleaning service for institutions and households. It was an age when wash day, usually Monday, involved hard work for women. Clothes had to be sorted, soiled linen soaked, and then rubbed by hand or beaten with a 'dolly' in a tub of soapy water. Mechanical washing, at a price, was available at the Sanitary Laundry. Sixty years later many people in Sevenoaks could wear clothes made of synthetic materials that were easy to wash at home in electric washing machines.

laundries

The 1891 census shows a number of women launderers living in the terraced houses of working-class areas such as the ***Shambles, Six Bells Lane, Redmans Place*** and ***Hartsland***. These women probably worked in one of the laundries in the town or took in washing from the big houses in the area. Several laundries were established in Hartsland: the Sevenoaks Sanitary Laundry, built on the site of the old gas works; the Oak Laundry, dating from 1895, in Bethel Road. There was also a laundry at the bottom of Sandy Lane and a steam laundry, Enstons, in Hollybush Lane.

John Dawson Laurie (1872-1954)

Businessman, stockbroker, and Lord Mayor of London. Laurie was the son of Alfred J. St George McAdam Laurie, who lived at ***Rockdale House*** in Sevenoaks town centre. In 1896 Laurie began work in the family firm in the City of London, and he also joined the local ***Volunteers***. During the ***First World War*** he was Provost Marshal of the 2nd Army on the Western Front, achieving the rank of Lieutenant-Colonel in the West Kent Regiment. After the war Laurie returned to work in the city. He became a City Alderman and was knighted in 1936, being elected Lord Mayor in November 1941. Laurie was made a baronet in 1942. He was a leading freemason; he never married. Sir John was elected a member of ***Sevenoaks Urban District Council*** and served one year as chairman. After his death ***Rockdale*** House was sold to the Sevenoaks District Old People's Housing Association and became sheltered accommodation for elderly people.

Ignatius Lazzari (b.1847)
Father Lazzari was the leader of the Roman Catholic Mission in Sevenoaks from its inception in 1880 until 1892. A priest of the Rosarian Order in Pompeii, he had been tutor to the son of a local family, the Buchanans, who were instrumental in funding and establishing the new Church of St Thomas of Canterbury at the junction of Granville Road and what, later, became Gordon Road. In his 12 years as Rector of the new parish, Lazzari was able to raise funds and open a temporary ***iron church*** and later, in 1883, a brick-built replacement. He opened an elementary school in the St John's Hill area, and in a campaign against drink in 1881 formed a short-lived branch of the Catholic Total Abstinence League of the Cross. Lazzari was also eager to hear 'the sound of music in the streets' of Sevenoaks, and he suggested, via the *Sevenoaks Chronicle*, that he would teach 'any who would wish to learn music with a view to the forming of a class for the practice of brass or stringed instruments'. Lazzari left Sevenoaks to undertake a new mission near Chatham. Remarkably, copies of his Order's magazines, still clearly addressed to him, have arrived regularly at the Granville Road presbytery to this day.

Leisure Centre
When the old ***swimming*** bath at Eardley Road was demolished, a new swimming pool was built in 1985 on the present Leisure Centre site at Buckhurst Lane. In turn, this centre was extended in 2000 to include a new pool, sports halls, gym and other facilities which, along with the refurbished ***library***, added to the cultural quadrant of the town. The site, in common with all ***Sevenoaks District Council*** leisure facilities, is operated by Sencio Community Leisure, a non-profit distributing trust formed in 2004.

Liberal Party
Whigs in west Kent pressed for political reform in the 1820s-30s. By the 1850s the local Liberal Party had a political agent and there were also Liberal clubs. Between 1868 and 1920 the Liberal Party regularly formed the national government. At four general elections in the 19th century a Liberal candidate was elected for the West Kent or Sevenoaks constituency. By the 1870s eminent local men such as ***Thomas G. Jackson***, ***James German***, ***Albert Bath***, and the Rev. ***John Jackson*** supported the Liberal Party. Liberals and their supporters waged vigorous campaigns against Tory dominance on the various local government boards and bodies. Local issues figured strongly in the by-election of 1902 when the Liberals, supported by the nonconformist vote, came nearest to defeating the Tories over the issue of the Education Bill. Only once in the 20th century have Liberals held the Sevenoaks seat, briefly in 1923. At that time the local party headquarters was in the centre of Sevenoaks, the last, at an address in the London Road, until 1966. In 1988 the Liberals merged with the ***Social Democrat Party*** to create the Liberal Democrats. The new party steadily built up its local government representation until between 1995 and 1999 not only did it control the ***Town Council*** but became the largest party on the District Council. Liberal Democrats then led an administration which was responsible for creating the Blighs Meadow shopping development and the Sevenoaks ***Leisure Centre*** as well as giving strong support to the Stag Theatre.

libraries
In the late 18th century Sevenoaks had a private lending library, and in the mid-19th century the ***Sevenoaks Literary and Scientific Society*** had created a lending library of over 1,000 volumes. By the 1890s there were a few private and subscription libraries, for example the Sevenoaks and District Library in the ***Odd Fellows Hall,*** 'open on Tuesday 6.30 p.m. to 8 p.m.', ***Salmons*** the printers subscription library in the High Street, and ***Sevenoaks Urban District Council*** also ran a subscription library in the Old ***Market House.*** The 'Free' Public Library was opened in The Drive in 1905, paid for by a gift of £3,000 from Andrew Carnegie the Scottish-American philanthropist, on land donated by ***Henry Swaffield*** next to the new ***Methodist Church.*** Edwyn Evans ***Cronk*** of Sevenoaks designed the two-storey red-brick building dressed with bath stone and with a grey slated roof. The ground floor contained the lending library; upstairs there was a magazine room and reference room. The public were invited to donate books and a librarian was appointed in 1906. ***George Bennett*** became librarian in 1920 and retired in 1966. He was followed by George Lawrence. Between them, they collected and preserved manuscripts, transcripts and documents vital to the history of Sevenoaks. George Lawrence opened branches in Bradbourne and St John's, and began a house-bound library service run by volunteers. In 1974, under local government re-organisation, responsibility for Sevenoaks library was transferred to Kent County Council.

As the number of books, documents and staff increased, it became clear that a larger building was needed. A site was found in Buckhurst Lane which was opened in 1986 by the local MP. The new building also provided accommodation for the ***Tourist Information Centre*** and the ***Citizens Advice Bureau.*** Less than 20 years later, Kent County Council decided the town library needed modernising and transforming into a cultural centre for the

44 Salmon's library. ***Salmon*** printed, engraved, published, bound and sold books. The firm also had a 'circulating library', paid for by subscription, in their shop at the top of the High Street, just above the ***old market place.*** The *Daily Telegraph*, advertised on the shop, was one of several London daily newspapers that could be bought in Sevenoaks. In the 19th century many provincial newspapers, such as the *Sevenoaks Chronicle*, carried national and international news syndicated by agencies which transmitted information by telegraph.

arts. The new-look library, renamed as Sevenoaks Kaleidoscope, opened in December 2006. The project cost £2.3 million, funded by the Heritage Lottery Fund, Kent County Council, the Arts Council and ***Sevenoaks District*** and ***Town Councils***. Sevenoaks Kaleidoscope had fewer books but a larger number of computers with access to online services, a refreshment space, a new art gallery, and an interactive museum.
Swan (1980)

lime
Lime was used for mortar for building work in stone and brick, but also as a fertiliser. It was quarried at various places on the ***North Downs*** and burned in lime kilns. These existed below modern Polhill since the 18th century (now a small industrial estate), while others, probably for agricultural purposes, were in ***Weald***. Pure chalk or limestone was heated in a kiln until its carbolic acid was driven off to produce pure lime. This, slaked with water, was made into a paste which when mixed with water and sand forms mortar; when the lime dries it sets the mortar. As a fertiliser, lime added carbonate of calcium to local sandy and clay soils.

Lime Tree Temperance Hotel
Temperance hotels developed in the mid-19th century when alcohol was relatively cheap and drunkenness a major scourge. In 1886 the Lime Tree Hotel embraced the Victorian craze for cycling when it became the headquarters of the local Touring Club. The Hotel later became known as the Lime Tree Commercial Hotel, and later simply the Lime Tree Hotel. It was very popular, with tennis courts and a croquet lawn in its grounds. When the hotel closed in the 1930s, the ***Sevenoaks News*** occupied the premises. The ***News*** was printed there until the building received a direct hit by a bomb in October 1940. After the ***Second World War*** the building was restored and the *Sevenoaks News* returned until 1966 when it was taken over by the Courier Newspaper group. The old hotel later became the home of the Butter Council before being renovated and becoming the Sevenoaks Business Centre in 1996.

Lime Tree Walk
Among ***Thomas Jackson***'s vast and diverse output of buildings, Lime Tree Walk, a street of workmen's houses, stands out as the only instance of local small-scale domestic architecture, which he had built in 1878-79, when his parents were living in Vine Cottage.

Early in 1879, Jackson recorded: 'The new cottages at Sevenoaks were nearing completion. I had tried to make them beautiful within the proper limits of cottage building; *not* the *cottage orné*, which is detestable, but with a kind of simple grace which comes from plain sensible construction.'
Jackson (1950)

Little Kippington
During the ***Civil Wars*** of the 1640s, the lands known as Little Kippington formed part of the ***Sevenoaks Park*** estate. Owned by William ***Lone***, a prominent Royalist, the lands were sequestered by Parliament. In 1652, Parliament sold the area known as Little Kippington to John Cogger. The description makes it clear that this was land to the south of the present

45 Lime Tree Walk: a watercolour by Roger FitzGerald. In his Recollections, published in a revised edition in 2003, Thomas Jackson recalled: 'My father's interest in workmen's dwellings, which I fully shared, now led us to break new ground in Sevenoaks. The sale of Vine Court by Multon Lambarde to a building syndicate sealed the fate of the old cottages on the Vine, and the same befell all the old cottages on sites that were attractive and conditions were put on all building estates prohibiting the building of anything but 'genteel' villas. The poor people were consequently pushed clean away from the town and a new suburb of little houses sprang up below the hill near the gasfields, a district closely built round with no garden grounds and nothing to make home attractive. It was to remedy this state of things and to do something to counteract the mischievous sorting out of classes into distinct districts for rich and poor, which always has the effect of creating two hostile camps, that we now set ourselves to work. When at last we heard of a field right in the middle of town on which no restrictions would be put we bought it and built twenty-four cottages. The result was that a great number of families were eventually well and cheaply housed on a beautiful site commanding lovely views and equal to any enjoyed by their well-to-do neighbours, and that workmen were close to their work instead of having to walk miles from home and back twice a day.'

Oak Lane, bounded on the west by Ashgrove Road. It was adjacent to, but not connected with, Great Kippington, then owned by the ***Farnaby*** family. The 1792 Kippington estate map, prepared shortly before the sale of Great Kippington to Francis ***Austen***, shows 'Cogger' still as the adjoining owner at Cross Keys.

local government

Before 1871 the parish ***vestry*** and the justices of the peace acting in the ***Quarter Sessions*** had a number of limited local powers in Sevenoaks. After 1834 the poor law became centrally directed from London but locally administered by guardians elected to the poor law union formed from a number of parishes. The boundaries of the poor law union also marked the area of a new rural sanitary authority established in the 1850s. In the next two decades, in response to local demands for improved public health and an adequate system of water supply and drainage, separate Sevenoaks urban and rural authorities were created with medical officers of health. The Highways Act 1862 led to the creation of Highways Boards funded by several parishes. In 1871 a local board was created, the town's first elected body, which took over some of the vestry's duties; Multon ***Lambarde*** was the first chairman, the offices in Argyle Road built in 1872.

Under the Education Act 1870 an elected school board was established in 1875 to manage new elementary schools, a responsibility taken over by Kent County Council in 1902. An elected County Council replaced the unrepresentative Quarter Sessions in 1889, although most county councillors continued to be drawn from the leisured classes. The piece-meal and chaotic system of local administration was changed by the Local Government Act 1894 which concentrated powers in an elected ***Sevenoaks Urban District Council*** (UDC) for the town, and a parallel Rural District Council with boundaries based on those of the Poor Law Union. The Act also gave rural parishes, such as Riverhead and Weald, elected parish councils. During the 20th century the UDC gained further powers. Reform and re-organisation were frequently discussed, but major change followed the Local Government Act 1972. A new larger ***Sevenoaks District Council*** was created in 1974, stretching from Edenbridge to Swanley, with a population estimated at 114,000 in 2010. A second tier of local government gave Sevenoaks and Swanley each a ***Town Council***, and there were 28 parish councils.
Keith-Lucas (1977); Lawson & Killingray (2004), 150-52

Lock's Bottom Farm
The farm, situated behind the wall of Knole Park on Seal Hollow Road, belonged to the Locke family until the late 16th century. The surrounding land was called Lock's Bottom land.

Lock's Yard
This yard was entered by a passage between numbers 98 and 100 High Street. The passageway still exists. The Yard originally contained seven cottages. Access to accommodation over the shops between numbers 100 to 106 High Street was gained by a staircase in the Yard. ***Jane Edwards'*** parents occupied number 98 High Street where her father ran a drapery business.

lodges
Owners of large estates protected the entrance to their lands by 'guardians' at gatehouses and lodges. Some of these lodges have been demolished such as the thatched roof lodge at ***Greatness*** but, being detached by some distance from the main house, many have survived even if the great house has gone. At ***Knole*** there are two sets of paired lodges, Plymouth Lodge and Knole Lodge. The ***Wildernesse estate***, which at its peak covered over 500 acres in Seal and Sevenoaks parishes, was at one time emparked, and had several lodges. The fencing around the park and gates allowing access by way of Park Lane are shown on a map of Gouldings Farm, Godden Green, dated 1778. There were timber clad lodges by the gates at either end of Park Lane in ***Godden Green*** and ***Seal;*** the former still exists but the latter was demolished in the early 20th century, after a replacement had been built slightly nearer Seal. This Edwardian building has trefoils on its bargeboards, a sign that Lord Hillingdon, then living at Wildernesse, had it built. A substantial lodge at the junction of Seal Drive and Seal Road, and single-storey lodges at the end of Wildernesse Avenue and, after the land between ***Seal Hollow Road*** and St John's Hill had been added to the estate, at the end of what is now Hillingdon Avenue were built by the

46 Greatness thatched lodge. A late 19th-century photograph of the lodge to ***Greatness House***. In all probability the reeds for thatching the cottage came from the stream on the estate. Thatched roofing, once common in Sevenoaks, by the 18th century was being replaced by brick tiled roofs which were cheaper and often had a longer life.

Camdens, who lived at Wildernesse from 1705 to 1860. These three all had the Camden crest, an elephant's head, on their walls. At the end of the 19th century the Seal Drive lodge was funded by the Hillingdons as a convalescent home for sick or deprived girls. Many of them went on to be domestic servants in various Hillingdon properties. There is an ornate Gothic lodge in Kippington Road which served ***Kippington*** House and the fine Grade II ***Park Grange*** Lodge of *c*.1869 which was the lodge for ***Park Farm***. One of the few survivors of the ***Montreal*** estate is the octagonal lodge at Lyndhurst Drive.

Lone family

The family owned ***Sevenoaks Park*** for 95 years. Richard Lone bought Sevenoaks Park in 1559 from Thomas Potkin. William Lone, a Roman Catholic and supporter of the King, lived at Sevenoaks Park at the time of the ***Civil Wars***. A prominent Royalist, in 1643 he helped to organise the local abortive uprising against the County Committee, which had taken over Knole. As a result, his lands were sequestered by Parliament. Sevenoaks Park was sold to ***Thomas Lambarde*** in 1654.

Long Barn, Weald

Probably a mid-14th-century building which was extended and adapted by various owners, including ***Vita Sackville-West*** and Harold Nicolson who bought it in 1915. They created the garden, developing ideas later to be used at Sissinghurst.

47 Longford Bridge in the 1900s. The name Longford indicates the difficulty of fording the ***Darent*** at this point when the river was high. The humped bridge made passage much easier for carriages, wagons, and people on foot.

Longford Bridge, Dunton Green
Before the Polhill road was constructed between 1834 and 1838, the road south from London to Sevenoaks came down Star Hill through Dunton Green, crossing the River ***Darent*** at Longford. The water at Longford was often wide and deep, and the road was frequently flooded. In 1636 a stone bridge was built to ease the problem. In 1637 the parishes of Sevenoaks, Chevening and Otford combined to finance the repairs needed at Longford Bridge. A mill on the River Darent, probably dating from medieval times, stood to the west of Longford Bridge. It was most recently known as Hamlin's Mill; it ceased work in 1947 and was demolished in 1987, the site being used for a car showroom.
Newman (2008)

M

main drainage
Before the 1880s Sevenoaks lacked a main drainage system to remove waste. Privies, and soil pits had to be regularly cleaned, and waste water lay on the surface; the result was ***smells*** and ***disease***. One 'sewer' in the 1870s emptied into Knole Paddock. Predictably there were demands for improved public health and a more pleasant town environment. The costs of constructing a main drainage system fell on the ***rates***, and therefore it was a political issue, opposed by some who had their own private systems of waste disposal or who were indifferent to the health and well-being of their neighbours. A main drainage system was constructed along the

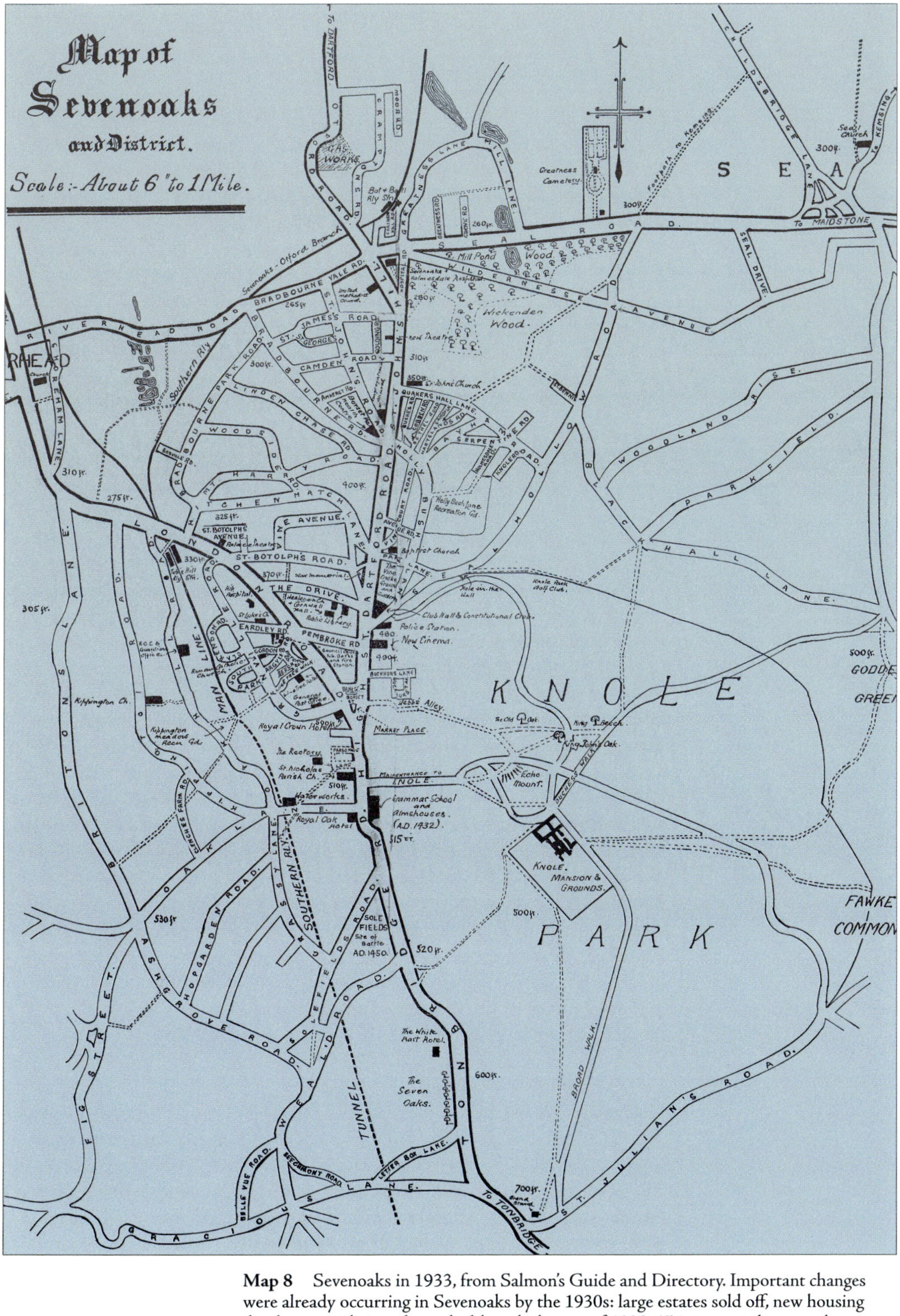

Map 8 Sevenoaks in 1933, from Salmon's Guide and Directory. Important changes were already occurring in Sevenoaks by the 1930s: large estates sold off, new housing developments being planned, although the war of 1939-45 interrupted many schemes.

Darent valley from 1878 onwards, but not without opposition, notably from Otford ratepayers.
Clarke & Stoyel (1975), 216-22

Manor House
A late Georgian square ragstone house on the Upper High Street, opposite ***St Nicholas*** and by the entrance to ***Knole Park***. It was built *c.*1800 as a dower house for ***Knole***, on the site of the medieval ***New Inn***. Manor House was acquired by ***Sevenoaks School*** in 1950.

manors
The manor was a territorial unit over which a local magnate had certain rights, administered through a manorial court applied to tenants on his own lands. The earliest known local manors developed from the estates of the Archbishop of Canterbury which included Otford, Halstead, Dunton (Green) and Preston in Shoreham. Parts of manors were gradually leased out so that by the 16th century they were effectively in private ownership, by which time the role of manorial courts had declined. The Kentish custom of gavelkind included partible inheritance in which all sons or, in their absence, all daughters, inherited equal shares, so that over time manors became divided among a number of people. Otford manor included Sevenoaks town centre. Two records mention a ***New Inn*** (Newyn): in *c.*1450 when it was leased to Richard Byrde for his lifetime, probably when ***Bourchier*** was Archbishop; and in 1517 when it was noted that it was in a prime position opposite ***St Nicholas***'s church. The New Inn was on the site of what became ***Manor House***. Further prime assets in Sevenoaks held of this manor are noted in a lease of 1530. A John Worseley was already lessee and yeoman of the Archbishop's slaughterhouse. In 1530 Worseley was leased some additional land which was said to be on 'the south of the town', and close to the highway between Sevenoaks and Tonbridge on one side and the Knole lands on the other. It was also close to a croft held by Master William Potkyn of London. The additional land was called Old Hawes, a term deriving from the word *hagae* indicating medieval plots within a town centre. These 'old' plots are likely to have been in the town centre in the ***Shambles*** area where the slaughterhouse was located. The plots were also next to some other land which Worseley also held, amounting to just over four acres. It can be envisaged that this land was used for the temporary grazing of animals destined for the meat market. Sevenoaks town centre and ***market*** was of limited size in the late medieval and early-modern period, but the large timber-framed house of the Archbishop's manorial bailiff (63-65 High Street) was located in the centre at the junction of the London and Dartford roads.
Du Boulay (1964), 37

maps
The earliest map of the Sevenoaks area is the Gough map *c.*1355 (named after an 18th-century antiquarian collector). Otford, then a significant ecclesiastical centre, is shown but not Sevenoaks. From the 16th century onwards estate plans were produced, e.g. ***Panthurst Park*** dated 1630. A new form of map in the 17th century was strip maps showing the course of major highways and ***turnpikes***, which were widely produced in the

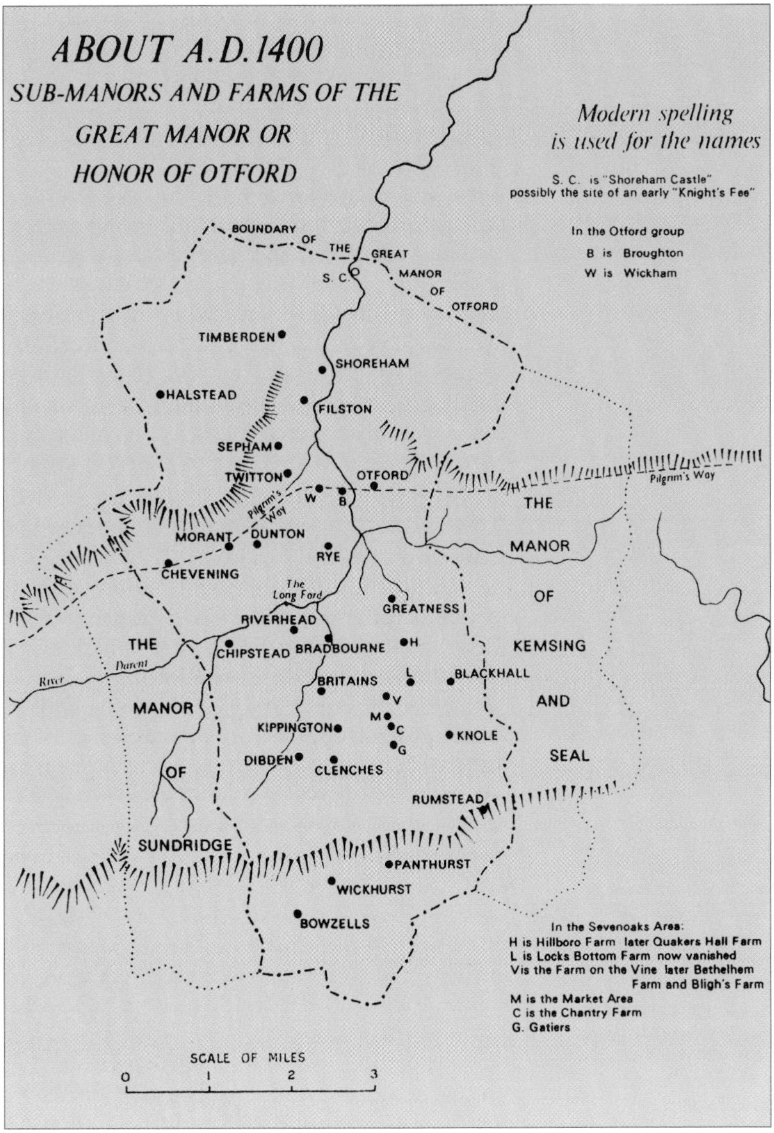

Map 9 The manors and parishes of the Sevenoaks area in late medieval times. Gordon Ward mapped 13 manors between the area of Greatness and Riverhill in the Elizabethan period.

following century. Philip Symonson's map of Kent, 1596, to the scale of half-an-inch to the mile, was a splendid piece of cartography, only superceded by the Andrews, Drury and Herbert map of Kent of 1769, at a scale of two inches to one mile, which showed 'Roads, Lanes, Churches, Towns, Villages' and 'every thing remarkable in the County'. ***Hasted***'s history of Kent contained local maps, including one of ***Codsheath*** – the Sevenoaks area. Kent, the county most vulnerable to French invasion, was officially mapped by William Faden for the Ordnance Survey (OS) in 1801. Local OS maps followed on a scale of one inch to the mile. Larger maps were created: 6 inches to the mile from 1840, and 25 inches to the mile by 1869. More detailed one inch OS maps were regularly revised to the 1970s and then abandoned for the current 1:5000 metric version. The map accompanying the ***tithe awards*** for Sevenoaks was surveyed and published in 1841. During the 19th and 20th centuries detailed plans and maps of parts of Sevenoaks often were drawn up when estates and lands were for sale and housing development.

Market House

The Old Market House in the High Street was built before 1554. It was pulled down and replaced in 1843 by the present Market House which was built in Regency style with an arcade below and a room above. The arcade was used for market stalls and the room above as a coroner's court and corn market. Its use declined when a new ***police*** station was built which included a court, and the corn merchants used the railway to go to the London Corn Exchange. In 1896, ***Henry Swaffield*** obtained the lease of the building from Lord Sackville and paid for alterations and repairs. He filled in the arcades and erected iron railings and gave the building to the Young Men's Christian Association for a reading room and social centre. The gift proved beyond the resources of the YMCA, and in 1901 the ***Sevenoaks Urban District Council*** took over the lease and used it for a public ***library***. After the new Library was built in the Drive in 1905, the Council sublet it to Kent Education Committee for use as a technical institute. When no longer required as a technical institute, it was converted in 1924 into a public lavatory, known locally as Tommy 'Skinner's Palace'. In the 1970s, the arcades were converted into shops.
Dunlop (1964); Richards (1901); Parkin (2009)

markets

The origin of Sevenoaks market goes back to the origin of the town itself. It seems to have sprung up naturally with no founding charter – later charters

48 The Old ***Market House***, pre-1554. This line drawing recreates what is known of the Old Market House as it probably was in 1554. It was octagonal, built of timber and tile on stone foundations. The upper part was used as a court room where some of the ***Wyatt*** rebels were tried and condemned to death.

49 Photograph of the market square *c.*1860s. The shape of this area of central Sevenoaks is largely unchanged. The man with the stove-pipe hat indicates the rough date when the image was taken. Cattle pens were erected outside the Chequers Inn. Although the cattle market ended more than 100 years ago, the ancient Saturday market still survives, trading on the site of the medieval market.

simply confirm existing rights. Sevenoaks lay on the ***droveway*** from Otford going down in to the Wealden forest at Penshurst where the pigs were pastured each year. This drove road gradually connected with other roads which were used by merchants bringing fish and imported goods from the coastal ports destined for London. The first market was probably held beside the ***St Nicholas*** chapel because markets were commonly held in churchyards in the Anglo-Saxon period. Later laws forbade the holding of markets in churchyards and it is thought the market moved from St Nicholas to the wide area of the High Street opposite Sevenoaks School. A wide area of an old high street is usually an indication of a market. From the 1280s documentary evidence shows that the market had moved northwards to where the road divides – to London in one direction and Dartford in the other. In between the two roads was a perfect market triangle, medieval markets were often triangular. It was a Saturday market and the stalls (seven feet by two feet) were set upon a grid system. Stalls were combined to form booths and eventually permanent shops. The ***Shambles*** area was where the butchers and fishmongers traded. Because of the market and the fact that the archbishops made ***Knole*** a palace, Sevenoaks became more important than Otford and Archbishop ***Bourchier*** is thought to have erected the first wooden ***market house*** in the 15th century. When Knole devolved to the Sackvilles, the rights to the market, such as fines and rents from shops, went to them. Much later, in the early

50 Cattle market by Tub's Hill station, 1990s. The animal market took place on Monday mornings. Sheep were brought in and penned. The auctioneer, with his clip board, stood on the wooden walkway above the pens. For many parents this was a poplar outing for young children who came to see the animals being sold. In the background, the Farmer's pub, another attraction after business was done.

19th century, the livestock market was split off from the general market and held once a month on a separate day (originally Tuesday, later Monday). At this time Sevenoaks was considered one of the great markets of Kent. It had survived when many other local markets, brought into being artificially with a charter as a money making exercise, had failed. By the latter part of the 19th century the local livestock market was failing, due to competition from Tonbridge and Ashford down the ***railway*** line. Sevenoaks' stock market ended in the early 20th century, but was revived by the Sevenoaks branch of the National Farmers' Union which re-opened the livestock market by Sevenoaks station in 1918, acquiring the rights from Knole. At the station site, as well as the Monday livestock market, a large general market was started on Wednesdays in 1965. When the market site was sold in 1999, the livestock market closed and the Wednesday market moved to the town centre.
Mitchell (1997); Parkin (2009)

Osborne Delano Marriott (1841-1913)
A medical doctor who practised in Sevenoaks from 1865. He trained in Glasgow where he was influenced by Lord Lister, who became a friend. Marriott moved to St John's Hill in 1867 and then later to the Old Vicarage in 1875, which remained his home until his death.

Catherine Martin (d.1861)
Catherine Elizabeth Martin is one of the few 'ordinary' women of 19th-century Sevenoaks to have a published biography. The Martins were members of the Wesleyan chapel. Catherine is remembered because her brother wrote a posthumous biography of her life which emphasised her devout Christian faith, her deep care for her neighbours and her 'holy zeal for the salvation of souls'. She died giving birth to her seventh child.
Field (1862)

Masonic lodges
Founded in Sevenoaks in the 19th century, in 1895 local Freemasons regularly met in St Nicholas parish hall in the High Street. Later the Masons moved into a former chapel in ***St John's Hill***.

Maywood

A large house in Bradbourne Road designed by ***Thomas Jackson*** for ***James German*** and built in 1874 on a five-acre site. The house was lived in by Lady Fanny Finch-Hatton in the early 20th century, when it was known as Hatton House. Just before 1914 it was bought by Percy Fawcett, a City solicitor, and he lived there with his family until house and site were compulsorily purchased in 1946 for use as a secondary school. New buildings to the north, and the house, became ***Hatton Girls School*** until 1976 when the School moved to a new location on Bradbourne Vale Road and its place taken by Sevenoaks Primary School, the house becoming the Sevenoaks adult education centre.

51 Maywood house in the 1930s. 'Maywood' commanded a grand view north over the ***Vale of Holmesdale*** and the ***North Downs***. This photograph, with the pony-drawn grass mower, was taken in the inter-war years, when the house was still a private home. The lawn, with its flower beds, is now a football pitch.

Members of Parliament

The Sevenoaks constituency was formed from the old West Kent constituency in 1885. The area and the population of the constituency have changed over the years. Sevenoaks has been represented by ***Conservatives***, except in 1923-24 when Ronald Williams (1890-1971) for the ***Liberals*** won the seat in a straight fight from the Tories by 609 votes. In a by-election in 1902 a major issue was the Tory Education Bill which was strongly opposed by many nonconformists; the Liberals failed to gain the seat but they severely dented the Tory vote.

Sevenoaks MPs

Sir *Charles Henry Mills*	1868-85
Charles Mills	1885-92
Henry William Forster	1892-1918
Sir *Thomas Jewell Bennett*	1918-23
Ronald Williams	1923
Herbert Styles	1924-29
Sir *Hilton Young*	1929-35
Sir *Charles Ponsonby*	1935-50
Sir *John Rodgers*	1950-79
Mark Wolfson	1979-97
Michael Fallon	1997-

men's organisations

Many of the clubs and organisations in Sevenoaks before the mid-20th century catered only for men. A few continue. Sevenoaks Round Table was founded in 1952 with 16 members. For 60 years the social club was a vibrant centre for men and helped the local community through fundraising efforts. The Sevenoaks Lions, a service organisation which raises money for charity, was formed in 1970. The Probus Club of Sevenoaks was set up in 1972 to provide a regular meeting point for retired professional and business men. The first Annual General Meeting and lunch was held in Blighs Hotel in January 1973. Sevenoaks Rotary Club belongs to the world-wide Rotary organisation founded in 1905 by Paul Harris, a lawyer, who wished to capture in a professional club the same friendly spirit he had felt in the small towns of his youth. Rotary's popularity spread, and by 1921 clubs had been formed worldwide. The Sevenoaks club was formed in 1933 and since then more than 70 well-known local businessmen have been the club's president. An evening club, Sevenoaks Amherst, was formed in the 1970s. TocH was an inter-denominational Christian organisation founded by the Revd Philip ('Tubby') Clayton in 1919, based on his experiences of running a wartime soldiers' club. A Sevenoaks branch was founded in 1928.

Merlewood

A large house in ***Mount Harry Road***, demolished in the 1960s, originally the home of ***Samuel Bevington***. Merlewood had a lodge (which remains) and a large garden, much of it woodland. During the ***First World War*** it was used by the Army. It was later taken over by ***Sevenoaks Urban District Council***, demolished and became the site of houses that form Merlewood Close.

Methodism

Methodism developed from the Christian evangelical revival in the 18th century, partly inspired by the preaching of John Wesley, a minister in the established church who visited Sevenoaks on 11 occasions between 1753-77. At Wesley's death in 1791 there were more than 72,000 members of Methodist societies and several hundred thousand adherents. In the early 19th century Methodists, although divided into Wesleyan Methodists and other 'connexions', formed new and large nonconformist denominations. Reunion came about in 1932. The first local meeting place of the Methodist Society was the home of Mrs Amy George, Hills Yard, ***Redmans Place***, in 1753. When members outgrew the house, they moved to a rented upstairs room in the 'Granary' in Coffee House Yard, London Road. In 1774 a chapel was built in Hills Yard. This remained in use until a new Wesleyan Methodist chapel, designed by W.W. Pocock, was built between Bank Street and Dorset Street in 1853 at a cost of £900. This first chapel was used as a store and then demolished in the 1960s. The Bank Street chapel served as the meeting place until 1904, a Sunday school building being added in 1862. In March 1904 the Methodists moved to their present building in The Drive. The building was largely financed by ***Henry Swaffield***, as were also the neighbouring ***Cornwall Hall*** and the Retreat ***almshouses***. Built of Kent ***ragstone*** with Bath stone dressings, unusually for a Methodist church it has a prominent spire. The interior has a gallery, granite pillars and a modern pipe organ. In 2010 a new glass vestibule was added to the front of the building.

Judd (1932); Killingray (2004)

52 Sevenoaks Methodist church. This photograph was taken just after the building was completed in 1904. It stands at the top of The Drive, a road newly made on the old ***St Botolph's estate***. Although early Methodist churches and chapels were fairly simple, nonconformists later adopted the style of the Gothic revival.

Edward Meyerstein (1863-1942)

London stockbroker and philanthropist. Meyerstein was born in Kent. He made his money dealing in South African gold. From 1912 until his death he lived at ***Morants Court***, north of Sevenoaks. In the 1920s Meyerstein offered £100,000 and 15 acres of ***Montreal Park*** for a new ***hospital***, but subscribers to the hospital rejected this generous offer, saying the money 'was "tainted" having been made in the City'. Rebuffed in Sevenoaks, Meyerstein gave money to hospitals in London and elsewhere in west Kent, particularly those catering for the needs of children. He was knighted in 1938, and also served as a High Sheriff of Kent.

Edward Miall (1808-81)

Congregational minister, journalist and politician. Miall was born in Portsmouth, served a church in Leicester from 1832-40, and then moved to London where he founded and edited *The Nonconformist*, a weekly newspaper. Three years later he formed what became known as the Liberation Society which campaigned for religious liberty and the disestablishment of the Church of England. Miall supported a range of

radical and nonconformist causes, eventually being elected to Parliament for Rochdale and later for Bradford. In the late 1870s Miall came to live in Granville Road, Sevenoaks, where he died.
ODNB (2004)

Middle Classes Union
A nationwide anti-socialist organisation formed in 1919 by a number of Conservatives, including MPs,'to withstand the rapacity of the manual worker and the profiteer'. The MCU was in part a reaction to the Representation of the People Act of 1918, which gave all working-class men the vote, and raised fears that ratepayers would bear the costs of post-war social welfare and educational reforms. In the Sevenoaks local elections in March 1920 the MCU won three seats (one held by ***Gordon Ward*** until 1922), a major issue being opposition to local government expenditure on a new road by the ***war memorial*** on ***The Vine***.

Militia Act 1757
The Militia Act created a more professional military reserve for home defence in the counties of England and Wales. Effectively a territorial army, men were selected to serve by ballot and they could be billeted in private houses. Resistance to the Act occurred in various towns across the country. In Sevenoaks a mob assaulted the Justices and demanded the lists of men to be balloted. Believing that the Rev. ***Thomas Curteis***, also a Justice, had a copy of the list they besieged ***St Nicholas Rectory*** and broke the windows. Curteis had fled to ***Knole*** for safety. The mob attacked Knole, but was repulsed by armed men from within the great house. Some 20 rioters were arrested. The ringleaders were heavily fined and imprisoned, most others received small fines. A West Kent Militia was embodied in 1778, expanded during the Napoleonic wars, and reconstituted as ***volunteers*** in 1859 when war with France threatened.

Mill Pond Wood
Nine acres of traditional woodland on a prominent sandy ridge between Seal Road (A25) and Hillingdon Avenue, close to Pinewood Avenue. The ***Sevenoaks Urban District Council*** purchased the land to be used as a public open space. The Wood is the site of a prehistoric funerary tumulus or barrow dated to 2400-1500 BC, partially excavated in the 1890s by Lewis Abbott who discovered it to be over 30 yards in diameter with an outer ditch three yards wide surviving below ground. In the centre he found traces of a cremation burial. In the make-up of the barrow, and in the surrounding area, Abbott found hundreds of worked flints from the Mesolithic period (8000-4000 BC) showing that the barrow had been constructed on a much older site. It is a scheduled monument.

Rear Admiral Henry M. Miller (1830-1902)
Miller was born in Exeter and entered the Royal Navy in 1851, serving in the Baltic during the war with Russia. Promoted to captain in 1870, he retired as a Rear-Admiral in 1887, having married the year before. Miller came to live in Sevenoaks and was elected to the new ***Sevenoaks Urban District Council***, serving as its first chairman from 1894-1900.

Charles Henry Mills (1830-98)
A member of a wealthy banking family, and a partner in Glyn Mills & Co, Mills was Conservative MP for West Kent from 1868-85. He married a daughter of the Earl of Harewood. Mills was knighted in 1872 and raised to the peerage in 1886 as Lord ***Hillingdon***. In that year he bought the ***Wildernesse*** estate from the ***Camdens***, land which straddled Sevenoaks and Seal. At his death Mills's estate was valued at £1.4 million. His eldest son Charles William Mills (1855-1919), also a partner in Glyn Mills, Conservative MP for Sevenoaks from 1885-92, succeeded to the title. The family were generous benefactors to the Sevenoaks and Holmesdale Cottage ***Hospital*** in the 1870s. The 3rd Lord Hillingdon sold the Wildernesse estate in 1925.
ODNB (2004)

53 *Montreal House.* An early 19th-century print of the great house of the Amhersts. The house was built on the hilltop above the fish ponds, using stone from the recently demolished ***Brook Place***. Built in a Palladian style with a main house of two storeys, flanked by single-storey wings on either side, it had seven large reception rooms, 27 bedrooms and four bathrooms.

Montreal House, park and estate
When ***Jeffrey Amherst*** returned in triumph from North America in 1764, he set about replacing his old family house, ***Brook Place***, with a grander mansion which he called Montreal House after his achievements in Canada. Amherst acquired more land to make a park, stretching from the back of the Harvester pub to ***Brittains Farm***, along Worships Hill to ***Bessels Green***, and along Coldharbour Lane to ***Salters Heath***. Amherst died childless and the estate was inherited by his nephew, William Pitt Amherst (1773-1857), 1st Earl Amherst, who significantly enlarged it by buying more land. His son, also William Pitt Amherst (1805-66), the 2nd

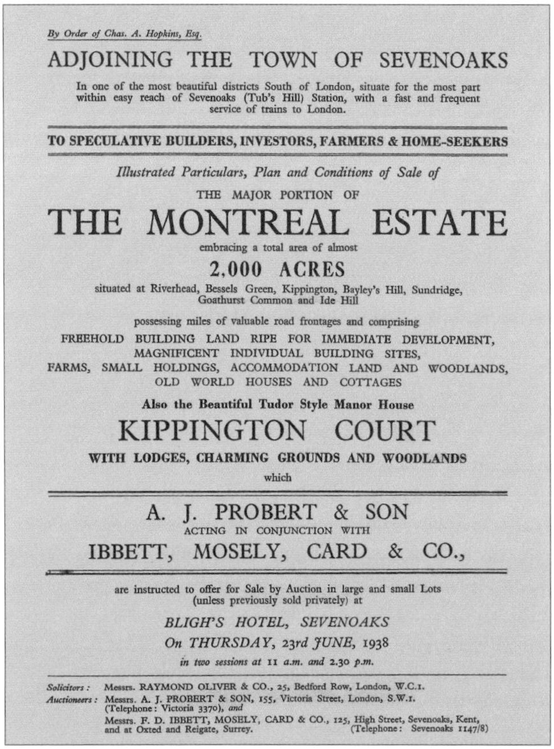
By Order of Chas. A. Hopkins, Esq.

ADJOINING THE TOWN OF SEVENOAKS

In one of the most beautiful districts South of London, situate for the most part within easy reach of Sevenoaks (Tub's Hill) Station, with a fast and frequent service of trains to London.

TO SPECULATIVE BUILDERS, INVESTORS, FARMERS & HOME-SEEKERS

Illustrated Particulars, Plan and Conditions of Sale of

THE MAJOR PORTION OF

THE MONTREAL ESTATE

embracing a total area of almost

2,000 ACRES

situated at Riverhead, Bessels Green, Kippington, Bayley's Hill, Sundridge, Goathurst Common and Ide Hill

possessing miles of valuable road frontages and comprising

FREEHOLD BUILDING LAND RIPE FOR IMMEDIATE DEVELOPMENT, MAGNIFICENT INDIVIDUAL BUILDING SITES, FARMS, SMALL HOLDINGS, ACCOMMODATION LAND AND WOODLANDS, OLD WORLD HOUSES AND COTTAGES

Also the Beautiful Tudor Style Manor House

KIPPINGTON COURT

WITH LODGES, CHARMING GROUNDS AND WOODLANDS

which

A. J. PROBERT & SON

ACTING IN CONJUNCTION WITH

IBBETT, MOSELY, CARD & CO.,

are instructed to offer for Sale by Auction in large and small Lots (unless previously sold privately) at

BLIGH'S HOTEL, SEVENOAKS

On THURSDAY, 23rd JUNE, 1938

in two sessions at 11 *a.m. and* 2.30 *p.m.*

Solicitors: Messrs. RAYMOND OLIVER & CO., 25, Bedford Row, London, W.C.1.

Auctioneers: Messrs. A. J. PROBERT & SON, 155, Victoria Street, London, S.W.1. (Telephone: Victoria 3370), *and*
Messrs. F. D. IBBETT, MOSELY, CARD & CO., 125, High Street, Sevenoaks, Kent, and at Oxted and Reigate, Surrey. (Telephone: Sevenoaks 1147/8)

54 A handbill for the auction of the Montreal estate, 1938. The auction catalogue described Montreal House and part of the estates as freehold building land ripe for development. It included land at ***Riverhead, Bessels Green, Kippington***, Bayleys Hill, Sundridge, Goathurst Common, Ide Hill as well as ***Kippington Court***. Earlier Montreal Road had been tarmaced (1931). In 1938 Lyndhurst Drive was laid out, Marlborough Crescent 18 years later.

Earl, bought yet more land. By 1910, when Hugh Amherst, the 4th Earl (d. 1927), inherited the estate it was running into financial difficulties, and he sold some of the land to raise cash.
The first auction was held in October 1920, at Cornwall Hall. The aim was to sell 485 acres of 'The outlying portions of the Montreal Estate', principally located in Ide Hill. Many of the lots did not reach their reserve price and were withdrawn. At the next auction in April 1924, 800 acres of the estate were put up for sale, but only 16 out of the 48 lots were sold. In 1926, ***Julius Runge*** bought 2,650 acres, the bulk of the remainder of Montreal estate, in order to safeguard it from development. He died in 1935 and his heirs auctioned the estate the next year. The auction included the 194 acres of Montreal Park including the house and a chain of seven lakes. The land was sold to a syndicate headed by a property speculator, Bernard Thorpe. Thorpe gained planning permission to develop 160 acres and sold it on to William Fasey and his company Salway Hill Estates. Montreal House was demolished. In 1937 Thorpe and his associates bought another 2,306 acres of the Montreal estate, which they sold on to Charles Hopkins, a London hotelier. Hopkins proceeded to auction 2,000 acres he had purchased. Prior to the 1938 auction, 314 acres between Riverhill and Riverhead, was sold to T.E. Nash, a builder from St Albans. He intended to develop land between Brittains Lane and Back Lane into a new urban community with high density housing, the Nash Development. When he was refused planning permission due to ***Green Belt*** policies, he built the houses on Redlands Road, Croft Way, Downs View and much of the housing on Brittains Lane. All that now remains of the old Montreal estate is the ***ice house***, the vandalised summer house on Salter's Heath, the octagonal old Lodge House at the entrance to Montreal estate in Lyndhurst Drive and the ***Amherst Obelisk***.
Nunnerley (2000)

Morants Court
First recorded in a land grant of 1293, Morants Court became an estate of over 600 acres by 1594. The house was owned by Price of Westerham in the 18th century, then by the Tonge family throughout the 19th century. ***Edward Meyerstein*** bought it in 1912. The earliest part of the house is early 15th century, with many additions, a large extension being added by Meyerstein. After his death it passed to various owners, part of the land being lost to motorway development in the late 1970s.

John Morton (c.1425-1500)
Morton, Archbishop of Canterbury, 1486-1500, and a cardinal from 1493, came from a modest Dorset gentry family. He studied at Oxford, entered

royal service, but survived the political turmoil of the late 15th century to succeed ***Bourchier*** at Canterbury and become Henry Tudor's chancellor. As Archbishop he spent significant sums on ***Knole***, probably being responsible for extending the accommodation areas on the south side in the 1480s. He died there of the plague in 1500.

motor vehicles

The earliest mechanical vehicles on local roads were steam-driven haulage engines which, although rapidly declining in number, remained in use until the 1940s. The development of the motor vehicle transformed almost every aspect of people's lives, especially as personal car ownership increased after 1960. The earliest cars and lorries were driven either by electric battery or an internal combustion engine; after 1908 the latter gained dominance. The first cars in Sevenoaks appeared in the 1890s, being restricted to two mph. within the town and four without. Carriage makers with engineering skills built motor cars for sale, for example George Humphrey & Co, at 166 High Street, in 1908 advertised as 'automobile engineer & coach builder', 'bodies built, painted, trimmed, etc', a 'Michelin tyre depot', where 'dissolved acetylene & sioca cylinders' could be exchanged. At the same time Hely & Co., on the London Road, sold petrol (to be taken away in a can) and tyres. The first motor bus services began in 1913. With the growth in motor and bicycle traffic, dirt roads were given tar macadam surfaces, a process that began in the town and on main roads, gradually being extended to most streets and lanes by the 1930s. Early petrol-driven vehicles carried spare

55 Motor charabanc outing in the 1920s. For many years the major bus hire company in the town was W. Davis and Sons of ***St John's Hill***. In the inter-war years and after the war until the early 1960s, it was common for local firms, institutions, and Sunday schools to hire a coach for a summer outing to the seaside or for a day out to a popular tourist place. Coach hire continued in the age of mass motor car ownership, for educational and social occasions, and also for elderly people. The baby is Elsie Marnock, who died in 2011.

fuel, but from 1920 garages with pumps served motorists. By then some houses were also being built with garages for cars, one of the first being the ***Baillie Scott*** 'Seal Hollow House' in Quaker Close. The increase in road traffic through the town led to demands for a ***Sevenoaks by-pass***, built in 1968-70. In the last four decades of the 20th century the car influenced the town and the patterns of many people's lives: parking places, wider roads, traffic lights and directional signs, the closure of the Westerham ***railway***, the journey to work and school, and domestic shopping at out-of-town shopping centres on the Otford Road and at Dunton Green.

motorways
The M25 from Sundridge to Westerham was built in 1976-79, following part of the course of the former railway line. Work on the Swanley to Sevenoaks part of the London orbital motorway was delayed due to opposition from the Darenth and North Downs Action Group (DANDAG), with more than 1,000 members, which argued for a different route that would protect the North Downs. The motorway was completed in 1982, linking up with the M26 from Wrotham to Sevenoaks constructed 1974-80.

Mount Harry Road
Mount Harry Road lies within what was once the ***Bradbourne estate***. The area was bought by Henry Hughes in 1840, who, it is suggested, named one of the wooded hills, where he built a summer house, after his son Harry. Change came with the ***railway*** when it became possible for people to travel to work in London. The demand for large family homes on the slopes surrounding the station led to the development of Mount Harry Road. The large red-brick houses surrounded by extensive gardens remained largely unchanged until the ***Second World War*** when some were used to house evacuees and to billet soldiers. After the war redevelopment resulted in impracticable buildings such as ***Merlewood*** being demolished and the building of smaller houses and some new roads. This continued into the 21st century with the last of the Victorian houses, at the very bottom of the hill, being redeveloped.

music
Various kinds of music have been performed in Sevenoaks over the centuries. In the 1840s the Sevenoaks Choral Society performed at the Crown Hotel with the help of professional musicians from London. Church music was also popular with congregational hymn singing and choirs leading services. The Sevenoaks Philharmonic Society had it origins in 1897 when Wilfred A. Taylor (d. 1922) founded the St John's Choral Society. Singers and instrumentalists separated during the war years and a Sevenoaks and District Orchestral Society was formed in 1944. Twelve years later members of the Orchestra and singers from the Choral Society formed the Sevenoaks Philharmonic Society Choir, which often cooperated with the Sevenoaks Symphony Orchestra. The Sevenoaks Music Club was formed by Ethel Breething in 1933, the first concert being performed in the ***Cornwall Hall***. The outbreak of war interrupted the Club's activities until 1943 when three concerts, one by Peter Pears and Benjamin Britten, were put on in ***Walthamstow Hall School***. These were a huge success and the

Club was re-launched. After this, regular concerts were held in the School dining room until the Cornwall Hall became available again for concerts. In 1958 a Silver Jubilee Concert was given by Joan Sutherland. Informal concerts were a regular feature of the Club, held in members' houses, school halls, and other venues. Music was provided by members and ranged from solo to performances of major works. From the outset the organisers tried to engage promising young artists before they became too expensive. As a result of this the Club accumulated an impressive list of eminent musicians who have visited over the years. Other choral groups in the town include Temenos (founded 1998) and the Cantate Choir (2002).

Small orchestras existed in the town in the 19th century. The Sevenoaks Symphony Orchestra was founded in 1946, bringing together local musicians, with a professional conductor and leader. The Orchestra, set up as a charity, aimed to make live orchestral music available locally. Three subscription concerts were put on each year, focusing on 19th- and 20th-century masterpieces thought attractive and enjoyable for audiences while at the same time being interesting and challenging for Orchestra members. The Orchestra offered an annual family concert, performed bi-annually with the Sevenoaks Philharmonic Society, and also put on concerts of lighter classics at Hever Castle in aid of charity. The Lydian Orchestra was founded in 1976 by June Clements (d. 1996) to give local talented young musicians the chance to play together, many of whom have gone on to professional careers. The Orchestra celebrated its 30th anniversary with a Paris tour. The Three Arts Festival, founded in 1951, brought together many musicians in the area.

N

National Association of Decorative and Fine Arts Societies
Founded in 1968, NADFAS set out to promote the advancement of arts education and appreciation and the preservation of Britain's artistic heritage. These aims were achieved through lectures on the fine and decorative arts, study days, visits and tours, the giving of grants, and volunteer activities such as Church Recorders, Heritage Volunteers and Young Arts. The first Society in Sevenoaks was started in 1972 by Rosemary Tammadge, and evening meetings were held at Sevenoaks School. In 1986 a second Society, that met in the afternoons, was started by Judith Hammer.

Vincent New (1906-94)
The artist and engraver Vincent New started his career in Otford where his father had bought a house and land on Pilgrims Way. Inspired by the scenery, he sketched and painted the Darent Valley and its villages. In the 1930s, New produced a series of drawings of the area for the ***Sevenoaks Chronicle***. During the ***Second World War*** he served in Naval Intelligence as a draughtsman, his career for the next 24 years, during which time he continued to work freelance. In 1993 Vincent New donated his drawings, paintings and Albion printing press to Sevenoaks ***Library*** and ***Museum***.

New Beacon School
The New Beacon emerged from the Beacon school in St John's, moving in 1900 to a new site on Brittains Lane. The poet and novelist Siegfried Sassoon was a former pupil.
Barty-King (2000)

New Inn
In 1481 the New Inn (Newyn) stood on the site of the ***Manor House***. The building was included in the land and property bought by ***Thomas Bourchier*** that year. The inn had a garden and a croft (enclosure) called Dambelesfeld which could be sub-let by the lessee at a profit. The leases indicate that the inn and its lands were a desirable asset which were usually granted as a favour to one of the Archbishop's 'servants', or household member: in 1517 this was William Cokk, and previously it had been John Grebby. Inns of this period, typically sited on main roads, provided a drinking room on the ground floor where beer and sometimes wine were consumed and business deals, such as the arranging of credit or the carriage of goods, were organised. The building probably ceased to be an inn before the end of the 18th century.

newspapers
The first English newspapers were published in the 17th century. One hundred years later there were two Kentish newspapers and a growing number of London papers, including *The Times*, which were read by a few people in Sevenoaks. Early newspapers were relatively expensive; paper was costly and until 1861 newsprint was taxed, partly to prevent the spread of 'seditious' ideas. Sevenoaks first newspaper was the *Sevenoaks Advertiser*, first published in May 1840. The four-page miscellany of literature and local affairs sold for one penny; 750 copies were printed each month by James Payne, a stationer. The newspaper carried advertisments for tenders for flour and bread for the ***workhouse***, the sale of a fire engine with 80 foot of hose for £10, and a notice from Mr Bligh of the ***Rose and Crown*** that he had superior horses, ponies and carriages for hire, and also a quiet pony for a lady to ride. The last edition was in December 1843. Other short-lived local newspapers were published in the mid-19th century: the *Sevenoaks Gazette*, 1855, *Sevenoaks Telegraph*, 1886-1900, the *Sevenoaks Express*, which was Conservative, 1863-1902, the *Sevenoaks Free Press*, 1874-79, the *Sevenoaks Herald*, also Conservative, established in 1877. Some Sevenoaks news was also reported in newspapers published in neighbouring towns.

Unlike other local newspapers, the *Sevenoaks Chronicle* survived. Founded in February 1881 by William Wicking, whose printing presses were in the old ***Post Office Yard***, it was an eight-page newspaper that cost one penny, with advertisements on the front page. The editorial offices were at 66 High Street (now Horncastle's shop) and remained there until moving to 54 High Street. In the first issue the editor declared that 'we shall exert ourselves for the benefit of the ratepayers and inhabitants, endeavouring to restrain extravagant expenditure'; its politics were 'independent Conservative'. The *Chronicle* became part of the Kent and Sussex Courier Group in 1922 and was printed at Tunbridge Wells. With the exception of two brief printing strikes it has appeared regularly ever since. By then the Courier Group (including the *Sevenoaks Chronicle*) had been taken over by Northcliffe Newpapers (publishers of many daily and regional newspapers). New offices for the *Chronicle* were opened in conjunction with the Waitrose development in 1983.

The *Sevenoaks News* was a weekly newspaper founded on Jubilee Day 1936 by Donald Hooper, formerly the manager of the local branch of the *Kent Messenger*. At the time it was the only newspaper printed in Sevenoaks. Hooper acquired the former ***Lime Tree Hotel*** in Lime Tree Walk, bought a semi-flatbed press and launched the newspaper in opposition to the *Kent Messenger* and *Sevenoaks Chronicle*. The *News* quickly built up a healthy circulation and survived the bombing of the printing works in 1940. Printing moved briefly to Tonbridge until the works were restored and an editorial office established at 49 London Road. Upon Hooper's death the newspaper was taken over by the Courier Group and became a mid-week publication alongside the *Sevenoaks Chronicle* under the combined editorship of Bob Ogley. The last edition appeared in 1981.

North Downs
The range of chalk hills to the north of Sevenoaks which run from east to west into Surrey. The highest point locally is west of Knockholt at 760 feet. The Downs have dry valleys and are wooded. The relatively poor soils have been mainly used for grazing, although in both World Wars certain areas were ploughed to grow crops.
Brandon (2005); Tuson (2007)

William Brook Northey (b.1807)
Northey lived at ***Vine Lodge*** in the 1850s with his wife and two daughters. He was responsible for reconstituting the Vine Cricket Club in 1848 after it had been dormant for 17 years. He also helped establish the Sevenoaks ***Volunteer*** Rifle Corps in 1859.

Nouaille family
Peter Gabriel Nouaille II was born in 1724 to a second generation French Huguenot family living in Spitalfields, London. His father, Peter I, was a successful silk trader and Peter II followed in his footsteps. His son, Peter III, married Elizabeth Delamare, also of a Huguenot family, in 1760. She inherited her father's wealth, and a mill at ***Greatness*** from her Uncle Abraham. Peter III developed the Greatness site as a silk mill, built cottages for his mill workers and Greatness House for his family. He also owned further land and property including St John's Lodge, which later became the family home, and the over 400 acres of Greatness Farm. Peter III died in 1809 at Greatness aged 86, but was buried at Christ Church in Spitalfields where his great-grandfather first arrived as a refugee from France and set up the family silk business. Peter IV (1776-1845) married Anne ***Woodgate*** in 1801. They had five children, none of whom married. Peter V, last of the male line, continued the family tradition of supporting the local community and was on the committee that brought the first ***railway*** to ***Bat and Ball***. His sister Annie was a generous benefactor of ***St John's School*** and Church. She used to travel up to Sevenoaks in a low trap pulled by two ponies and was reputed, on occasion, to have been trundled up to the town in a wheelbarrow by her gardener. Peter V died

in 1864 but Annie lived to the age of 89, dying in 1897 – the last of the family.

nurseries/market gardens
Market gardening was one of the small-scale industries in Sevenoaks in the 19th and early 20th centuries. William Seale is listed in the 1857 directory as 'nursery and seedsman, the Vine'. R. Neal & Sons had a nursery on ***St John's Hill*** in the 1920s, land sold for housing and the future Wickenden Road area. Turner's Nursery, on Weald Road, was established on land originally owned by the Sackvilles. The title was transferred to William Spurrell in 1935 for the purposes of a plant nursery and to erect a house for the caretaker of the business. It was active until the 1970s, with a retail garden shop composed of elderly greenhouses overlooking the ***Vine***. When the business was sold houses were built at Turner's Garden, and new apartments on the site of the old shop.

O

Oak End
This grade II listed house in the Upper High Street is thought to date from the 14th century, part of ***Sevenoaks Park*** estate. Substantial Georgian additions to the house were made in the mid-18th century.

Oak Lane
An old road leading west off the Upper High Street. The area at the bottom of the hill was known as Flow Fields; it often flooded in winter and was used for skating.

Rowland Oakeley (1899-2001)
Oakeley was the footpaths' warden for the ***Sevenoaks Society*** who walked miles every week over the footpaths with his Yorkshire terrier. He instituted and led bi-monthly country walks. In 1973, the ***Sevenoaks Society*** began publishing his walks; eventually there were four books, with a total of 44 walks. Oakeley worked closely with the District Council's Footpath Warden to create a permanent record of the area's 750 or so paths, and was largely responsible for persuading Kent County Council to set aside funds for building footpath bridges; some 40 were built in our area.

Odd Fellows Hall
The Odd Fellows, a friendly society founded in 1810, offered health insurance and was a burial club. Soon after, a Sevenoaks branch opened with a building in Coffee House Yard, also known as the Assembly Rooms. In 1910 the Odd Fellows celebrated their centenary with a concert at the Club Hall with Lord Sackville in the chair. Tickets were six pence.

Charles Ogle (1851-1878)
Architect and war correspondent. Ogle was the son of John Ogle who ran a boarding school at St Clere and then from the early 1880s in Sevenoaks. Charles studied at his father's school, then trained to be an architect. In

1877, while in the Balkans, he became a temporary correspondent for *The Times*, reporting on the wars with the Turks. During the Greek-Turkish war he was murdered by Turkish irregular troops at Makrinitsa in Thessaly. Popular sentiment in Greece claimed Ogle as a 'martyr to the cause of Greece and humanity'. A British-Turkish commission of enquiry concluded that Ogle had met his death 'due to his own imprudence'. This did not satisfy John Ogle, or Liberal parliamentarians, and there was a popular demand in Britain, including a petition from Sevenoaks, for a further enquiry. This reported in 1882 but was inconclusive. John Ogle became a philhellene and an active member of the Greek Committee which campaigned for an enlarged Greece. In Thessaly Charles Ogle is regarded as a hero. The town of Volos has an Ogle street, and Ogle's grave and memorial in Makrinitza is maintained and annually decorated.

Old Harpsichord Factory
A building at the top of Bradbourne Road, originally a bakery, but used from 1957 by John Feldberg (d. 1960) and his widow Ann until 1980 as a workshop to make harpsichords. Altogether 272 instruments were made and sold and used by distinguished performers. Since the works closed the building has been a commercial office.

56 ***Old Post Office.*** The old post office in the Upper High Street has been the subject of frequent drawings, paintings and photographs. This drawing is by the local artist ***Vincent New***. The building is timber-framed with tile hung walls and a brick tile roof. For many years it was the main 'tuck' shop for boys from ***Sevenoaks School***, who covered the walls and ceilings with their signatures.

Old Post Office
This is in the Upper High Street and was one of the few surviving sub-Post Offices in the town. Originally a 16th-century inn called the 'Three Cats', it was divided into the Old Post Office and private houses. The ***Frith*** family lived there in 1520.

Otford Palace
The Archbishop of Canterbury *c*.820 had a manor house at Otford. His successors expanded it to become one of the largest in Kent. By the 13th century, Otford Palace was the centre of a vast bailiwick with lands stretching deep into the Wealden forest. The original Saxon timbered manor house was replaced by a moated palace built of local ragstone. In *c*.1514 Archbishop ***William Warham*** rebuilt the palace with Tudor brick to a scale unprecedented in England. The vast size served to spur an envious Cardinal Wolsey to build Hampton Court as a rival to the magnificence of Otford Palace. King Henry VIII also laid envious eyes upon the building, and Warham's successor at Canterbury, ***Thomas Cranmer***, reluctantly handed the palace over to his royal master. When Queen Elizabeth inherited the estate she was unwilling to spend the vast sums necessary for its upkeep. The poorly guarded palace had the lead stripped from its roof, and the subsequent damp rotted its timbers. Within a few decades the abandoned building was being pillaged for its brick and ragstone. By 1600 the palace was

57 Outram's shop in the London Road. In 1880 James Outram (d.1927) opened a saddler's business in the ***Bishops House*** building. The shop, which later expanded into sports and travel goods, traded until 2001, when it was sold and turned into a fish restaurant.

derelict. All that remains is the ruined north-west tower.
Shelton (2003)

Outram's shop in the London Road
In 1880 James Outram (d.1927) opened a saddlers business in the ***Bishops House.*** building. The shop, which later expanded into sports and travel goods, traded until 2001, when it was sold and turned into a fish restaurant.

Henry Owen (b.1852)
Daniel Grover had seen the possibilities for development in the ***Hartsland*** area in the 1840s. After his death his properties were put up for sale and Henry Owen bought his builder's premises, residence and freehold corner plot of building land at the top of ***St John's*** Hill for £1,880 at auction in 1881. He and his family moved into the house, called 'The Limes' and Henry Owen took over the builder's yard, where Henry Owen advertised as 'Sevenoaks Steam Joinery Work. Contractor, slate & timber merchant. Dealer in building materials'. The houses

he built were large ragstone semi-detached buildings, suitable for the middle-class residents of the time. His advertisements for houses for rent in the ***Bayham Road*** area appeared frequently in the *Sevenoaks Chronicle* in the early 1880s.

Nathaniel Owen (1627 -1705)
Owen was a ***Quaker*** who lived in the house now known as Quaker's Hall Cottage. He was a prosperous wool and linen merchant and minted his own ***tokens***. Owen was heavily fined for refusing to bear arms and imprisoned in 1661 and again in 1669. Released in 1672, he was fined and his warehouse of linen goods impounded for holding a Quaker meeting at his house in 1675.

Robert Owen (1771-1858)
Owen was born in Wales. He became a successful cotton manufacturer renowned for his enlightened ideas and the model working conditions at his New Lanark mill on Clydeside. In his *A New View of Society* (1814-18), Owen advanced utopian socialist ideas, arguing that environment could transform character and that co-operative planned villages helped to promote social progress. Owen was one of the 'founders of British socialism'. From 1852 he lived at ***Sevenoaks Park*** with his secretary.

P

Packhorse Road, Bessels Green
In October 1934, parkland of 23 acres surrounding ***Chipstead Park*** estate was sold at auction in one lot for £9,750. London and Home Counties Property Investment Ltd built 32 houses in Packhorse Road.

Samuel Palmer (1805-1881)
Palmer lived and painted in the Sevenoaks area for much of his early life, living in Shoreham in the 1820s to 1840s with the artist John Linnell, his mentor and father-in-law, and other family and friends. His love of the Kent landscape, and especially the pastoral scenes in the ***Weald*** and ***Underriver***, led to many sketches and watercolours of the district. His sensitive lines and soft tones captured the rolling hills, verdant woods and calm rural scenes of a pre-industrial world. Many of his paintings of the Underriver area have been located by both a local historian and an artist, for example, *The Golden Valley* (*c*.1833-4) shows the bright golden landscape of the harvest season and was probably painted from the hills above the village.
Barton and Tong (1995)

Panthurst Park
The Park occupied the south flank of the sandstone ridge. In early documents the land is referred to as 'Panters'. In the 15th century the Park, along with ***Whitley Forest***, belonged to Lord Say and Sele, then it passed to the Archbishop of Canterbury, being surrendered to Henry VIII by ***Cranmer*** in 1538. In the second half of the 16th century it had a succession

Map 10 A map of ***Panthurst Park***, 1630. Panthurst was bought by Thomas ***Lambarde*** in the early 17th century. The area of over 400 acres may have been enclosed in the previous century. Most fields are named, their acreage enumerated, in some instances their use indicated, and many have drawings of domestic animals. The major trees shown in the hedges were a source of timber for construction. These early 17th-century field patterns remained largely unchanged to modern times. On the east of the map the sharp bend on ***Riverhill*** can be seen, the road being labelled as 'the way from Tonbridge to London'.

of owners, or lessees, who enclosed further land. The Park ceased to be a ***deer park*** by 1570.

parish boundaries

The boundaries of many original English parishes, including those of ***St Nicholas*** Sevenoaks, were determined by early medieval times. Parish boundaries were marked at intervals by stones, and traditionally on Rogation Sunday (the fifth Sunday after Easter) the boundaries would be walked ('beating the bounds') to ensure that these were in place. Parish boundaries had a new importance after the 16th century as the ***vestry*** had responsibility for administering the parish, and deciding who was born there and thus entitled to poor relief. St Nicholas parish was divided steadily through the 19th century as new parish churches were built and the role of the vestry declined in administrative importance.

parish registers

A major administrative reform by the Tudor state was the introduction in 1538 of parish records of baptisms, marriages, and burials. These were written on loose pages, and only in 1597 were they ordered to be recorded in bound registers kept by the clergy. Local clergymen were required to transcribe the pre-1597 records into the new registers. Not surprisingly some early records were lost. The Sevenoaks records began in 1559, but the Vestry copy of the bound registers did not start until 1600. In making entries of baptisms, marriages, and burials, it was not uncommon for clergymen, or parish clerks, to add brief personal notes. Until 1752 most parish registers began the new year, not on 1 January but on Lady Day 25 March. In that year Great Britain moved from the Julian to the Gregorian calendar (coming in to line with much of Europe).
Ward (1931), 116-121

Park Farm

Park Farm along with nine acres of land was sold to Sir George Berkeley in 1869-70. He built the large grey stone mansion which he called 'Park Grange' on the site. The house was later sold to ***Charles Plumtre Johnson*** in 1911. ***Sevenoaks School*** acquired the bulk of the property through the Johnson Trustees in 1948. The substantial estate has provided playing fields, staff houses and boarding accommodation for Sevenoaks School.
Scragg (1993)

Park Place

Park Place stood at the southern end of Sevenoaks, the present site of Park Grange. It had several owners, the ***Lones*** and the ***Lambardes*** in the 17th century. Lambarde replaced the old Tudor house with a new ragstone building.

Parliamentary elections

Until 1832 the land tax returns indicated which men were entitled to vote in parliamentary elections. Electors had to be aged 21 and over with 'property and income' in Sevenoaks; they did not have to live in Sevenoaks. In 1840 there were 136 men in Sevenoaks parish with a right to vote, their names recorded in a printed Poll Book. Many members of the propertied classes opposed extending the franchise fearing that this would weaken their power and result in irresponsible government. The right to vote was fought for and gradually achieved by Reform Acts passed in 1832, 1867, 1884, 1918, and 1928. All adult men, and women aged 30 and over, gained the vote in 1918; women of 21 and over were given the vote in 1928. Until 1884 many constituencies returned two members.

> *Electoral violence on The Vine, 1868*
> *Until the secret ballot was introduced in 1872, general elections were often corrupt and violent affairs with voting done publicly. As a child, John Fortescue saw the turmoil of the 1868 election on the Vine: '... then the proceedings became lively. The crowd began to rock and sway in an ominous fashion, and the yells turned to the smothered growl of hounds worrying a fox. Presently the police rose to their feet, and falling in marched across the ground 30 or 40 strong in columns of four.'*

Edward Parry (1863-1943)
In 1911, Parry who became a judge at the early age of 31, came to live in 'Clarendon', a large red-brick villa in Granville Road. He practised in the London courts, retiring in 1927 with a knighthood. Parry was also an author and playwright. In 1905 his play *What the Butler Saw* was produced at Wyndham's Theatre.
ODNB (2004)

Paygate
The site of a toll gate on the Sevenoaks to Wrotham ***turnpike*** at the junction of Seal Road and Seal Hollow Road. Long after the turnpike had disappeared the place was commonly known as 'Paygate' with local buses terminating there in the 1930s.

Pepita (Josefa Ortega) (1830-1871)
Lionel Sackville-West, 2nd Baron Sackville, met a Spanish dancer named Pepita in Paris in 1852. Born in the slums of Malaga, Pepita, who was already married, soon became his mistress. During their 19-year relationship, Pepita had five illegitimate children with Lionel. Pepita's grand-daughter, Vita ***Sackville-West***, wrote *Pepita* (1937), a biography of her mother and grandmother.

Pest House
The Pest House, later called the Fever Hospital, was situated on the east side of ***Oak Lane***, north of Fig Street. It is marked on the ***Tithe Award*** map of 1841. Another pest house, at Starvecrow, stood close to Fawke Common. Any person believed to be suffering from a contagious ***disease*** such as smallpox, typhus, cholera or scarlet fever was taken to the Pest House. Navvies digging the ***railway tunnel***, living in insanitary huts with toilets shared between several families, increased the number of people taken there. In 1865 smallpox was so rife the Pest House could not accommodate them all. The Pest House was leased by the Local Board from the Churchwardens and Overseers in 1874

58 Paygate cottage. One of the lodges at the entrance to the Wilderness park.

and passed to ***Sevenoaks Urban District Council*** in 1894. It closed in 1902 when the Council built nearby the Oak Lane Isolation Hospital. Dr ***Gordon Ward*** complained in 1930 that patients got inadequate attention due to an influx of 16 cases of scarlet fever and lack of equipment to deal with such a large number. In 1948 the Isolation Hospital was taken over by the National Health Service and became known as the Oak Lane Hospital. By 1956 it had become a hospital for geriatric patients. In 1972 the hospital was sold to Kent County Council who converted it into a home for children with disabilities, The Croft, which has since closed.

Pett family

William Pett of Riverhill gave, with others, 15 acres of land at Hollybush, known later as ***School Lands***, to ***Sevenoaks School*** in 1510. Richard then John, his successor (died 1593), owned much land at Riverhill and Otford. William Pett (1710-86) is the earliest recorded ***cricket*** bat maker in Kent. His bats, very different from modern ones, were designed to look more like hockey sticks. John Frederick Sackville, 3rd Duke of Dorset, purchased 11 of his bats in 1766 at two shillings and sixpence each. One of Pett's bats, made in 1745, is now in the local ***Sevenoaks Museum***. Amos Pett (1827-1916), one of William's descendants, was a basket maker with a shop at 121 High Street, and also Collector to the Local Board. Behind his shop there was a yard which was called Pett's Yard.

Petty Sessions
These were regular courts held by justices of the peace to try minor offences without a jury. Modern magistrates' courts are a continuation of that system. In the 19th century Sevenoaks was one of 16 petty sessions in Kent.
Landau (1984)

pew rents
It was common practice in both Church of England and nonconformist churches to raise money from pew rents. Members of the congregation annually paid for a pew, and prices varied according to position. The income went towards maintenance of the church building and sometimes to supplement the minister's income. Some people opposed the system as a tax that deterred church attendance. However, it continued well into the 20th century. For example, in 1851 rents were paid for 173 out of a total of 266 seats at the Wesleyan ***Methodist*** chapel, while ***St Mary's Riverhead*** had 400 free of 600 seats. By 1905 all 700 seats at ***St Nicholas*** were free, but at ***St Mary's Kippington*** 116 of the 414 seats were rented, while at ***St John's*** of 600 seats 150 were rented. The practice slowly died out, largely because it became too expensive to administer.

photographers
There were a number of photographers working in Sevenoaks in the mid- and late 19th century. In the 1855 *Directory*, ***C. E. Corke***, the Jeffery brothers, and James Stanger are all listed. Later on R. Wicks worked at the St John's Photography Gallery; W. Edmond Wallis at the Cranbourne Photo Company, 74 High Street; and H.G. Inskipp was also in the High Street. Photographers also made *cartes-de-visite*, or calling cards, measuring 2.5 by 4 inches with a photograph, which were widely used from the late 1850s to the 1870s. Photography became a popular activity after the invention of the Kodak box camera and returnable film in the 1890s. In 1924-1925 a Sevenoaks and District Photographic Society met at the Cornwall Hall, although by the 1930s it appears to have declined. The present Sevenoaks Camera Club was founded in 1952. In the first decade it thrived but by the early 1970s membership had declined. Membership continued to fluctuate for some years, but increased with the advent of digital photography in the 1990s.

place names
Many place names have a rich history, in some cases indicating the use or value of land. For example 'chart' often indicates poor waste land, '-den' a grazing place, 'shaw' a small area of woodland. Field names may also indicate geography, size or customary use: 'chalky', 'quarry', 'six acre', 'Hop Garden', and 'Saw Pit field'. Sevenoaks probably gained its name from a distinctive group of trees, ***Riverhead*** indicated the settlement's position on the ***Darent***, while ***Longford*** was a crossing point on that river.
Watts (2003); Wallenberg (1934)

Plymouth Drive
A road constructed in the early 1930s and named after Mary Sackville (1792-1864), from her first marriage in 1811 to the Earl of Plymouth

(1789-1833). The childless Mary inherited ***Knole*** on the death of her mother, Arabella, 3rd Duchess of Dorset in 1825. Mary was widowed and then married, in 1839, William Pitt, 1st Earl ***Amherst*** (1773-1857), who came to live at Knole.

Polhill

The name of the main road (A21) that descends the ***North Downs***, and which takes its name from local landowners, the Polhills, who owned ***Chipstead Place*** from 1711 to 1829. The hill, part of the Sevenoaks to Farnborough ***turnpike***, was built with a gradual gradient between 1834-38. The Polhill Arms, built at the same time, stood at the top of the hill, and a straight road led on to Badger's Mount.

police

For centuries the policing of local law and order and dealing with nuisances of various kinds was the responsibility of a constable subject to the parish ***vestry***. Serious unrest was invariably dealt with by calling on the military. Kent was late in agreeing to a County constabulary, the uniformed force eventually being established with headquarters in Maidstone in 1857. In a transitional period, to 1872, local policing continued to rely on the parish constable overlapping with a few County constables. A police station with magistrates court was built in the High Street in 1864, at the cost of £3,000; the local force then was a superintendent and six officers. In the early 1970s a new station and court was built at Morewoods, the original building in the town centre being converted into apartments. Police skills were extended in the late 19th and early 20th centuries, and the 'beat' was supplemented with the bicycle, and later motor vehicles, and improved communications. By the start of the 21st century the police had an office in Akehurst Lane, off the High Street, but this closed in June 2010 and the police office moved to the ***Sevenoaks District Council*** offices in Argyle Road.
Ingleton (2002)

politics

It is important to see 'politics' as more than the activities of the major political parties. Political activity has been part of public life in Sevenoaks for many centuries. It involved 'parish pump politics', issues such as allegiance to patrons and opposition to wealthy land owners, disputes over access to land and to water supply, who paid local ***rates*** and how they were spent, and who was entitled to vote in local and parliamentary elections. For example, ***education*** has been a political issue in Sevenoaks since 1870, but so has the building of new houses and roads, waste disposal, pollution, burial sites, and the ***Green Belt***, all of which involved campaigns by rival lobbies and groups.
Killingray (2009)

ponds

Up to about 1840, people in Sevenoaks depended on wells, pumps and ponds for their ***water supply***.

There was a caged pond in the High Street, opposite the ***Old Post Office*** at the junction of London Road and the High Street. According to the *Sevenoaks Advertiser* of March 1841, this was formerly a large horse pond filling up half the roadway, bordered by stone banks and a post and rail

fence; Box said that scolding women were ducked here. The pond was filled in by 1860. Behind the ***Royal Crown Hotel*** were three ponds in Crown Meadow. More ponds were to be found at ***Bethlehem Farm***; the top of Pembroke Road; the foot of ***Tubs Hill***; at the top of ***Hitchen Hatch Lane***; the Long Pond, used for skating in cold weather, where The Drive met the High Street; and Bull Barn Pond in the fields of ***Covell's Farm***.
Box (1927)

Charles Ponsonby (1879-1976)
Member of Parliament for Sevenoaks 1935-50. Educated at Oxford, he became a solicitor. Ponsonby served in the ***First World War*** with the West Kent Yeomanry whose war history he subsequently wrote. He was a member of the wartime government 1940-45, as parliamentary private secretary to Anthony Eden at the Foreign Office.

population
The number of people living in Sevenoaks, both town and parish, is not known until the first official census of 1801. It is estimated that there were 900-1,000 people in the town in the decades 1560s-70s. An estimate by Gregory King in 1695 suggested that 1,572 people lived in the parish. Historical demographers calculate population size by counting the number of houses and assessing each household as 4.5 people. The pre-19th-century population, although small, increased and declined as a result of poor harvests, ***disease***, and migration in and out of the area. Life expectancy was short and infant mortality rates were high through much of the 19th century, nationally only declining dramatically after 1911. In 1801 Sevenoaks was a small rural town and remained so for much of the century. Population increased more rapidly from the 1860s with the coming of the railway. Also important was improved public health, aided by a supply of clean water and modern sanitation which had more impact on life expectancy and infant mortality rates than individual medical care. During the 20th century the largest growth in population came with new housing developments – in the years 1931-39 (+11 per cent), and also in the decade 1971-81 (+10 per cent). By the early 21st century there was a new and growing challenge: an ageing population. Increased life expectancy posed serious problems of caring for the elderly, and further dedicated homes were built for the aged in Sevenoaks.

Sevenoaks – census figures

1801	*2640*	*1911*	*10953*
1811	*3444*	*1921*	*10915*
1821	*3942*	*1931*	*10484*
1831	*4709*	*1941*	*no census*
1841	*5061*	*1951*	*14866*
1851	*4878*	*1961*	*17645*
1861	*4695*	*1971*	*18247*
1871	*5949*	*1981*	*17212*
1881	*8305*	*1991*	*18075*
1891	*9341*	*2001*	*18159*
1901	*9741*		

59 Pillar box. This 19th-century pillar box with its crown and V.R. – 'Victoria Regina' – belonged to the Royal Mail, one of the great institutions of the State. Built into a wall in Bayham Road, this box was thoughtlessly destroyed in 2010. The number of letters handled by the ***Post Office*** declined after the 1990s as electronic mail increased. By then the one penny letter of 1840 had increased in price many times over as the Post Office sought to maintain its universal service.

postal services

A public letter carrying service was established in 1635; Sevenoaks was an immediate beneficiary with a Stage Post at the Bull Inn, ***Chipstead***. Before that date only State Papers were carried, all other correspondence relying on private messengers. A Crown monopoly for the delivery of mail and the supply of horses was established in 1657. Regular weekly services were set up and Post Boys were employed for each Stage. London mail for Sevenoaks was taken to the Letter Office in Southwark, brought by stage to Chipstead where the local post master arranged for letters to be forwarded to local towns and villages. In 1676 the ***Post Office*** was moved to the ***Chequers Inn***, Sevenoaks. From 1750 the mail stage and mail carts used the new ***turnpike*** to London, the journey taking up to 10 hours. In the early 19th century the ***Post Office*** moved via the Crown Inn, the Dorset Arms, and the Wheatsheaf to the High Street and finally to South Park. In 1837 the Post Office was given a monopoly on mail delivery. The introduction of the penny post, the famous 'penny black stamp' of 1840, reduced the cost of postage to anywhere in the United Kingdom and resulted in a great increase in the number of letters handled annually by the Post Office.

Pillar, or letter, boxes were first introduced by the post office in Jersey in 1852 on the recommendation of a Regional Surveyor's clerk, the aspiring novelist Anthony Trollope. The public liked them; provided postage stamps had been purchased in advance, there was no need to walk to a Post Office to post letters securely. The first boxes in London arrived in 1855. The first in Sevenoaks was the Town box at the bottom of ***Tubs Hill*** in 1870; by 1873, more boxes, at Upper Tubs Hill, ***St John's*** Hill, ***Vine*** and ***Sevenoaks Common*** had been installed and by 1881, Granville, making six in all. Stoneville Park appeared in 1882; by 1886 Bayham Road and Lower High Street had been added. A list in the Sevenoaks Telegraph *Directory*, 1901, shows 19 Town boxes with only one freestanding 'pillar box', others being wall boxes and lamp boxes attached to lamp standards or telegraph poles. Today, over 100 years later, there are some 70 boxes in postcode area TN13 alone. The Victorian Ludlow box in the Old Tuck shop opposite ***Sevenoaks School*** is still there. Since 1990 several Victorian and Edwardian boxes have been replaced with modern Queen Elizabeth boxes.

Mail was first brought by rail via Tonbridge to Sevenoaks in 1844. Thereafter regular daily mail services developed with several deliveries each day. This increased with the arrival of the two railways lines to Sevenoaks in the 1860s. By 1891 there were daily deliveries at 7 a.m., 11 a.m. and 6 p.m., with an early morning delivery on Sundays. Late 20th-century structural changes in communications, particularly the advent of email and private selective delivery services, resulted in an end to the Post Office monopoly in 2005. By the early 21st century postal deliveries were reduced to six days a week and many post offices had closed.

Donald (1992)

postcards

The first picture postcards in Britain were issued in 1894. ***Salmon*** was an early pioneer of postcard printing with 12 black and white photographs of the town and district. This was soon followed by coloured cards of local scenes. The Essenhigh ***Corkes*** were amongst those who at the turn of the century provided photographs and watercolours for Salmon. C.E. Corke had privileged access to Knole which proved of immense value. His watercolours and photographs and those from Alfred Quinton, who produced 2,300 views for Salmon, helped turn a local printer into a national postcard publisher.

Post Office
The original Sevenoaks Post Office, established in 1840, was at 58 High Street where Waitrose now stands. An alleyway led from the street into ***Post Office Yard***. By 1895 sub-post offices were at the ***Old Post Office***, in the Upper High Street; at the top and also the bottom of ***St John's*** Hill, and on ***Tubs Hill***. The entire High Street postal business moved to South Park in 1897, and in 1970 was replaced by a new building with a large sorting office.

Post Office Yard
Behind the town ***Post Office*** in the High Street was a yard accessed under an archway. Inside the yard there were three wells, Nash's Mineral Water factory, a ***forge***, the printing press for the *Sevenoaks Chronicle*, and the ***telegraph*** office and ***telephone*** exchange. The printers moved in 1916 and their place taken by Parris's ***bakery***. The Yard was demolished in 1981 to make way for Waitrose.
Terry (2000)

Pound
The ancient Parish Pound, a small area of fenced grassland just west of the ***Vine*** in Pound Lane, was provided for temporary custody of stray animals. Livestock kept on common or open fields without hedges and fences would stray into the town where they caused nuisance or damage. Rooker says that the history of the pound, or pinfold, is first recorded in a memorandum book of 1663 which stated that the Pound Keeper was paid one shilling to 'cry in the town' that all horse traffic in Knole Park was to cease. In 1815, a letter from the Agent of Knole to the Duchess of Dorset stated that the Pound Keeper had been fined nine shillings for releasing nine pigs from the Pound without a proper warrant.
Parish (1999)

poverty
Low or irregular wages, sickness, widowhood, old age, and misfortune meant that a large part of England's population in the past lived in poverty. In medieval times assistance for the poor came from charitable donations and religious institutions. With the Dissolution of Monasteries and chantries in 1536-40 the poor were often reduced to begging and stealing. The growing number of poor vagrants was seen as a threat to social order and an Act of 1572 provided for the punishment of beggars coupled with relief of the impotent poor. Further Acts of 1597-1601 created a relief system run by each parish and paid for by ***rates*** levied on local landowners. Able-bodied paupers could be put to work; children into apprenticeship schemes; the aged and sick often given support in their own homes, an ***almshouse***, or in a local ***workhouse***. The Settlement Act 1662 determined the ways in which a poor person could claim to be legally settled in a parish

60 The animal Pound, in Pound Lane. Early in the 20th century, ***John Rooker***, the minister of ***St Nicholas***, rescued the Pound from decay and put it in good order at his own expense, although afterwards he asked for donations to help him meet the expense of £28 10s. 11d. ***Sevenoaks Town Council*** now has responsibility for this small patch of land.

other than where they were born. This 'old' poor law system lasted to 1834. The extent of poverty in 17th-century Kent can be calculated from the ***Hearth Tax*** of 1664 from which the poor were exempt. Across the county one third of the population lived at subsistence level; in Sevenoaks parish, with 1,467 people, 600 were poor of which 350 lived within the town. Certain Kent towns developed industries and became less reliant on agriculture, but this barely happened in the Sevenoaks area. The poor in rural Sevenoaks could move away, although the Settlement Acts meant they could also be returned to their parish of origin.

An unpredictable agricultural economy from the mid-18th to the mid-19th centuries, along with population growth, poor harvests, the repeal of the Corn Laws in 1846, and mechanisation, all disadvantaged agricultural workers. The number of poor increased, particularly in the decades after the Napoleonic wars, placing an increased burden on parish ratepayers. In 1834 the Poor Law Amendment Act abolished the old system and introduced a centrally directed one based on unions of parishes. The poor were actively discouraged from seeking relief by a harsh regime in the new

Sevenoaks Union workhouse, although the elderly poor and the sick in Sevenoaks tended to receive outdoor relief in their own homes. In the 19th and early 20th centuries, when the population grew rapidly, Sevenoaks had a permanent core of paupers, a high proportion in the workhouse being agricultural labourers and children. The Sevenoaks clergy saw this as a problem and sought means to alleviate temporary unemployment in the 1860s and 1870s. Several churches ran boot and clothing clubs, and, after 1890, jumble sales which provided cheap clothes. Although the number of people nationally in receipt of relief fell in the decades 1850 to 1900, by the latter date over 25 per cent of the elderly were poor. The Old Age Pension Act 1908 helped those aged over 70 years, but in 1911 one third of men and half the women inmates in the Sevenoaks workhouse were elderly. Private charity continued to supplement aid to the poor and the unemployed, for example the Sevenoaks Relief Committee formed during the trade depression of 1908. In April 1930 the Boards of Guardians were abolished, union workhouses renamed public assistance institutions and the administration handed over to local authorities. They continued in this form until the introduction of the National Health Service in 1948, when the Sundridge workhouse became a hospital for the elderly. It finally closed in 1998, was sold, and converted into luxury apartments. During the Depression of the early 1930s, Sevenoaks had 414 men unemployed and with little chance of finding work. Modern poverty is often disguised; in the early 1990s there were more than 2,000 unemployed people in the area.

preparatory schools
Private 'prep' schools have come and gone in Sevenoaks during the last two centuries. Most took boarders. Proprietors advertised that they would prepare boys, from gentry and middle-class homes, for entrance to 'public' schools at the age of 13. One of the first established was Sevenoaks Academy (1796-1885), a school for young gentlemen in the Red House, owned by John Baptiste Anquetil. Anquetil had previously taught at ***Sevenoaks School***, his father being a refugee from the French Revolution. In 1841 Vine House Academy had 25 boys as boarders. The Rev. ***John Jackson*** turned from the ministry to teaching and in 1867 he and his wife opened Scottiswoode House School in ***St John's Hill***. It advertised: 'Young Gentlemen range from 5 to 14 years of age; the Little Boys are carefully prepared in a separate Department. The situation is high, dry and bracing near the Vine Cricket Ground and Knole Park'. Four years later Lonsbury College, also on St John's Hill, claimed to afford 'a liberal and practical education to the sons of the gentry and middle class inhabitants residing in Sevenoaks and the immediate vicinity'. The Avenue House School, styled 'The High School for Boys', which arrived in Sevenoaks from Braintree in 1886, in an advertisement in Salmon's *Picturesque Views of Sevenoaks*, proclaimed that in 1894 and in 1898 a pupil from the School was awarded first place in Book Keeping at the Cambridge Local Examinations. At the census of 1891, there were 25 boys boarding at the School, ranging in age from nine to 15 years. The School, demolished in 1934, stood on Avenue Road between Dartford Road and Vine Court Road. In 1910 St Aldates, The Beacon in St John's Road, and Beechmont School, stated that they were 'for Gentlemen's sons'. One school with boys and girls was Kippington House, leased as a school for girls and small boys between 1919 and 1938;

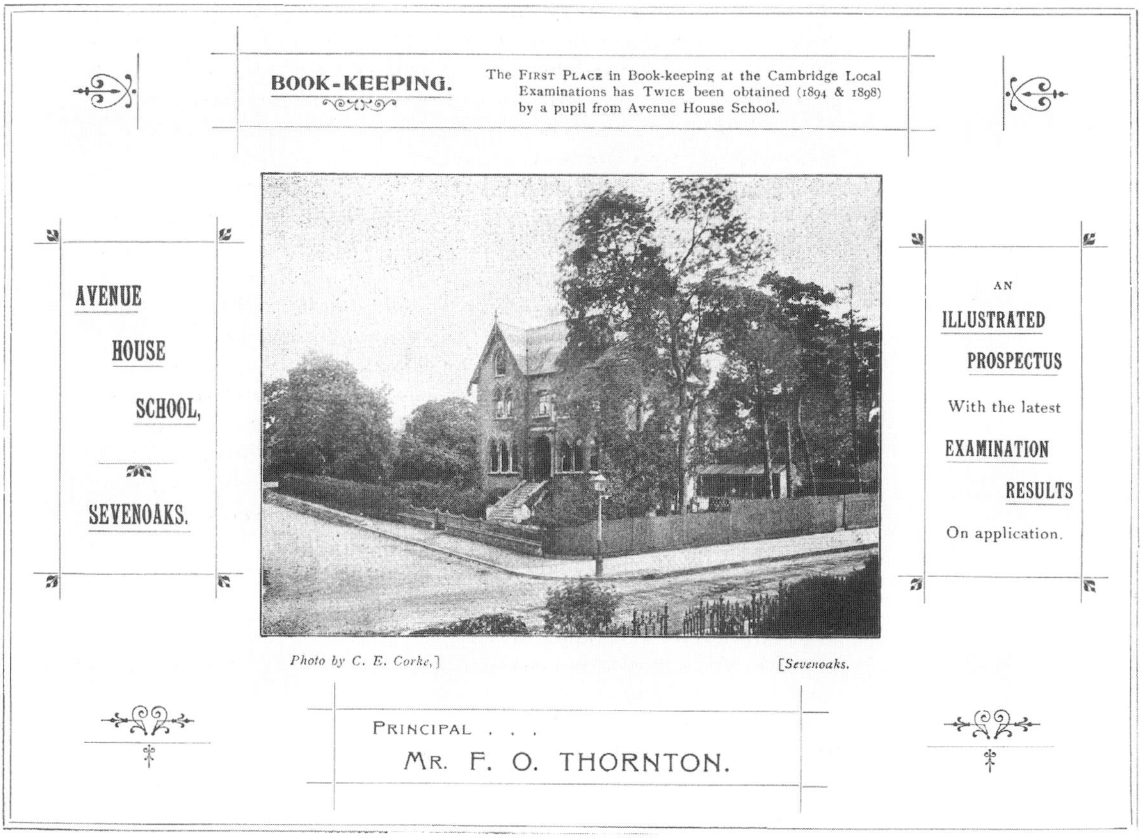

BOOK-KEEPING.

The FIRST PLACE in Book-keeping at the Cambridge Local Examinations has TWICE been obtained (1894 & 1898) by a pupil from Avenue House School.

AVENUE HOUSE SCHOOL, SEVENOAKS.

AN ILLUSTRATED PROSPECTUS With the latest EXAMINATION RESULTS On application.

Photo by C. E. Corke,] [Sevenoaks.

PRINCIPAL . . . MR. F. O. THORNTON.

61 Avenue House School. Preparatory schools were often run as commercial undertakings. Many were small businesses, their success dependent upon satisfied parents. It is not surprising that so many in Sevenoaks came and went. The prospectus, like this one for Avenue House, sought to persuade parents and guardians that the school had a good record of educating children to the required level in order to enter a 'public' school.

its prospectus called it 'A school for girls of gentle birth'. Another was Oak School in Hitchen Hatch Lane which advertised for pupils in the *Sevenoaks Chronicle* in 1930, as a Preparatory School for Girls and Boys 'near the station and bus routes'. Girls' preparatory schools were also founded after the 1870s to provide a genteel education. Vine College advertised in Salmon's *Directory of Sevenoaks* in 1881 as a boarding and day school for young ladies 'where pupils receive a sound education in English, French, Music, Drawing and Painting'. Bradbourne College, advertised in the *Sevenoaks Chronicle* in 1910 as a boarding and day school for girls, occupied a large Victorian house at the junction of Bayham Road with Quaker's Hall Lane. The school moved to Bayham Road in 1904-5 but closed in 1978 and was replaced by a block of flats. St Bega, Dartford Road, in 1910 announced itself as 'the Home school for the daughters of Gentlemen'. That year Wykeham House, in Eardley Road, was 'a private school for girls'. The Farnaby Girls Preparatory School ran briefly as a 'day and boarding school' from 1949-56, in Farnaby House, on the site of what is now Farnaby Drive.

Winchester House prep school was started in 1936 by Percy Wilson in a house in ***Granville Road*** with just four boys. Wilson had served during the war with John Norman whose family owned ***New Beacon School***. In 1945 the school moved to a large Victorian family house in ***Hitchen Hatch Lane*** with a two-acre garden. After 1963 the school expanded its building and the number of pupils, but decline set in and the school closed in 1985, the site being developed for housing and named Winchester Close. There were other 'prep' schools which survived into the 21st century: the ***New Beacon*** emerged from the Beacon school in St John's; ***Sevenoaks Preparatory***, was founded in 1919, ***Solefields*** in 1948, and the ***Granville*** for girls in 1945. Most of these school had the ultimate aim of getting their students into prestigious 'public' schools at 13, or a local grammar school at eleven.

Presbyterian church
Early in 1941 a small group of Sevenoaks residents began to explore the possibility of establishing a Presbyterian church. Services were held initially in a wooden hut in ***Granville*** Road and later at the Cheyne Hospital. By 1940 a site was found at the corner of Kippington and London Roads and a church was completed in 1964. Most Congregational and Presbyterian churches amalgamated nationally in 1972 as the United Reformed Church, but both churches continued in Sevenoaks. The Presbyterian Church on London Road became known as the Christ Church United Reformed Church. *Killingray (2004)*

Primrose League
The Primrose League was a political organisation founded in 1883 to promote the ***Conservative*** cause and to uphold the British Empire. Named after Disraeli's favourite flower, the League also had a Ladies Grand Council formed in 1885. In its early years the Sevenoaks habitation, as local branches were called, was led by Lords ***Stanhope*** and ***Hillingdon***, members of the ***Amherst*** family, and local gentry such as ***Multon Lambarde***, with the solicitor William W. ***Knocker*** as honorary secretary. There were 528 League members in the district by 1888. In 1890 League membership throughout Britain exceeded one million, including many women. League membership declined after the First World War and the body was finally wound up in 2004.

public houses
Before the development of public houses in the 18th century, beer was supplied by alehouses. Beer was brewed on the premises, often by women known as alewives or brewsters. Anyone who wanted to sell ale had to apply for a licence at the ***Quarter Sessions*** or the ***Petty Sessions*** and declare that they would not keep a 'disorderly house'. Aleconners were appointed to inspect beer for quality and price, four being listed for Sevenoaks, Riverhead and Weald in 1841. In 1830 an Act permitted beer houses to open on payment of a small annual sum; the number increased steadily in the next 30 years. Public houses also grew in number. Outside the home and the church, they were a major source of leisure and entertainment, but also the source of drunkenness. Nonconformist churches in particular and ***temperance*** organisations often opposed the licensing and location of 'pubs'. The development of the ***cinema*** and other leisure attractions reduced the attraction of public houses, and many closed. Television further hit pub trade, although many went over to serving food. For example the Vine ceased to be a pub and became a restaurant in 2006.

Within the town the Black Boy was in existence in 1701, as was the Pied Bull, also known as the 'Coffee House', once called the Swan, and soon to be renamed the Dorset Arms (a Sackville title). There were several 'Crown' inns: Old Crown, the 'first Inn on the right hand on the Road leading from London', according to a press notice of 1730; the Lower Crown, where cock fights took place, 1739, and the Second Crown, kept by Jenny Morley, which also served as a 'post-house', mentioned in the press in 1727. The ***Rose and Crown*** was often known as the 'market pub'. The Coachmakers Arms in the Upper High Street was built in the early 18th century as a private house, turned into a beer house in the early 19th century, became the Coachmakers Arms in the 20th and has now returned to being a private house. Sixty yards north of ***Six Bells Lane*** was the Bricklayer's Arms, whilst the Plumbers' Arms, a seedy ale house according to ***Gordon Anckorn***, stood on a site in the London Road next to the old ***jail***. The ***Oddfellows*** and Foresters Arms (*c*.1891-1955) was connected with the local branches of the friendly society of that name. The Holmesdale Tavern in the High Street, bought by John Bligh in 1862, boasted five bars. It was demolished in the 1960s.

In the St John's area by 1920 there were ten public houses: the New Inn, Castle, Rifleman, Elephant's Head, Railway Tavern, Bat & Ball, Man of Kent, Compasses, Camden Arms and Greyhound. Only the New Inn and the Rifleman survived to 2011. At Tubs Hill there were the Farmers (previously the ***Sennocke Hotel***), and the Railway and Bicycle, both demolished 2006-10. There were also pubs on the roads out of Sevenoaks: the White Hart on Sevenoaks Common, and the Halfway House on the

62 Rock and Fountain pub. The Rock and Fountain on Tubs Hill, which closed in 1959, was a 'doss house' where travellers could have a night's lodging for a few pence. When this photograph was taken the pub was a tied house, to the Dartford Brewery Co. The then landlord was E. Turner; his name is given in large letters when it was usual for the name to be written in small print on the lintel frame of the main door.

London Road north from the town, both of which existed in the 18th century.
Anckorn (1984); Fowler (2003); Paynes Almanac (1841)

public parks and gardens
The meaning of the word 'park' has changed over time. One of its early uses was for an area of enclosed land, such as the ***Knole Park*** and ***Montreal Park***. The gentry imitated by enclosing their land with walls and hedges. Many Victorians reformers thought of open areas for public use, for re-creation, and these were increasingly provided by local authorities and philanthropists by the late 19th century. ***Knole Park***, although private, was open most of the year to the public. The first public park in Sevenoaks, 'The Vine Pleasure Gardens', was bought by the Local Board in 1893, and opened at regular hours with music frequently played from the ***bandstand***. A decade or so later the ***Sevenoaks Urban District Council*** purchased the 12 acres of Holly Bush as a recreation ground for the town, an area once known as ***School Lands***. Half the purchase price of £4,750 was donated by ***Francis Swanzy*** who performed the inaugural ceremony when the new pavilion was opened in 1914. Later playing fields along with ***tennis*** courts and ***bowls*** were laid out. In 1989 The ***Sevenoaks District Council*** developed the grounds with an outdoor bowls green and indoor bowls centre, tennis courts, children's playground, an all-weather ***hockey*** pitch (which replaced the cricket pitch), a café, and a large flat area of grass for informal play. Many children referred to the local recreation ground, with its swings, slides, and roundabouts, as the 'rec'. The 11-acre Knole Paddock sports fields was bought from the ***Knole*** estate in 1929 by the Sevenoaks UDC. At the same time, Kent County Council purchased the adjoining nine-acre Raleys Field. Both are now owned by ***Sevenoaks Town Council*** and used for cricket, football and rugby, plus a small gym owned and operated by the Sevenoaks Town Council. The Pavilion is leased to Sevenoaks

63 Rheinbach Gardens. One of Sevenoaks's smallest public gardens is at the top of Bradbourne Road. It was purchased by **Sevenoaks Urban District Council** in 1926, when the neighbouring Dorset House was demolished. Originally know as Upper St John's garden, it was renamed Rheinbach gardens in 2007, the sign presented by the mayor of the German twin-town the next year.

Rugby Football Club, land at Lower Raleys Field is leased to Sevenoaks Clarendon Lawn ***Tennis*** Club, and the Indoor Cricket School, built in 1951, is leased to the Association of Kent Cricket Clubs.

A quieter park was Kippington Meadow, a three-acre park, originally part of the ***Kippington estate***, given to the town in 1913 by the Rev. Percy Thompson, son of ***William J. Thompson***, 'as an open space in its state of natural beauty'. In the 1970s another playground was created in the old sand pit at Pontoise Close. The Upper High Street gardens, adjacent to ***Six Bells Lane***, originally a vegetable garden of 0.14 acres, was made into a flower garden in the 1930s by Joan Constant who lived in the Old House opposite. In 1949 she gave the garden to the town in memory of her parents.

Hollybush Residents Association (1999)

Pump House

Also known as 'Walnut Tree House' or Cottage and the 'Arboretum', this large brick-built property house stood on the London Road where the West Kent Housing Association building now is. It had a public water pump outside – hence diarist ***Jane Edwards*** called it the Pump House. Occupants over the years included Heley, the Sevenoaks coach builder, and the Kippington Church Institute. In 1910 the photographer ***Charles Essenhigh Corke*** moved there from 39 London Road and built a studio for painting in the garden. An interesting cultural figure who lived in the property from 1872-79 was Geraldine Jewsbury (1812- 80), novelist, critic, and close friend of Jane Carlyle. These two were early pioneers of the women's movement. Geraldine was also friendly with Miss ***Herries*** who lived at ***St Julian's***. Jewsbury's six novels pre-date her Sevenoaks period but she wrote articles and her reviews for the *Athenaeum* in the seclusion of the house and garden. Later the Arboretum (so re-named by the ***Essenhigh Corkes***) became a coal office for ***Quinnells*** and a café. Despite pressure for the property to be restored rather than demolished, this historic house fell victim to the developers in 1973, having stood empty since 1968.

punishments

In the 18th century there was a ducking stool by the pond at the top of the High Street, opposite the present-day Horncastles shop. Scolding wives would be lowered and ducked in the muddy water. Near the ducking stool was a cage or lock up where offenders would be put. The ***jail*** was in the London Road (present numbers 16-18), and a scaffold for hangings on ***Gallows Common***.

Box (1927); Knapfla (1994); Conley (1991)

Q

Quakers

There have been Quaker Christians – the Society of Friends – in Sevenoaks since the 1650s, a prominent member being ***Nathaniel Owen***. Their presence in the northern area of the town led to it being called ***Quaker's Hall***. The Society of Friends bought the present Quaker Meeting House in Hollybush Lane in 1958. Built in 1870 and known as Knole

Cottage, at one time it had been used as a sanatorium by ***Walthamstow Hall School.***
Draper (1993 and 1995)

Quaker's Hall area
Thomas Hilder from Seal bought the northern section of the ***Hillborough*** estate in 1748. When his son Thomas inherited in 1760, he built a new house, Quaker's Hall, a short distance from Quaker's Hall Cottage. Timbers were used from a barn in the grounds which had been 'adzed and charred' to prevent dry rot. These are still visible in the 'new' house which is Grade II listed. The association with ***Quakers*** resulted in the new house being known as Quaker's Hall, although in the title deeds it is named as Hillborough House. Quaker's Hall Cottage in Bayham Road, part of the Hillborough estate, was owned in the 1650s by the Quaker ***Nathaniel Owen.***

quarrying
From ancient times people have quarried for useful stone in the Sevenoaks area. In medieval times ***ragstone*** was quarried as a building stone; in the early modern period ***lime*** was taken from the ***North Downs*** for agricultural purposes; from the 15th century brick earth was used for making ***bricks*** and tiles; and in the 18th to 20th centuries gravel was increasingly

64 Quarry men. There were many quarries in the Sevenoaks district. These men produced gravel for road building.

Map 11 Quarries and brick works since the mid-19th century. For many centuries ragstone, sand, lime, flints and gravel have all been excavated locally for building and for a variety of industrial and commercial purposes. The process often scarred and altered the landscape, although there were many small workings that left little trace. A careful reading of the landscape can often identify former workings. Victorian brickworks employed large numbers of men, women and children. Much of Sevenoaks's townscape is witness to their labours.

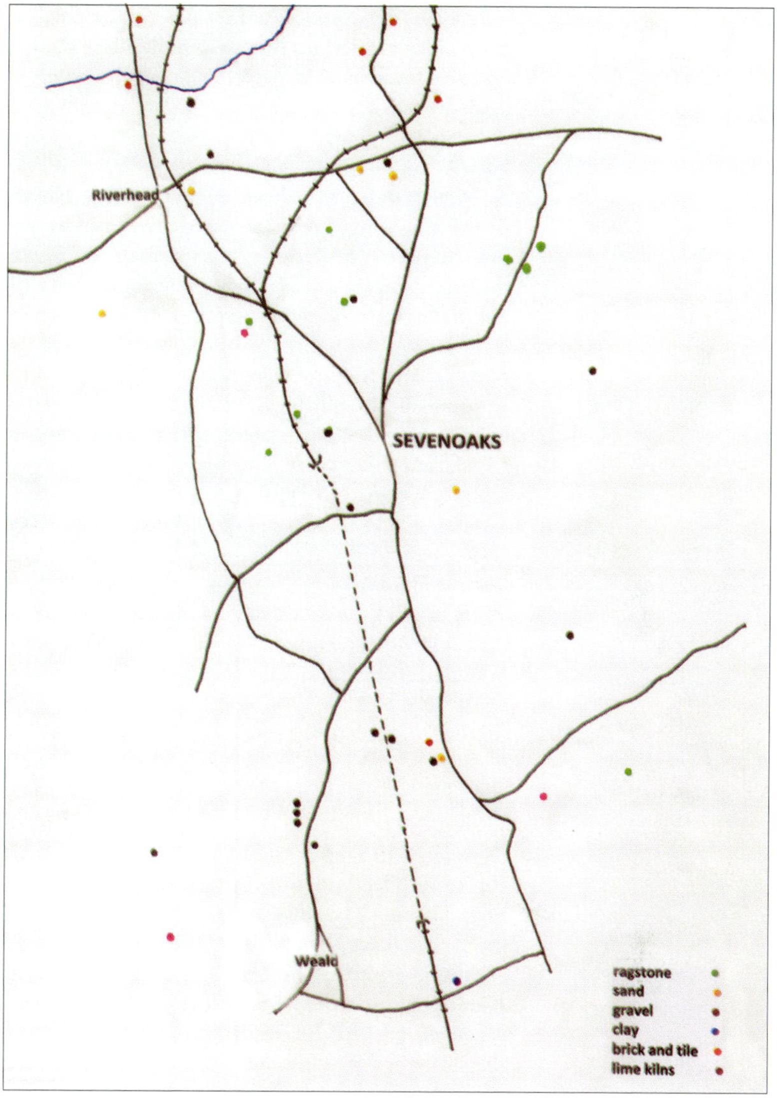

excavated for road building. Large- and small-scale quarrying has changed the local landscape, most notably excavations at the brick works at ***Dunton Green*** and gravel extraction north of the A25 at Bradbourne where large lakes have formed. Some former quarries served as ***rubbish*** tips, for example the old brick fields on the Otford Road. Some former quarries can be easily identified (e.g. at ***Dry Hill***) or located on old OS maps; road names are another clue. The Bradbourne quarry was opened by Tilcon in 1971 for sand extraction on land rented from Redland; it closed in 1981. The 280-acre Sevenoaks Sand Quarry, which stretches from the railway line east of the Bat and Ball station to Childsbridge Lane and the M26, was first worked in 1928. It is now owned by Tarmac who bought the quarry from Tilcon in 2000. Currently 200,000 to 250,000 tons of dark and fine sand are quarried each year for use in the building and construction industries. The sand is extracted from the larger of the two lakes and also from a dry sandbank. After extraction it is washed, screened to remove dirt and grit, and either bagged in the bagging plant or taken away in 20-ton loads by trucks.

Quarter Sessions
The Quarter Sessions were regular courts that tried serious offences. Originally they were presided over by justices of the peace for the County but in Tudor times they extended their role beyond law and order to include a variety of local matters such as roads and bridges, commerce and the maintenance of the poor, enforcing conformity to the Church of England and punishing Sabbath-breaking. For judicial purposes Kent had two Quarter Session courts, one at Maidstone and the other at Canterbury. Disputes between the two divisions led in 1814 to the creation of a Court of General Session, attended by Justices from across Kent who met in Maidstone. This body administered the County until the creation of Kent County Council in 1889.
Landau (1984); Conley (1991); Elizabeth Melling (2004)

Quinnell family
The Quinnells were carriers and furniture removers, established in 1814. Later they dealt as ***coal*** and coke suppliers. For many years the firm operated from Quinnell's Yard in Bradbourne Road, now the site of an apartment block.

R

ragstone
Ragstone, also known as greenstone or Kentish rag, was extensively quarried in the Sevenoaks area. Many large buildings were constructed of rag: ***St Nicholas, Knole,*** the ***almshouses*** at the top of the town, and it was commonly used in the 18th and 19th centuries for walls around parts of ***Knole park,*** and the ***Montreal*** estate (where more expensive dressed stone was used), and for private houses. Ragstone was often reused, for example the stone in the ***Sevenoaks School*** library came from a demolished building. Many late 19th-century houses were faced with the stone, for example the polygonal rag used on many of the larger houses in the Hollybush and ***Bayham*** Road areas.

railways
The first railways in Kent bypassed Sevenoaks. The South Eastern Railway's main line to the coast, finished in 1844, followed an existing route as far as Redhill, then turned east across the Weald to Tonbridge and Folkestone. Another line ran further north to Chatham, passing through Swanley, opening in 1860 and later became the London Chatham and Dover Railway. But Sevenoaks traffic, both passenger and freight, had to go by road to Tonbridge (from 1842 four trains a day, a journey by road and rail of more than three hours, a single second-class fare of six shillings). Over the next 15 years, various abortive schemes for a line through Sevenoaks were produced, without success. Eventually,

the engineer ***Thomas Crampton***, and a group of local landowners, put together a package for a new line up the Darent valley from Swanley to the first Sevenoaks station at ***Bat and Ball***, although the original intent was that it should terminate in Riverhead. It was opened in May 1862 as a nominally independent company, although operated by the Chatham line. By then the South Eastern had got approval for its own direct line from Lewisham to Tonbridge, with a second Sevenoaks station at the foot of ***Tubs Hill***. It was an expensive line to build, involving deep cuttings and the long Polhill tunnel through the North Downs, and an even longer one under the greensand ridge to the ***weald***, during which the builder ran into an unexpected underground stream. This brought about a change of contractor, but also provided a good ***water supply*** to the town. The new line was opened in 1868, and a link between the two rival companies' stations was opened the following year. An extension from Otford Junction to Maidstone followed in 1874. Railway building required the compulsory purchase of land and resulted in cuttings, embankments, and bridges that dramatically changed the local landscape. It also required an army of navvies, men temporarily housed in moving camps that often posed a threat to local social stability.

The original Sevenoaks line via Swanley never made money for its promoters, and its service to London was poor compared with the more direct route via Orpington, which soon developed a good express service to the City and, later, to Charing Cross. By 1872, Sevenoaks was an attractive commuter town and new housing developed near Tubs Hill station. Competition between the two rivals led to the collapse of the Chatham company and the amalgamation with the South Eastern and Chatham Railway (SECR) in 1899. In turn the SECR merged with

65 A 19th-century satirical print about the railway. The date of this print is unknown, but it probably dates from the 1880s. The implication is that railway travel was slow and unreliable. The opposite was the case. Railways were generally safe, tied the country together, and moved large numbers of people and huge quantities of goods at speed from place to place. Historians argue about how much railways aided economic development, but there is little doubt that they did have economic consequences.

two others into the Southern Railway in 1923. The new company began to electrify its Kent routes (reaching both Sevenoaks stations in early 1935); and this policy continued after the war under the nationalised British Railways, when lines to the coast were electrified in 1962. After privatisation, South Eastern Trains took over the services, but the line through Otford to Blackfriars and beyond was later allocated to First Capital Connect.

The final link in the Sevenoaks railway system came with the opening in July 1881 of the line from ***Dunton Green*** to Westerham. Operated by what was commonly called 'a pull and push locomotive', it was a feeder for the main London trains. The original scheme to extend the line from Westerham to Oxted by 1890 was never realised. With falling passenger numbers the line was finally closed in October 1961 to much local opposition.

Tubs Hill station, a mainly timber building, was demolished in 1975 and replaced.

White (1992); Gould (1999)

railway tunnels

The long ***Polhill*** tunnel under the North Downs, and the Sevenoaks railway tunnel, were constructed as part of the new line to Tonbridge. The Polhill tunnel, one mile and 850 yards long through chalk, was relatively easy to build. The workers or 'navigators' were housed in temporary accommodation at ***Bogs Island, Dunton Green,*** where the pub called the Miners' Arms used to preserve their memory. The Sevenoaks tunnel, which runs for one mile and 1,691 yards through the greensand ridge under the western end of the ***Kippington estate,*** was more difficult to cut. Work began in 1863 against considerable opposition from local landowners. It needed tall towers to site the line accurately, and these were later followed by tall ventilation shafts. Despite initial surveys, the builders soon ran into unexpected underground ***water*** where the clay soil joined the underlying greensand. As a result the works were flooded, and the original contractor, ***John Jay,*** had to surrender the contract. The workers were poorly housed in huts in White Hart Wood, and a temporary iron chapel was built for their use on ***Tubs Hill.*** The tunnel was eventually completed and the line opened throughout in 1868.

Leeds (2000); Marx (1867/1990)

railway accidents

The ***railway*** through Sevenoaks has seen two major train crashes. The first was in 1884, when a signalling error led to a collision between two goods trains at ***Tubs Hill*** station; the driver and fireman of one of them were killed. A worse accident occurred in 1927, when an express passenger train headed by one of the new 'River' class tank engines was derailed just south of the bridge across the Shoreham road at Riverhead. The carriages were thrown to both sides of the track, 13 passengers were killed and many injured. An enquiry later found that the ballast was badly laid and the track had shifted. This, added to the high centre of gravity of the side-tanks of this locomotive, led to violent oscillation and finally to the derailment. All the 'River' engines were withdrawn and later rebuilt as tender locomotives.

66 Building Sevenoaks tunnel. This watercolour by an unknown artist shows work on the north end of the Sevenoaks tunnel in 1868. The railway from Charing Cross to Sevenoaks was reputed at the time to be the most expensive line ever built, costing £9.5 million; the Sevenoaks tunnel cost one million pounds.

An account by Sir Jonathan Hutchinson FRS (1828-1913), who saw the tunnel being built through the sandstone ridge in 1867:

> *'As yet the bottom level [of the tunnel] had not been reached everywhere but the ground was broken in many different places and deep clefts were being carried down: at several there were shafts some 300 feet deep; so deep in fact that we could be just see a candle at the bottom which looked like a dim star. At the top of each shaft was a steam engine by which the material was being drawn up. The rope used was of wire. The rock, clay etc was brought up in a small wheel carriage which fitted on a railway at the top and was at once wheeled off on its arrival; the water came up in a large tub and was turned out into troughs. ... The men at the bottom were standing knee deep in water but this an informant said was not the worst of it, the water constantly dripping upon them being a much greater annoyance. We saw two men come up in the bucket; they were both very weak, pale and cold looking.'*

Raley's Corner
The bend in the narrow main road at the 'top of the town' by ***Six Bells Lane***. It is named after a bakery on the corner called Raley's.

Thomas Percy Ratcliff (1874-1952)
T.P. Ratcliff, 'The Man in White', widely known as the 'father' of community singing, was born in Faversham. He lived in the United States, and when war was declared in 1917 he assisted recruitment drives by leading singing in public cinemas during intervals between films. He returned to Britain after the War, from 1941 onwards living in Sevenoaks High Street and being employed as a temporary singing master at ***Sevenoaks School***. Ratcliff's chief claim to fame was the worldwide recognition he gained in the inter-war years as the conductor *sans pareil* of massed community singing occasions, such as Cup Finals at Wembley Stadium, as well as at major military tattoos. Dressed completely in white he commanded large crowds. Ratcliff was also the editor of the *News Chronicle Song Book*, which enjoyed enormous popularity during the hey-day of the Community Singing movement and for a long time afterwards.

rates
The main source of local taxation was rates levied on property, mainly lands and houses. The revenue collected was used to meet the costs of local administration, including provision of poor relief, law and order, and the maintenance of roads. In the 19th century the role of government steadily increased both at central and local level, thus requiring more revenue and greater supervision.

Rectory Lane
A short lane off the Upper High Street immediately north of ***St Nicholas Church***, originally leading to the ***glebe lands*** that stretched down into the valley and to Glebe Farm, immediately to the west of the church. One of the Glebe fields, known as Quarry Field, was a possible source of ***ragstone***. It may have been the source of the stone for the new boundary wall constructed by the stonemason John Marchant when, in 1810, the churchyard was extended westwards into part of the glebe land given by the Rector. By 1818 the first part of the lane served as a grand entrance and carriage sweep to the ***St Nicholas Rectory*** set in ample landscaped gardens, including a pond to the north of the house. By 1869 the line of the lane and walls was clearly established, with a footpath over open fields down to Oak Lane. In 1931 A.D. ***Laurie*** bought much of the glebe land. He sold the farm in 1938; the new owner demolished it and built a modern house on its footprint. A sizeable part of the rectory garden was sold in 1960 and houses built in what became St Nicholas Drive.

Red House
Now number 50 High Street was built in 1686 for Thomas Couchman of Tooting. The famous pharmacist Dr ***Thomas Fuller*** owned it from 1688 until his death. It was then owned by John William Cranston until 1743, when it was purchased by Francis ***Austen***, already agent to the duke of Dorset, and the founder of a firm of solicitors to which ***Knocker*** and Foskett are direct successors. An engraving of the house appears in Harris's

67 A postcard of ***St Nicholas church*** from ***Rectory Lane***, *c*.1900. This photograph, taken around the end of the 19th century, and made into a coloured postcard, looks towards the west end of St Nicholas. The kissing gate on the right is on a footpath to ***Oak Lane***. The traditional five-barred gate was to let wagons and animals through to Rectory farm.

History of Kent (1719), from which it is apparent that the present door case was not an original feature; also the three dormers on the street frontage were then five. Francis Austen improved the domestic facilities. Francis lived long enough to welcome his great-niece, Jane Austen, to the Red House in 1788 when she visited with her parents and sister Cassandra. Latterly he shared his legal practice with John Fellowes Claridge, who on Francis's death in 1791 entered into partnership with his son Francis Motley Austen and also served as a JP. The legal practice continued under various guises – Austen & Claridge (*c*.1785-1838); Austen, Claridge and Holcroft (1838-1841); W.F.Holcroft (1844-1864), Holcroft and Knocker (1864-1884), and so on, but apparently in other premises, for from 1796

In June 1751, Francis Austen was visited by his aunt Mary Tilden; she wrote: 'I hired Horse & man & went one day to Sevenoak while Neice Hooper was there. Nephew fine; House & gardens were very delightfull; he shew'd me all the Offices where Brewing, Bakeing, Washing &c [are done], Coach House, Grainery, where to dry Hopps &c. which he built himself, & lastly his Cellars, well stored with the best Wines & other good liquor. I told him I wisht I was his Housekeeper, I should live well, and afterwards advised him to marry again and enjoy all his good things with a good Wife. I almost think Cousin Austen has laid out as much in Buildeing and making things convenient in his House as the whole Purchase was at first, it being sold very reasonable as I have heard.'

to 1885, the Red House was occupied by a school for young gentlemen known as the Sevenoaks Academy. It became the premises of Knocker and Foskett in 1935.

Redman's Place
A narrow cobbled street which ran from the High Street to the back of the modern Waitrose store. Redman's Place was reached under an archway which still exists on the east side of the High Street between numbers 78 and 80, Warrens and Brewers. It was originally called Harvey's Yard or Printing House Yard. The insanitary houses had no ***main drainage***. ***Water*** came from a well and pump in the yard. The 1891 census lists shoemakers, an upholsterer, servants, shop boys, a groom, a glazier, a dressmaker, a farm labourer, a coach builder, postmen, a tea dealer, a laundress, a char woman, a carpenter and a bricklayer living in the 16 terraced houses in the street. In 1961 the houses were demolished under a slum clearance order.

Religious census 1851
The only official national census of attendance at places of religious worship was conducted on Sunday, 30 March 1851. The returns, taken the same day as the official census of population, provide a snapshot of one aspect of religious activity. The local figures, especially for ***St Nicholas***, are vague, and indicate that more than 1,500 people attended a service at one of the three established churches (in Sevenoaks, Riverhead, and Weald), with 460 at the ***Methodist*** chapel, and 750 at the ***Baptist*** church in Sevenoaks and the chapel in ***Hartsland***. This was a better turnout than across much of England, the national figures indicating that only half the population attended any place of worship, and that the numbers worshipping in the established church were in decline compared with those going to nonconformist places of worship.
Roake (1999), 128-31

Frank Richards (b.1868)
Born in Kent, Richards came to Sevenoaks as a journalist for the *Sevenoaks Chronicle*, which he later edited. In 1901 he published his *Old Sevenoaks*, illustrated by his friend ***Charles Essenhigh Corke***.

Riverhead
The origin of the name Riverhead may come from the Anglo-Saxon *hrither + hyth* – 'cattlewharf', or *rither* meaning a hill. It was the centre of the ***Codsheath Hundred***, the Hundred occupying the high ground where ***St Mary's*** Church now stands. The village was a 'Liberty' of Sevenoaks parish until 1894 when ***Sevenoaks Urban District Council*** was established and the village gained its own parish council. At the time Riverhead was a village of modest size clustered round the crossing of the Sevenoaks to London and the Maidstone to Reigate roads. The village, surrounded by farm and parkland, had about 300 dwellings, half in the village and half in the scattered settlements. ***Montreal Park*** was to the south, the park wall forming a boundary to the village centre, ***Chipstead Place*** to the west and ***Bradbourne Park*** to the east. After the opening of the ***railway*** stations at ***Bat and Ball*** in 1862 and ***Tubs Hill*** in 1868, the village grew steadily to accommodate new commuters.
Mills (1994); Anon (2002)

68 Protesters in ***Riverhead*** demand the enforcement of the speed limit through the village, 1920s. After 1920 the number of ***motor vehicles*** steadily increased in Sevenoaks. ***Roads*** were numbered and the A21 through Riverhead and the town carried more passing traffic. There were speed limits, charabancs restricted to 12 mph in built-up areas. But a great deal of local traffic consisted of horse-drawn carts and wagons. It was an uncomfortable mix, and the people of Riverhead objected to their quiet village being disturbed by speeding motor cars. It was a political issue, and they acted.

69 ***Riverhead*** infants' school 2002. The school formerly stood in the centre of the village. In 2002 it moved to a new and unusual building on ***Worships Hill***, designed by Roger FitzGerald, which generated much interest. The building has a curved roof with sedum growing on it, which turns different colours with the seasons. Sedum needs virtually no soil, making the roof structure lighter, and it does not need to be cut. Sedum also supports wildlife, and delays rainwater run-off, reducing the load on drainage systems. All the classrooms face the parkland to the south, getting the best of the sunlight and natural ventilation, while the hall, entrance, and staff areas all face Worships Hill, buffering the children from the noise and danger of a very busy road. The entrance is a like a giant triangular shape, in red, the school colours. The hall is a big blue cube. The doors to the classrooms are all different, and vision panels are set at the average eye height of the pupils, so the children can easily see through and the adults have to bend down. There are very low windows to the library, so the pupils can see out when they sit on the floor listening to a story.

Riverhill
The hill down the sandstone scarp to the south of Sevenoaks. The name comes from the Anglo-Saxon 'rither', hill.

Riverhill House
A house originally built in the late 16th or early 17th century standing just off the main road and below ***Riverhill*** with extensive views south across the ***weald***. Among early owners of the house and small estate were the ***Petts***, their presence commemorated by Petts Style, on the boundary with ***Knole Park***, and a field called Petts Piece. In the 17th century it came into the possession of the Beseech family, Richard Beseech being a yeoman farmer. His land passed to the Children family in 1665 and they were responsible for building the core of the present house of locally quarried ***ragstone*** on the site of the Tudor farmstead. From the Childrens the house passed by marriage to Henry ***Woodgate*** in 1781, large landowners to the south. Woodgate, in partnership with Children, lost heavily when their private Tonbridge Bank failed in 1816. He left Riverhill House, which was let to the Buckleys, who had two children, the daughter dying in infancy, the son killed as a 17-year-old ensign at Waterloo in 1815. The Woodgates in 1842 sold Riverhill House to ***John Rogers*** who began the process of laying out a specialist garden and enlarging the house. Riverhill House has remained in the hands of the Rogers ever since. In 2009 the owners, benefiting from the advice and publicity of the 'Country House Rescue' programme on Channel 4 television, adapted the gardens for wider public access.
Woodgate (1910); Jenkins (2003)

road names
The earliest road names are medieval in origin. Some roads were named because they were directional: the London, Tonbridge, Dartford, and Seal roads, and Shoreham Lane. Others indicated a change in the terrain: Bayley's Hill (known as such in 1650), ***Tubs Hill***, and ***Seal Hollow Road***. Some roads were named after the locality, for example ***St John's Hill*** and Road, and Wilderness Avenue. Most local street names date from Victorian times when new residential roads were laid out, often named after local landowners and developers (Polhill, after the ***Polhill*** family, Cramptons Road after ***Thomas Crampton***), national figures (Cobden Road, Gordon Road), or after a physical feature (Sandy Lane, Quarry Hill, ***Riverhill***). Road names have also changed, Madams-Court Road, as it was called until the early 19th century, becoming Star Hill, and Sandy Lane becoming Bullfinch Lane. Parts of roads also had distinctive names, for example in ***Hartsland***, four dwellings on the west side of Prospect Road were known until the 1940s as Hortus Place. As can be seen from the early census enumerators' returns and street directories, houses in most streets were not numbered until the development of the modern ***postal service*** in the mid-19th century. Small houses might be identified by a terrace name, such as Cedar Terrace; larger homes were named by owners, and were often subject to change. Many of the large houses built on the new estates of ***Kippington*** and ***Greatness*** were not numbered but only had names.

In the late 20th century new roads have been named after a builder's daughter (Blair Close), a local figure (***Baden-Powell*** Road, Riverhead),

70 Dartford Road looking north, *c*.1905. A coloured postcard of one of Sevenoaks's main roads at the junction of ***Mount Harry Road***. There is little traffic, the occasional horse and cart, a couple of cyclists, and gas street lamps. The late Victorian houses are separated from the road by front gardens, hedged and fenced, with gates. On the skyline is the silhouette of the ***Congregational*** church at the top of ***St John's Hill***.

71 London Road looking north, *c*.1900. Another coloured postcard, produced by ***Salmon***, of a local scene at the top of ***Tubs Hill***, as the road descends towards the railway station. To the modern eye it is easily recognised by the lie of the road, the roofscape, and the houses with the projecting upper bay windows. It might look idyllic but Sevenoaks was home to many people who struggled on low incomes, lived in poor conditions, and whose children died from tuberculosis, diphtheria, influenza, and measles.

a former ***nursery*** (Turner's Close), and the owner of a small factory (Morel Court), and to continue the name of large houses that previously occupied the site (e.g. Egdean Walk, ***Merlewood***, and ***Carrick*** Drive).

roads

The oldest roads in Sevenoaks are the early medieval drove roads, the present London and Dartford roads which meet in the town and along which animals were driven from the ***North Downs*** and the ***Vale of Holmesdale*** into the ***weald***. From 1555 each parish was responsible for maintaining local highways, paid for by local ***rates***, and with local people providing the labour. The Highways Act of 1835 introduced a new system

with paid overseers for groups of parishes. In the 18th century the major north-south and east-west roads through Sevenoaks became ***turnpikes***. However, most roads and tracks had natural surfaces that were dusty in summer and muddy and rutted in winter; the clay weald was especially difficult to cross even when roads were improved. In Sevenoaks a common sight during dry weather was the water cart to lay dust on the roads. The great change in roads came with macadam surfaces which were steadily applied to most public roads in the 20th century.

Rockdale

Built as the home of the ***Laurie*** family in 1875, the three-storey ragstone building belonged to Alfred J. St George McAdam Laurie, who in the 1890s had the first telephone in the town with no. 1. His son, Sir John Dawson Laurie, lived at Rockdale but after his death the house was sold in 1951 to the Sevenoaks and District Old People's Housing Association, and was converted for accommodation for 'old men and women who had come to the end of their tether and could no longer live on their own'. Since then flats for people aged over 60 to rent have been built on the Rockdale site: The Pleasaunce in 1959, Rockdale Gardens in 1968, Beatrice Wilson flats in 1985 and Stable Court in 1992. Rockdale Housing Association also recognised the need for leasehold properties and therefore built 28 apartments (Webbs Meadow and Constant Meadow) in Akehurst Lane. In 2009 planning permission was granted for the construction of a new 48-bedroom care home and to convert and extend Rockdale House into leasehold flats.

John Rodgers (1906-93)

Elected MP for Sevenoaks in 1950, Rodgers was the sitting member for the next 29 years. From York, he became a lecturer at Hull University but quickly turned to the world of advertising, eventually rising to be deputy chairman of J. Walter Thompson. Rodgers used his commercial skills in various government departments during the ***Second World War***. In Parliament he was among the One Nation group of Tory MPs intent on modernising the party. Rodgers was pro-European but had little concern for office, briefly serving as Minister for Regional Development and Employment 1958-60. In the words of his fellow MP Geoffrey Rippon, he was 'a happy man who in a long life did many good things'.

John Rogers (1807-67)

Rogers came from a family of Wiltshire cotton cloth merchants who by the early 18th century had established themselves in London. John Rogers, an avid botanist and plant collector, was a correspondent of Charles Darwin, and became a Fellow of the Royal Society in 1839. He married a daughter of Henry Thornton of Clapham. Rogers saw ***Riverhill House***, liked it, first moved his family to ***Vine Lodge*** in Sevenoaks, and then bought the property from the ***Woodgates*** in 1842. He exploited the acid soils of the garden on the sheltered south-facing sandstone hill, growing various rare plants and trees brought to Britain from Asia and the Americas. His horticultural activities were carefully recorded in his gardening notebook. Rogers died of cholera in Switzerland.

Roman Catholics
From the 1560s onwards Roman Catholics (like other religious dissenters) were persecuted by the State. The major Roman Catholic family in Sevenoaks in the 16th and 17th centuries were the ***Lones***. The Compton Census returns of 1676 stated that out of 900 adults in the parish only eight were 'papists' (and 20 nonconformists). Although a relatively small minority, Catholics were seen as disloyal because they acknowledged an Italian ruler, and as such they were prevented from holding public office until 1829. Within Kent opposition to Catholic emancipation was very strong. Hostility towards Catholics declined very slowly through the 19th century, increasing in 1850 when the Roman Catholic church re-established its system of bishops in England. The Roman Catholic church of ***St Thomas*** was opened in Sevenoaks in 1880, followed by a church school.
Dobson (1978); Bell (1996)

Romans in the Sevenoaks area
There are numerous recorded Roman sites in Kent and signs of considerable activity in areas surrounding Sevenoaks. However, Sevenoaks itself is almost a blank with only two finds recorded, one a fourth-century Roman coin found in 1933 in Buckhurst Avenue, the other a Romano-British cremation urn found in ***Kippington*** Road in 1973. Whilst the coin may be the result of a stray loss, the cremation is of more significance, suggesting settlement not too far away. The lack of information is perhaps not surprising. Romans, or Romano-Britons, settled in the fertile river valley of the ***Darent*** which provided an easy line of communication, and not on the poor soils of the sandstone ridge. The villa at Lullingstone, and other elite dwellings in the Darent valley from Otford to Farningham, bear witness to this. Many minor ***roads***, as yet unrecorded, probably existed to link outlying farms and villas, such as the one at Plaxtol, east of Sevenoaks, to settlements and roads. Many of these roads may have been merely tracks, possibly of pre-Roman origin. The road passing the Iron-Age hillfort of Oldbury in Ightham is reputed to be of early date. This route passes near the area of Seal Chart where a substantial Roman-British cremation cemetery was found in 1835, containing at least 60 urns, burnt earth, ashes and calcined stone. This, again, indicates the presence of a settlement nearby and not far to the west, directly on the old route, a Roman well was discovered in 1907. Two sites are recorded in Stone Street, east of Sevenoaks, one suggesting the location of a farmstead or villa. Nearer to Sevenoaks, close to the parish boundary, is the site of another cremation cemetery at One Tree Hill where a number of urns were found in 1888. West of Sevenoaks there is also a scattering of Roman sites: pottery, two cremation sites and a gold coin at Brasted and an interesting site at Sundridge with not only pottery, but bloomery slag as well, indicating that metal working was being carried out.
Williams (2010)

John Rooker (1859-1936)
The Rev. John Rooker was Rector of Sevenoaks from 1907 to 1920, the first evangelical minister of the parish church. After ordination he served

his first curacy at ***St Mary's Kippington*** from 1884-86. Rooker had a keen interest in the history of the area, writing articles that appeared first in the *Sevenoaks Chronicle*, and then published as *Notes on the Parish Church of St Nicholas* (1910). He also wrote accounts of his travels in the Middle East. Rooker was a political ***Liberal***, endorsing Lloyd-George in the general election of 1918 and standing as a Liberal Party candidate for the Urban District Council in 1920.

Rose and Crown Hotel
A former double-bayed ***coaching*** hotel in the High Street, at one time called the Commercial Travellers and Farmers Inn. It had a long connection with the ***market***. On market days the sheep and cattle pens would reach as far as the doorway and, inside, rooms became the headquarters for the day for buyers and sellers. The gardens extended to what is now Buckhurst Avenue. The hotel closed in 1936 and was demolished the following year.

Royal Crown Hotel
This inn stood at the corner of South Park and London Road, was originally a ***coaching*** house on the route between London and the South Coast. It had an enormous ballroom which was the social centre of the town from the mid-19th to the early 20th centuries. Dinners, dances, meetings and auction sales were held at the hotel. The garden extended to 12 acres, with views over the valley towards Ide Hill.

Royal Oak Hotel
In the Upper High Street, a ***coaching*** inn on the route from London to the South Coast. It was formerly called the Black Bull, and before that the Bull and Brush. ***Jane Edwards*** in her Diary (1863) called it a 'large and respectable inn where balls were held'. The former Royal Oak Tap next door was a ***forge***.

rubbish dump
The area of the ***Vestry estate***, once known as Old Ladds Hill, a brick field formerly owned by ***Thomas Crampton***, was sold to a Southwark vestry for use as a rubbish dump in the late 1880s. For many decades it served as a major tip. When full a further rubbish dump was developed in another former ***brickworks*** on the west side of the Otford Road, acquired from Durtnells by ***Sevenoaks Urban District Council*** who operated it as a household refuse tip until the waste disposal function was transferred to Kent County Council in 1974. The tip was subsequently capped with clay and closed down. A new public rubbish disposal site was then opened at Dunbrik.

rugby
Rugby was first played formally in Sevenoaks in the 1920s. In 1924 Sevenoaks School played its first game and in 1925 Sevenoaks Rugby Football Club was founded. Its first pitch was in ***Hitchen Hatch Lane*** and the sides changed in the ***Sennocke Hotel***. The first home game, against Lensbury in October 1925, was won. Soon after the club moved to its present ground at Knole Paddock where, under covenants established when the ***Sevenoaks Urban District Council*** acquired the land from

72 The ***Royal Crown Hotel*** in the upper London Road: a late 19th-century photograph. The Royal Crown was once the centre of much of the social and cultural life of the well-to-do of Sevenoaks. The hotel was demolished in 1935 to make way for the Odeon ***cinema***. The ***Stag*** theatre complex now occupies the London Road side of the site, and the ***post office***, built in 1975, stands on the South Park side. Crown Fields, a small housing development, was built in the former gardens of the hotel

Knole, it had the right to the use of two pitches in perpetuity. The 1930s was a golden period for the club with players representing Kent and the London Division and playing in England trials. In 1947 the club arranged with the Vine Cricket Club for the use of its pavilion for changing and post-match hospitality and then in 1952 there was the official opening of the first club house, a wooden building, on a piece of land between Knole Paddock and Raleys Field. In 1959 the first venture into junior rugby began with an U21 side, quickly followed by an U18 side and, in the school holidays, U18 and U16 schoolboy sides. From the mid-1960s the club was regularly fielding six sides, mainly playing block fixtures against clubs from the South East. In 1966 the club had its first tour to Pontoise, Sevenoaks's twin town. Development since has been rapid: in 1978 a new clubhouse was built, mini rugby was started; in 1984 the club had its first coach; and in 1987 league rugby was introduced with Sevenoaks in Kent 1. More than 25 ex-juniors have played junior international rugby and in 2000 David Flatman became the club's first full international followed four years later by Andy Titterell, who also became a British Lion. In

2003, the club had the honour of one of its members, Robert Horner, being President of the RFU in the year England won the world cup.

Julius Joseph Runge (1879-1935)

Runge came from a prosperous German Jewish family. He made his money from sugar and was the first Managing Director of the newly amalgamated Tate and Lyle in 1921. In 1926 he leased ***Kippington Court*** for a short while before buying it. An immensely wealthy man, he purchased a major part of the ***Montreal estate*** from the 4th Earl of Amherst, with a view to protecting it from commercial development. He first bought Middlings Wood, some 35 acres of land between Kippington Road and Brittains Lane, and in 1925 put in an offer of £85,000 for 2,650 acres, the bulk of the remainder of the Montreal Estate. Covenants were placed limiting development to detached properties which were 'artistic and pleasing', in order to protect the estate. Within six months of his death, his executors sold the estate and the developers moved in.

Rye road

Also known as 'the fish road' which until the 16th century offered the quickest route from the coast to London. It came through ***Salters Heath***, or Mackerels Plain as it used to be called, to ***Chipstead***. Strings of packhorses brought baskets of fish landed at the port of Rye. There was a fish market in Chipstead where the fish was bought by the Royal Purveyor for the Court and by London merchants.

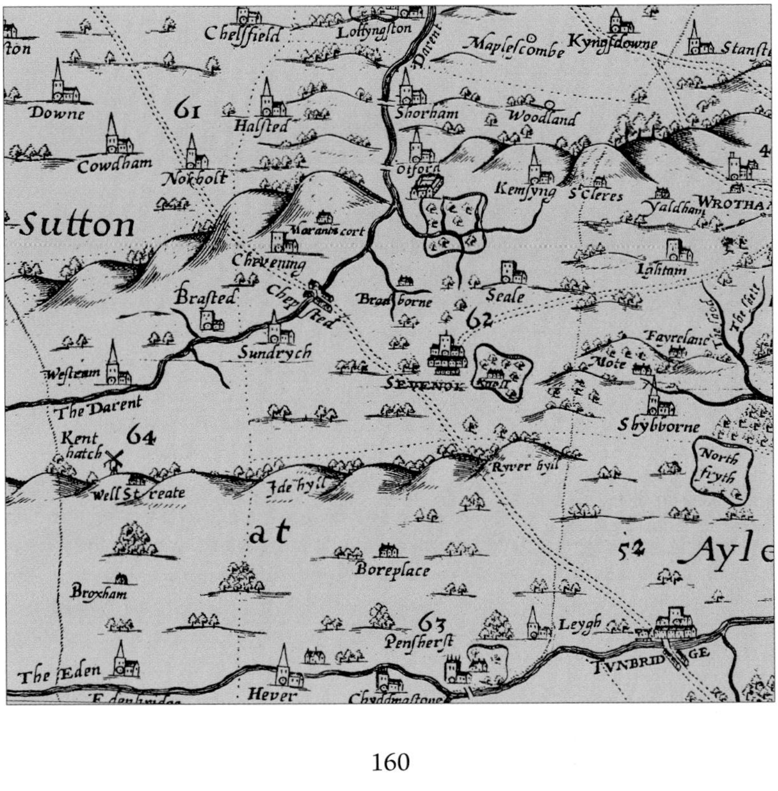

Map 12 The ***Rye Road*** in 1596, shown on Philip Simonson's map of the County, described as 'A New Description of Kent'. The map, drawn to the scale of half-an-inch to the mile, shows the Rye Road crossing the Medway at Tonbridge, then via ***Riverhill*** to ***Chipstead***, after which it climbs the ***North Downs*** to Knockholt and on to London. The other road running east from Sevenoaks is ***Seal Hollow Road***. Simonson also shows the ***deer parks*** at Penshurst, Knole and Otford.

S

Vita Sackville-West (1892-1962)

Victoria (Vita) Sackville-West was born at ***Knole***. As the only child of Lionel Edward Sackville-West, 3rd Baron Sackville, and his cousin, Victoria Sackville-West, her upbringing was privileged and solitary, and the chief companion of her childhood was the great palace of Knole. In her prolific garden writings, Sackville-West acknowledged that the 26-acre walled garden gave her the idea of a garden long before she created her own gardens at ***Long Barn*** in ***Weald*** and Sissinghurst Castle with her husband Harold Nicolson, whom she married in 1913. Knole's aristocratic associations and its historical backcloth helped to develop Sackville-West's literary taste and define her temperament. Her first publication, *Chatterton*, was printed privately in Sevenoaks in 1909, when she was seventeen. According to her biographer, Victoria Glendinning, Vita spent hours in the attic at Knole acting out the Chatterton drama. When her father died in 1928, by primogeniture the house and the title passed to Sackville-West's uncle, Charles (1870-1962). The loss of Knole affected her for the rest of her life, and what she called her 'atavistic passion' for her childhood home is clearly displayed in her book *Knole and the Sackvilles* (1922).

Brown (1985); Glendinning (1983)

St Botolph's Road

In the 1640s the City of London parish of St Botolph-without-Bishopsgate bought from Sir Ralph ***Bosville*** 80 acres of land in Sevenoaks. The purpose was to produce rent which each year would 'clothe four poor men of the parish'. Several tenants rented the estate and by 1852 the lease was secured by Samuel ***Bligh***. Sevenoaks's population grew with the coming of the railway in the 1860s, and the St Botolph vestry sought to increase the value of their asset by constructing a new road and leasing land for housing. St Botolph's Road was built in 1877 but remained unused as there were difficulties with the Charity Commissioners over leasing building plots. Twenty years later the estate was sold to the British Land Company which put in two new roads, The Drive and Pembroke Road, and house building began in St Botolph's Road. The final part of the St Botolph estate, owned by the Bishopsgate Foundation, was the ***Sennocke Hotel***, built opposite the railway station in 1868.

Killingray (2004b)

Map 13 The St Botolph's estate in 1841. For over 300 years the London parish of St Botolphs-without-Bishopsgate owned property in Sevenoaks. The land extended from the old Blighs farm house (the modern Oak Tree) in the High Street north-east to the site of the mainline railway station, an area originally of over 80 acres bounded by the Dartford Road and *Hitchen Hatch Lane*. Tree names indicate size or the nature of each field.

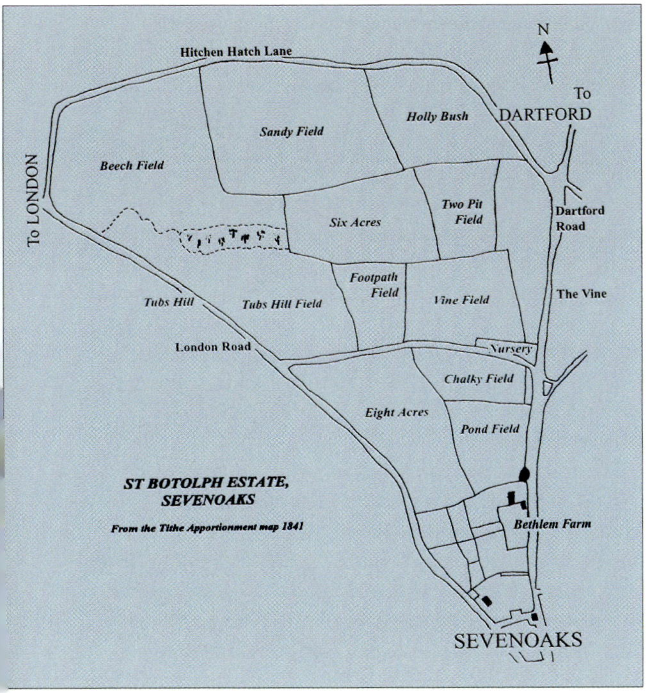

St Edward the Confessor, Weald
The Roman Catholic church of St Edward was built in Weald in 1965 by the Castelli family, who for several years lived at ***Long Barn***. Although it had seating for 100 people, the shortage of priests meant that services had to be limited to a mass on Friday mornings.

St George's Weald
The old parish of ***St Nicholas*** extended well south of Weald village. In winter time and wet weather parishioners, particularly the poor, faced a long uphill journey to the parish church in Sevenoaks. To 'ease' the situation, St George was built as a chapel of ease in 1820 'for the accommodation of the Poor in the Weald in the parish of Sevenoaks'. The ***ragstone*** building was enlarged in 1839 and ***Thomas Jackson*** added a chancel in 1870. A small church school was also built 1836-42. Weald became a separate parish in 1861. In the last ten years an extension has been added to the church building.

St Hilary's School
A private day school for girls founded by Mrs Dorothy Packman, a woman of high ideals and spiritual outlook. The school started as a small kindergarten in a private house in Seal in 1942. Two years later the school moved to the large house, known then as Park View, in Bradbourne Park Road and the name St Hilary's was adopted. In 1992 St Hilary's merged with ***Walthamstow Hall*** to become the junior department of that school.

St John Ambulance Association
The Association was formed in Britain in 1877, dedicated to teaching medical first aid and providing ambulance services. The Sevenoaks headquarters is now at ***Bat and Ball*** in the ***iron church***, originally the temporary ***Roman Catholic*** building, brought to this site from Granville Road in 1884.

St John the Baptist church
In the mid-19th century as a small community began to develop at ***Hartsland*** and ***St John's***, ***Thomas Curteis*** the Rector of ***St Nicholas***, had a chapel of ease built on ***St John's Hill***. Opened in 1858 the building was constructed of ***ragstone*** and stood on land donated by the Marquis of ***Camden***. The church derived its name from the medieval St John the Baptist Hospital, which stood further down the hill, near the ***Bat and Ball*** crossroads. Nearby stood the Shrine of Our Lady of Greatness which also had its Holy Well, called the ***St John's Well***. In 1862 the first ***railway*** station in Sevenoaks opened at Bat and Ball, generating further demand for housing and also encouraging industrial growth. To accommodate the needs of the expanding population the north aisle and baptistery were added in 1878, when St John's also became a parish in its own right. In 1900 a magnificent red-brick church was planned but, with the ***First World War*** looming, only the first stage was completed, adding the present east end and Lady Chapel built in red brick. The adjoining parish room was completed in 1910.

St John's
A triangular area of north Sevenoaks bordered on the west by ***Bradbourne*** Road, on the east by ***Hartsland,*** and by the A25 to the north. Much of the area was developed for housing in the decades between 1840 and 1880, with further infilling in the early and mid-20th century.

St John's Health Clinic
Set up by Dr ***Carnarvon Brown*** in 1914 and run by a voluntary committee for its first 10 years. Hundreds of Sevenoaks mothers and babies attended on a regular basis.

St John's Hill
The northern continuation of the Dartford Road, as it descends towards the ***Vale of Holmesdale.*** Until the mid-19th century is was often referred to by local people as ***Workhouse*** Hill because of the presence of that uncomfortable reminder of poverty and distress which stood on the west side at the junction with the present Camden Road. The shops and pubs at the top and the bottom of the hill – Upper and Lower St John's – were built in the late 19th century.

St John's National Mixed School
An elementary school built in ***Quaker's Hall Lane*** in 1873 for the children living in the ***Hartsland*** and adjoining areas. The school became a primary school in the mid-20th century. It was demolished in 1978, and replaced with a block of flats, now called 'Old School Court'.
Nigel Yates, Robert Hume and Paul Hastings (1994), plates 10 & 11

St John's School, Bayham Road
Built in 1877 as Sevenoaks Public Elementary School for Infants. When it enlarged to take boys from ***Cobden Road School,*** it became known as Bayham Road County Primary School. The pupils from ***St John's National School*** in Quakers Hall Lane joined the St John's School when their school was closed.

St John's Well
Until recently there was no proof of the position of St John's or Our Lady's Well, despite several references. ***Gordon Ward*** mentions 'St John's Well' in his *Sevenoaks Essays* (1931) as being 'recently covered in'. The spring was found again after research by the vicar of ***St John's church*** in 2008. It is sealed by a large stone slab and located in a private garden.

St Joseph's Catholic (Mixed) School
In 1882, a school for the children of the parishioners of ***St Thomas's Church*** in Granville Road was built at the southern junction of Prospect Road and Cobden Road, where now stand modern semi-detached houses. Financial constraints, coupled with the small number of Catholic pupils and the inconvenient distance from the church, led to the closure of the school in 1900.

St Julian's
In 1819 John Charles ***Herries*** leased the site of St Julian's, one mile south of Sevenoaks in a commanding position overlooking the ***weald.***

He commissioned a new house and garden from the architect John B. Papworth, duly completed by 1821 using ragstone from the estate. John Charles shared the lease of the property with his cousin Robert Herries. Over the next few years J.C. Herries, now a High Tory MP, extended the estate and bought the lease from ***Multon Lambarde***. By the 1830s the two cousins decided to remodel and extend the house and they asked the architect James Pennethorne to undertake this work. Pennethorne's plans were submitted in late 1835 and the work was completed two years later. Over the next few decades the Herries extended their 200-acre estate southwards and bought further land. The Herries sold the estate in the 1940s and it became a country club.
Bates and Killingray (2003)

St Luke's parish church
Within the parish of Sevenoaks, the new independent parish of ***St Mary's Kippington*** was established in 1877. As the parish was bisected by the ***railway*** cutting, ***William Thompson***, owner of the ***Kippington estate***, aimed to provide churches in both halves of the parish and, as a temporary solution, utilised the small ***iron church*** in Granville Road which had been erected in 1878 for worship whilst St Mary's was being built. Plans by John Thomas Lee to build a more permanent, red-brick church in Granville Road were modified for a new site in Eardley Road, acquired in 1902 from the proprietors of the nearby Children's Hip Hospital. In July 1903 phase one began; in 1908 phase two was started with the building of the nave, to which a third bay was added in 1912-1913 to accommodate the children's carriages from the Hospital. In this period St Luke's enjoyed a measure of devolution as a 'daughter' church within the parish of Kippington. From the 1940s onwards, St Luke's was largely the responsibility of the curate at St Mary's, for whom the parsonage was built in 1954-1955. An application for parochial status was rejected in 1957 and, instead, in 1958 a Conventional District was established with its own minister, churchwardens and church council and financial independence. Also in the late 1950s the original church was completed to Frederick R. Pite's designs, including space at the west end of the church, a new choir vestry, new fittings and a permanent hall. Finally, in 1996, St Luke's became an independent parish with its first vicar. In 1998 the Millennium Project was launched to carry out further improvements to the church, to the designs of Malcolm Green, including a new parish office, disabled access, parish room, and new bell, all dedicated by the Bishop of Rochester in October 2002.
Killingray (2004); Newman (2003)

St Mary's Kippington
In 1864, ***William James Thompson***, a wealthy tea importer and churchwarden at the parish church of ***St Nicholas***, acquired the ***Kippington*** estate. Thompson resolved to set up a new church in his own parish in order to meet his evangelical convictions, which he considered were not being fulfilled at St Nicholas. The first place of worship was the temporary '***Iron Church***', situated on a plot in Granville Road, which was dedicated in April 1878. Later the same year the foundation stone of the new St Mary's was laid on a site in what is now Kippington Road. The

building cost £12,500 and is of Early English Gothic design built with seating for approximately 450. The consecration ceremony, presided over by Archbishop Tait, took place in 1880. Thompson's nine children included Henry, who served as Vicar of St Mary's 1895-1919. Most of the memorials in the church commemorate members of the founder's family.

St Mary's Riverhead
St Mary's was built in 1831 to a design by Decimus Burton on land provided by Lord ***Amherst*** and ***Multon Lambarde***. Initially a chapel of ease for ***St Nicholas***, it became a parish in its own right in 1864. Chancel and chapels were added in 1882 by Sir Arthur Blomfield. The building is approached by a long flight of steps to the west tower and overlooks the busy Riverhead Square. The church contains a mosaic reredos by Salviati given by Canon ***Burn-Murdoch***. St Mary combined with St John the Divine, Dunton Green, following the closure of the latter in 1985. A new parish hall was built to the north of St Mary in 1998.
Newman (1976)

St Nicholas church
A church has stood on the site of St Nicholas for at least 1,000 years. The first building was probably a timber thatched wayside shrine on the ***droveway*** to the ***weald***. From this humble structure developed a stone building, on the site of the present chancel. The earliest known record of Sevenoaks as a parish is in the ***Textus Roffensis*** *c*.1120. One hundred years later Sevenoaks was a small ***market*** centre, and the first Rector who is named had charge of what had become a more substantial building constructed from ***ragstone***. By the mid-15th century Thomas ***Bourchier***, Archbishop of Canterbury, owner of ***Knole***, may have been responsible for the further expansion of the perpendicular building that is the present St Nicholas. Little is known of how the Reformation affected St Nicholas; even less is known of the people who formed the congregation. All parishioners were expected to attend services, but clearly not all did. From 1538 the Bible had a central place in the church, and services conformed to the liturgy of the Prayer Book first introduced in 1549. ***John Donne*** was an absent Rector, leaving the 'cure of souls' to his vicar. Later, in the 17th century, two of the clergy, ***Nicholas Gibbon*** and Thomas Kentish, were ejected more for their political views than their theological ideas. During the 1660-70s box pews and galleries were constructed in the nave to provide seats for a growing town population. Even with clear windows this made for a gloomy building, which was also cold and damp in winter.

From 1716-1907 the ***Curteis*** family owned the advowson (reportedly gained in a game of cards) which gave them the right to appoint clergy to St Nicholas. In 1812-13 the 90-foot tower, which was 'in ruinous condition' and 'dangerous', was restored leaving the church with a debt for 60 years. The last Curteis as Rector, at his own expense in the 1870s, removed the box pews and galleries, installed open pews (the oak came from Knole) and new stained glass windows. When Curteis, who was High Church, retired, the advowson was bought by a Low Church trust. Since then St Nicholas has been in the evangelical camp. Curteis's successor was ***John Rooker*** who proved to be a very popular minister. Although the 20th century saw a

73 A modern watercolour of ***St Nicholas church*** by Roger FitzGerald. Unusual for an old parish church, the east end of St Nicholas stands very close to the main road. The position, and the dedication to the patron saint of travellers, offers clues as to its origin, probably as a shrine on an early medieval ***droveway***.

decline in church attendance, especially after 1960, the congregation of St Nicholas increased. By the 1980s the building was too small and limited for all the activities which included a large Sunday school and various youth groups. Several schemes to extend the building failed to meet with congregational or public approval, but the eventual solution was the construction of an Undercroft in the mid-1990s, soon paid for by church members. Since then St Nicholas has 'planted' two other churches that meet in ***Lady Boswell's School***.

Rooker (1910); Killingray (2004); Newman (1976); Cameron (1999)

St Nicholas parish hall

Although ***St Nicholas*** became an evangelical church after 1907, at the height of the Prayer Book controversy in 1927-28, some parishioners feared that this theological position might be lost. In order to preserve an Anglican evangelical presence in the town, a separate trust was established which built the St Nicholas parish hall in South Park (1928). The architect was Charles Cable. The parish hall was demolished and the land sold for flats in order to help pay for the building of the Undercroft at St Nicholas in the 1990s.

St Nicholas rectory

In the past two hundred years there have been three rectories for ***St Nicholas***. The first, now called 'The Old Rectory', is an 18th-century double-fronted house standing on the main road north of the church, rented out until sold in 1946. It served as the Rectory until a new building,

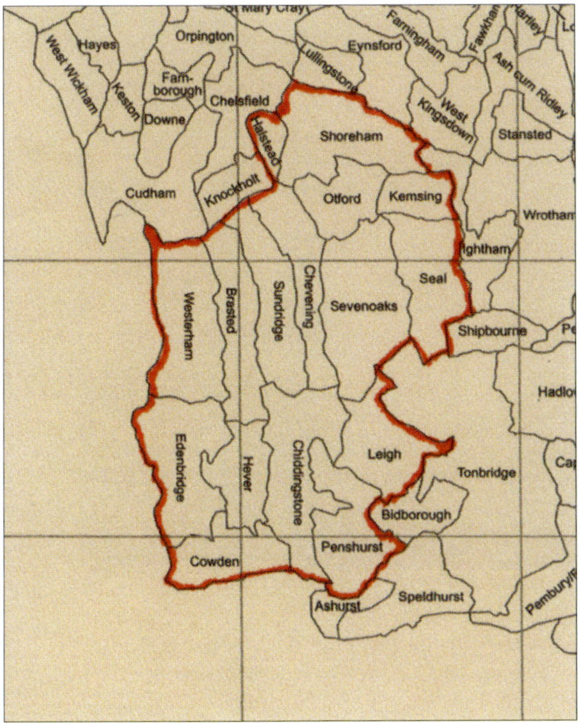

Map 14 The boundaries of St Nicholas Sevenoaks and adjoining parishes in 1850. For nearly a thousand years the boundaries of St Nicholas and the neighbouring parishes remained unchanged. Under the new Poor Law of 1834, 16 parishes were brought together into the Sevenoaks Union. Those boundaries also marked the authority of the Sevenoaks Rural District Council when it was created in 1894.

designed by Decimus Burton, was built in the middle of the Rectory grounds in 1831. This served successive Rectors but by the 1950s it was 'ravaged by dry rot' and condemned. It was demolished in 1959 with part of the Rectory grounds being sold off for housing (St Nicholas Drive), a new Rectory built (architect White), and the old stables converted into a dwelling.

St Nicholas Infants school
The school was established in 1835 at the entrance to Lime Tree Walk, later moved to 59 London Road. In 1885 the school house was converted to a classroom. The school housed 160 children in its early days. The school, which became part of ***Lady Boswell's*** opposite, was finally closed and moved to a new site in 1972.

St Thomas's Roman Catholic church
It took thirty years after the Restoration of the ***Roman Catholic*** hierarchy in England in 1850 before moves were made to build a Catholic Church in Sevenoaks. Initially a very small group of people had heard Mass in a private house in Granville Road. The small Catholic community, under the leadership of Father ***Ignatius Lazzari***, set about acquiring some vacant land in Granville Road and raising funds with a view to first erecting a temporary ***iron church*** and then, when funds permitted, a small brick-built structure to replace it. Father Lazzari must have cast his appeal widely because among the benefactors were the 15th Duke of Norfolk, the 3rd Marquis of Bute, a convert to Catholicism, and the Empress Eugenie, widow of Emperor Napoleon III of France, then living in Chislehurst. The first Mass was heard in the iron church on 20 October 1880; the replacement building was completed four years later. A further extension to the brick building, incorporating the apse and about one-third of the current length of the church, was completed and opened with great ceremony in 1896 by Cardinal Vaughan. A remarkably comprehensive report on the Pontifical High Mass was carried in the *Sevenoaks Chronicle* and also in a number of national Catholic newspapers. Throughout its planning and building stages it had been referred to as The Manning Memorial Church in recognition of the late Cardinal Manning who had lived as a boy at nearby ***Combe Bank***, at the time a well-known figure due to his work for the London poor and intervention during the 1889 dockers' strike. The final extension, bringing the building to its current length, was completed in 1926 to the design of Frederick Walters. The Father Tom Quinn memorial Porch was a late 20th-century addition. One well-known parishioner was Lady Victoria Sackville, mother of ***Vita Sackville-West***; her name appears in the parish records between 1912 and 1922. During the past 130 years, St Thomas has had just six Rectors or Parish Priests.
Bell (1996); Killingray (2004)

74 ***Salmon*** the printers composing room, 1899. Many print workers were highly skilled men who were able to secure employment and to negotiate reasonable wages.

Salmon

Salmon is the oldest established ***postcard*** and calendar publisher in Britain. The company was founded in 1880 when Joseph Salmon, who had been a bookseller in London, acquired a stationer's shop with a general printing business at 85 High Street, Sevenoaks. He continued the business in its existing form until he retired in 1898, to be succeeded by his son, also Joseph Salmon. By 1890, Joseph Jnr had become interested in the potential of printing and publishing pictorial postcards and he produced a collection of 12 black and white postcards of Sevenoaks and district. This was followed by a small collection of coloured postcards of local scenes. Such was the success of these early cards that in a very few years the range had been widened to include comic cards. Around 1912 Joseph Salmon also started to publish postcards featuring the work of Alfred Robert Quinton, a famous association that was to last until the artist's death in 1934. Also at this time Salmon started to publish a small series of local view pictorial calendars with coloured illustrations of English scenes. The earliest calendars were in a turnover style although as techniques developed both turnover and panel style calendars were produced in increasing numbers. By the end of the ***First World War***, the business had outgrown its original site in the ***Shambles*** and a new factory was built on ***Tubs Hill***. With subsequent additions and extensions this site has remained at the heart of the business ever since and now houses the printing works, sales office, stock warehousing and dispatch operations. The company has remained in the ownership of the Salmon family and today is run by Charles and Harry Salmon, the fifth generation of the family to be involved in the business.

Salter's Heath

An area of common land just north of ***Dibden***, customarily a place of salting fish on the main ***Rye road*** to London. It was enclosed in 1830.

Salvation Army
Founded in 1878, the Salvation Army opened its first Corps (church) in Sevenoaks in September 1887. Meetings were held in the old ***Baptist*** chapel in the London Road in the centre of town. The early Salvationists with their direct form of evangelism and social action often met harsh opposition; when they came to Sevenoaks they were abused and stoned by the 'rough element' of the town. The Salvation Army did not remain a consistent presence throughout the years. The Corps was still open in May 1904, but had closed by February 1905. It reopened in May 1919 and closed again in October 1966 after 45 years of worship, evangelism and community work in Sevenoaks. At that point the meeting hall was in the old Baptist church in Cedar Terrace, later the Kingdom Hall of the Jehovah's Witnesses. The Old House in Upper High Street was used as a home for retired Salvation Army officers in the 1950s. Sevenoaks Corps reopened once more as a Community Chaplaincy in 1989 and was given corps status in 1998, but found development and outreach difficult without a building of its own, closing again in 2004.

School Board
An elected School Board for the Sevenoaks area was formed in 1875. The Board erected ***Cobden Road School,*** the Boys School in Quaker's Hall Lane (1895), ***St John's National Mixed School*** founded in 1873, ***St Nicholas Infants School*** founded in 1835 (enlarged in 1880 and 1885), and ***St Joseph's Catholic School*** in 1882.
Richards (1901)

School lands
In 1510, Richard Blackboy, along with William ***Pett,*** William Potkin and others, gave 15 acres of land from the ***Hillborough*** estate, lying east of Hollybush Lane near the Vine, as an endowment for ***Sevenoaks School.*** Known as School Lands, the School was able to obtain an income from the land by leasing it for agricultural use. In the 1880s it was used as a cricket field by the School. In 1910 Sevenoaks School sold 12 acres of this land to ***Sevenoaks Urban District Council*** with a covenant that 'the land shall not be used for any purpose other than a recreation ground or such other public purpose or purposes as the Council may from time to time direct'; the area became known as Hollybush Recreation Ground. After the reorganisation of local government in 1974, ownership passed to ***Sevenoaks District Council.*** The remaining three acres of the School Lands were bought by ***Walthamstow Hall School*** in 1905.

Mackay Hugh Baillie Scott (1865-1945)
The Arts and Crafts architect designed houses of a traditional English nature but with spacious well planned interiors. Many of his designs were taken from indigenous older houses in the Sevenoaks area, with large chimneys, steeply pitched roofs, old peg tiles, local hand-made bricks, inglenook fireplaces and a wealth of oak joinery. He made efficient use of space in a small area, rooms being designed with much of the necessary furniture built in, bay window seating, dining recesses and inglenooks which created rooms within rooms. Baillie Scott understood the value of

75 The Dartford Road dentistry. The dentistry is the only dental surgery to have been designed by Baillie Scott and Beresford Hope. Purpose-built during 1926-27, the building is listed and still has many of the original features including the central atrium with an octagonal glazed dome and a blue and white fireplace. The practice was begun in 1927 by Sir Wilfred Fish, dentist to the Royal family. In the late 1930s it was bought by Bob Eustace, and continues as Eustace and Partners.

craft and the skills of good craftsmen. Many examples of his houses can be seen in Sevenoaks. 'Seal Hollow House' was designed by Scott in 1908 as a country house with a small estate for William Ashcroft-Thompson. It was a good example of what was then known as the 'Artistic House', two storeys of white roughcast with a tile roof. It has low sweeping roofs and dormer windows. Inside there was a billiard room, great hall, minstrels' gallery, servants' quarters and, unusually for the period, a garage. Leaded light windows, exposed beams, heavy oak doors and hand-made fittings were typical of the Arts and Crafts Movement. The house has since lost its billiard room, original garage and kitchen. Most of the garden has been sold and the modern houses of Quaker Close are built on the land. 'Tylers', built in 1937 in Oak Hill Road, was Baillie Scott's last commission. The layout is typical of his work with the entry facing north, and service corridors upstairs and downstairs. The brick hanging tiles and long sloping roof are banded to give a strong horizontal aspect. The front door is solid oak with studs and strap hinges, the porch contains a wooden mail box and settle. 'Witham' is one of several Baillie Scott houses built speculatively on

Baillie Scott houses in Sevenoaks

Blackhall Lane:	*'Godden House' (formerly 'Godden Grange'), and 'Kilnwood';*
Kippington Road:	*'Blue Bonnets' (formerly 'Barberries') and 'Greenways';*
Oak Hill Road:	*'Tylers Cottage';*
Seal Drive:	*'Byways' and 'Wildernesse Cottage';*
Seal Hollow Road:	*'Kent Cottage';*
Wildernesse Avenue:	*'Donyland Cottage', 'Whyteladies' and 'Wychden';*
Woodland Rise:	*'Downash', 'Little Croft', 'Little Garnstone Manor', 'Rise House' (formerly 'This Is It'), 'Maple House' (formerly 'Tanglin'), and Witham'.*

the ***Wildernesse estate*** in 1929. The layout is similar to his standard plans with the main rooms south facing. It reflects local building traditions with hanging tiles and long sloping roofs.
ODNB (2004)

Seal
The village and parish of Seal derives its name from the Anglo-Saxon word *sole* or *sol* meaning a 'muddy slough, a wallowing place' which probably relates to a local pond. The village straddles the A25 and by 1980 was almost joined to Sevenoaks by ribbon development along that road. Sited at the crossroads of ancient trackways, in the past the village provided travellers with accommodation in two coaching inns (both now closed), and had a local market dating from at least 1233. The local authority parish of Seal forms the eastern boundary of Sevenoaks from ***Greatness*** in the north and roughly follows the western edge of ***Knole Park*** down towards Hildenborough and ending at Great Hollanden Farm. The ecclesiastical parish of Seal, on which it is based, was originally part of Kemsing-cum-Seal, a typically long narrow parish extended from the ***North Downs*** and into the ***weald***. With its own church, Seal was *de facto* independent of Kemsing from Tudor times. In 1874 the parish officially became independent of Kemsing and within a few years itself was divided with separate ecclesiastical parishes based on Seal St Lawrence and St Margaret's Underriver churches.

Seal was a largely agricultural community until the 20th century, much of the economy based around providing labour and services for surrounding farms and estates, notably the ***Wildernesse estate***. At the beginning of the 19th century the parish population of 993 was second only to Sevenoaks at 2,640 in the old ***Codsheath*** Hundred but, with no direct access to a ***railway***, the population did not increase as fast and by 2001, with just under 2,500, had fallen well behind others such as Otford and Kemsing. However, with the increase in private ownership of ***motor vehicles*** after the mid-20th century, like other villages around Sevenoaks, it attracted commuters working in London and elsewhere in Kent.

Seal Hollow Road
Originally an ancient track, now the B2019, that forks east from the northern end of Sevenoaks High Street, to follow a shallow valley skirting the Knole estate and winding down to the Seal Road, the modern A25. Until the mid-18th century Seal Hollow, also known as the 'horseway', was the main road from Sevenoaks to ***Seal***, and on to Maidstone. During the heavy rains of autumn 1968 the ragstone wall of ***Knole Park***, on the east of the road, acted as a dam; under the weight of water it broke sending a cascade of flood water down Seal Hollow Road.

Second World War
When war was declared in September 1939 plans had already been made at national and local level to meet the emergency. A major concern was aerial bombing and the possible use of gas. Gas masks were distributed, and children evacuated from London to rural Kent where it was believed they would be safe from German air raids. In August-September 1939, Sevenoaks and surrounding villages accepted 7,000 evacuees. The

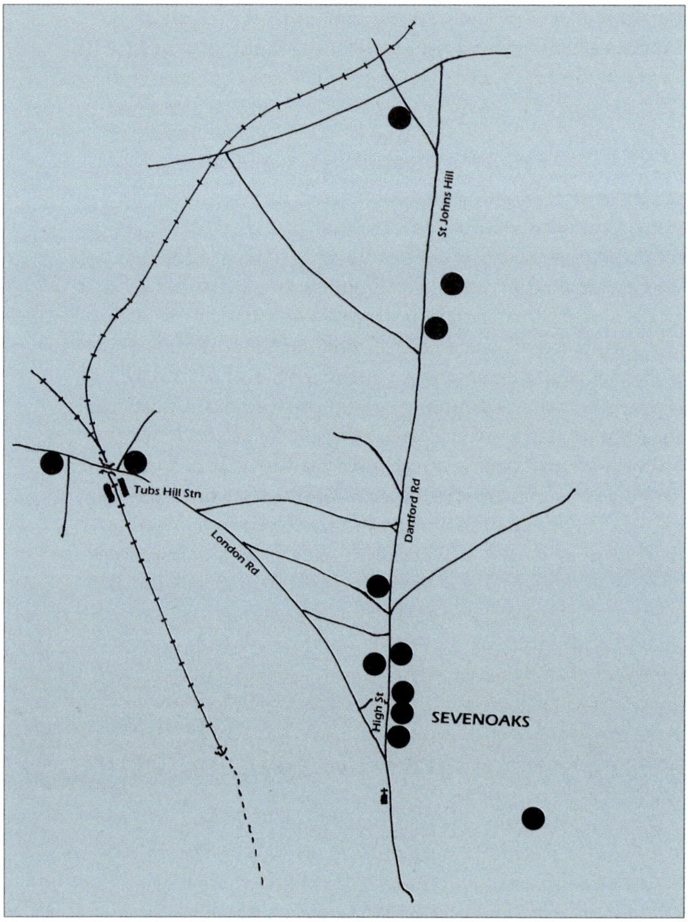

Air raid shelters constructed in Sevenoaks 1939

Methodist Church	St John's Hill
Greyhound Pub	St John's Hill
Camden Arms Pub	St John's Hill
Stanhays Garage	Dartford Rd
Heathfield Hotel	London Road
Sennocke Hotel	London Road
Buckhurst Lodge	High St
The Old Brewery	High St
Russell and Bromley	High St
S Young and Son	High St
Warrens Opticians	High St
Buckhurst Lodge	
The cart shed at Knole	

Robin Brooks, 'Sevenoaks goes to war', *Bygone Kent*, 1, 1 (1989). pp. 391-3.

Map 15 Public air raid shelters 1939. The threat of war resulted in the frantic building of air raid shelters of different kinds to protect people from bomb blasts. Many households had personal shelters in the garden (the Anderson) or the house (the Morrison). Many schools also had underground shelters. The red dots mark the public air raid shelters quickly created and located in shops, pubs, an old brewery, churches, two hotels, and the cart shed at Knole.

Underriver Embroidery, now in ***Sevenoaks Museum***, tells the story of the arrival of a group of children from Camberwell who were evacuated to Underriver in September 1939. A 'blackout' was imposed which resulted in an increased number of road accidents. Local houses were used as hostels for evacuees, for example Hill House in Seal Hollow Road, and ***Kippington Grange***. Land was requisitioned in Scabharbour Lane, ***Weald***, where the Gaza barracks were built. Shelters were constructed and air raid precautions supervised by uniformed Air Raid Wardens. At Lullingstone a decoy airfield was constructed in 1939-40 in an attempt to protect the RAF fighter station at Biggin Hill. Large local houses were requisitioned, for example ***Beechmont*** becoming a billet for women of the Auxiliary Territorial Service who serviced motor units in Knole Park. As preparation for a German invasion after the debacle of Dunkirk, pill boxes were built, and the army requisitioned land at ***Whitley Forest*** building tarmac roads, barracks and a parade ground.

Conscription was imposed, first for men into the armed forces, but subsequently for women, many of whom took the jobs formerly held by men, particularly in agriculture. A large part of the population was in uniform of one kind or another. Rationing was also introduced and

76 Evacuee children in cattle pens at Sevenoaks ***market, Tubs Hill***, August 1939. A London girl evacuee many years later recalled her experience of arriving at Sevenoaks: 'From [Tubs Hill station] we were taken to the cattle market which was just across the road from the station, we were then put into the cattle pens, ten children to a pen. The teachers had tears in their eyes as they looked at some of the little five and six year olds in those pens where the cattle should be, it didn't seem too bad for us older ones. From there we were taken by coach to Underriver, the boys went to Seal.' *West Kent Federation of Women's Institutes (1995)*

determined efforts made to increase food production (in 1939 Britain imported over 60 per cent of its food needs). War Agricultural Committees directed farmers to plough-up grass lands for wheat, barley and potatoes, and also promoted the use of tractors and other agricultural machinery. Householders were encouraged to grow vegetables in their gardens and ***allotments*** were created on playing fields and marginal land. Young Farmers' Clubs expanded; the one at ***Walthamstow Hall*** grew fruit and vegetables in the school grounds and raised animals for food.

In May 1940 Local Defence Volunteers were formed, later renamed the Home Guard, from men aged 17 to 65. The 20th (Sevenoaks) Battalion of the Kent Home Guard first met at Wildernesse Country Club and Knole Park Golf Club, and drilled at the ***Drill Hall*** in Argyle Road. Their role was to observe and report on all enemy movements and defend, in accordance with prepared schemes, certain roads, towns and positions vital to the protection of the area.

Many of the bombs that fell on Sevenoaks were arbitrarily dropped; the district had no military or strategic significance. The first serious bombing came on the night of 17 October 1940 when bombs hit Bosville Drive and the Club Hall together with houses in Buckhurst Lane and shops

77 Houses in Wickenden Road destroyed by a V2, March 1945. German V2 flying bombs, launched from moveable platforms, were rockets with warheads that flew at 2,000 mph. There was no effective defence against what were regarded as terror weapons; they could not easily be seen and usually were only heard when they exploded on impact. The V2 that struck Wickenden Road, three months before the end of the war in Europe, destroyed two houses, killed nine and wounded 13 people.

An evacuee, 12-year-old Josephine Bagley, recorded her involvement in the Underriver embroidery project:

'In the village lived a lovely lady named Lady Wilson, she invited us into her house to do some tapestry. It was a long piece of material like calico, and a long picture was drawn on it of 'us evacuees' leaving London and arriving in Underriver. We embroidered our initials at both ends. We went there sometimes once or twice a week. We would sit in her window seat with it across our laps.' Extract from The Memories of Josephine Moir, Sevenoaks Library

in the High Street, killing one man and badly injuring several people. A mine was dropped on open land in ***Knole Park*** with further bombs on houses in ***Lime Tree Walk***. On 1 November 1940, one high explosive and two oil bombs were dropped on London Road, ***Riverhead*** killing one person and severely injuring several others. German V1 'flying bombs' fell indiscriminately, ***Beechmont*** being hit in 1944. More serious were the much faster V2 rockets, one of which struck ***Wickenden*** Road in March 1945. Other raids in the area involved the loss of property. Official war casualties in the area of ***Sevenoaks Urban District*** registered 22 people killed, 59 severely injured, and a further 111 slightly injured; in the Sevenoaks Rural District there were 62 killed, 70 severely injured, and 188 slightly injured. In the Urban District 98 high explosive and 4,000 incendiary bombs were dropped whilst the Rural District saw 3,257 high explosive and 53,500 incendiary bombs. In addition the urban district saw five V1 'flying bombs' drop within the borders whilst the rural saw 137 V2s. These statistics also stated that the Rural Districts of Sevenoaks and Dartford were the most heavily bombed, whilst Shoreham was the most bombed village in the entire country.

In preparation for the D-Day landings in France, invasion army vehicles were stored among the trees in ***Whitley Forest***, many of them under camouflage covers. Some of today's footpaths run along those old tarmac army roads, while the circular brick tank at Five Wents, where five paths meet, was another army installation. At one point massed army vehicles for the invasion stretched along the road from Knole to the top of ***Riverhill***, shielded by the cover of trees.

The war years disrupted family life, patterns of work, children's schooling, the position of women, and changed diets. It also brought important social and political change: the Beveridge Plan for a welfare state, reform to the secondary ***education*** system, and a change of government in 1945 when electors overwhelmingly voted for the Labour Party.
Brown (1944); Franklin (1945); Moore (1989); Brooks (1989); Weald History Group (1999)

Sennocke hotel
Built in 1868 on the ***St Botolph's*** estate, this pub was variously called the Sennocke Commercial Hotel, Posting House, Sennocke Arms, and finally The Farmers. The hotel was built when ***Samuel Bligh*** secured a 99-year lease from the St Botolph's estate for a plot of land opposite the new ***Tubs***

78 The Farmers, 1990s. By 1988, when Mike Collings, the last of the 29 landlords, took over the hotel, it was 'in a very rundown state, dirty and shabby with few customers'. The pub, the last remaining building owned by the ***St Botolph's estate***, was closed on the decision of the trustees. Despite a vigorous campaign and a petition signed by more than 4,000 people to keep the pub open, it was sold in January 2006 and soon demolished.

Hill station. When the stock ***market*** was relocated from the centre of the town to where the ***BT building*** now stands, Parliament granted a petition for exemption from the Licensing laws in 1918, permitting the Sennocke Hotel all-day opening on market day. During the ***Second World War*** part of the hotel was used as an emergency fire station. In 1983, the hotel was taken over by John Farmer, who undertook major alterations and changed the name to 'The Farmers'.

Serpentine Road
A residential road, built in the late 19th century, named because of its twisting course intersecting Bayham Road and eventually meeting Seal Hollow Road. The upper part was originally called Circular Road.

Sevenoaks
Sevenoaks takes its name from a natural feature – seven, presumably sturdy, oak trees. Until well into the 19th century the town was often written as 'Seven Oaks'. Various suggestions have been made as to where the original trees stood. ***Dunlop***'s idea that this was near to ***St Nicholas*** church and the future ***Sevenoaks School*** seems as good a guess as any. Much later seven oaks were planted by the 3rd Duke of Dorset in the 18th century on the Tonbridge Road, opposite the White Hart Inn. Seven oaks were also planted at the north end of the ***Vine*** cricket ground to commemorate the coronation of Edward VII in 1902. Six of the trees were blown down in the hurricane of October 1987 and were replaced, the first being planted by Gloria Hunniford. Seven oak trees, a gift from Buckhurst Cricket Club, were also planted in 1984 at Raley's Field. The American oaks were seven trees planted in 1946 near the Vine Tavern to commemorate the town's gratitude to the American Forces during the ***Second World War***.

Sevenoaks Artisans' Dwellings Company
The acute shortage of working-class housing at reasonable rents, together with the absence of basic facilities in existing houses in the town at the

79 Seven oaks, Tonbridge Road, from an early 20th-century postcard. The seven oaks, symbolising the town, were planted south of Sevenoaks in the 18th century. They were felled in 1954, believed to be diseased, and seven replacement trees were planted by ***Vita Sackville-West*** and the chairwoman of ***Sevenoaks Urban District Council*** in March 1955. A gypsy caravan added flavour to a postcard, but few farmers or local authorities tolerated such itinerant travellers on their land. The H telephone pole seen here was common on trunk routes, while single poles usually carried phone lines to individual houses.

end of the 19th century, was frequently considered by the ***Sevenoaks Urban District Council***, and became known as the 'cottage question'. Reluctant to incur the cost of using statutory powers, the Council preferred private enterprise to provide a solution. However, the low level of affordable rents gave insufficient return on capital invested. There was a nationwide movement of people prepared to accept a relatively low return on investment in working-class housing that became known as 'five per cent philanthropists'; in 1903 the London and County bank declared an 11 per cent dividend. ***Alfred Laurie***, long concerned about the housing shortage, formed this Company in May 1903 and 'invited' local support, 22 shareholders quickly responding and each investing between £250 and £10; they included local benefactors ***Henry Swaffield, Frank Swanzy*** and also Joseph ***Salmon***. The Memorandum of Association provided, *inter alia*, 'to erect houses for artisans, labourers and others, with shops and other buildings deemed necessary in connections with a cottage estate'; the intention to form a self-contained estate reflected the influence of the contemporary Garden City movement. By 1904 a terrace of 20 houses was completed and occupied in ***Crampton's Road*** followed by another terrace of 19 in Moor Road (initially called Hales Road). A large plaque of the Company can be seen on each terrace. The Company went into voluntary liquidation in 1933.
Tarn (1973)

Sevenoaks bypass
Road traffic through Sevenoaks on the road to and from the coast steadily increased in the 1920s-30s, and returned rapidly once private motoring resumed after the end of the ***Second World War***. Long and frustrating

queues of traffic blocked the High Street every summer weekend. A bypass was proposed as early as 1922; but it was only in 1964 that work started on a new road 6.5 miles long to the west of the town, between the chalk downs at ***Polhill*** and the bottom of ***Riverhill***. It involved construction of 16 bridges and culverts, including one across the River ***Darent*** at ***Chipstead***, demolition of three cottages and the clearance of about 70 acres of woodland. Construction was delayed by a series of landslips on unstable ground near Gracious Lane, where the new road crossed the greensand ridge. The route had to be shifted a little, and the new bridge there rebuilt. The northern end from Polhill to the A25 was not affected and opened in 1967. It took another year to complete the damaged southern end. Ten years later the northern end was incorporated into the new M25 ***motorway***. The southern end was later joined to the new Tonbridge bypass, opened in September 1971, providing a through route round both towns. During the latter years, various schemes were put forward to provide a relief road to take traffic out of the town centre: a town plan of 1951, the Lock report 1959, the Buchanan plan of 1968, and finally Alan Bennett's scheme of 1971 for an '***eastern way***' that would cut through part of Knole Park, all of which were greeted with protests – and not implemented.

Sevenoaks Common

The Common lies south of the town on the greensand ridge; it is an area of common land which had developed into woodland through lack of grazing. Between 1949 and 1961 the ***Sevenoaks Urban District Council*** purchased 39 acres of the common land which is now owned and managed by ***Sevenoaks Town Council***. Another area of the Common further west is privately owned. The age of the trees, mainly beech, oak and ash, suggests that is has been woodland for at least 150 years. It was badly affected by the October 1987 storm when approximately 50 per cent of the trees were lost, although regeneration and replanting has resulted in strong recovery.

Sevenoaks Co-operative Society

Co-operative stores gradually spread in Britain from the 1840s. A co-operative society was formed in Sevenoaks in 1895 and the first store opened the next year, run by Fred Hooker, a Liberal member of ***Sevenoaks Urban District Council***. By 1903 it had premises in the High Street, more than 500 members, and similar stores were reported as operating in nearby villages. That year, when the Sevenoaks Tenants Association was set up, many of the people involved were members of the Co-operative Society.

Sevenoaks County School for Girls

In September 1950 the secondary girls school known as Hatton was established in new buildings, along with ***Maywood*** (Hatton House), between Bradbourne Road and ***Bradbourne Park Road***. Opening the School, originally named after Lady Fanny Finch-Hatton (1820-1909), Mary Soames, youngest daughter of Winston Churchill, described it as 'an absolute palace'. The majority of girls in the area attended and during the 1950s most left at the age of 15. The School moved to a new site north of the A25 in 1974 which cost £587,000, and was renamed Bradbourne School for Girls. In 2010 the School merged with ***Wildernesse School*** for Boys to become ***Knole Academy***.

Sevenoaks District Council
Sevenoaks District Council was set up in 1974 as part of a national reorganisation of local government. The Council was made up of ***Sevenoaks Urban District Council***, based at the Argyle Road offices, Sevenoaks Rural District Council in Oakhill Road, and part of Dartford Rural District Council in Swanley. The Council was based at these sites until 1986 when the main offices were centralised at the redeveloped Argyle Road offices. As well as Argyle Road, the Council has the Dunbrik Depot in Sundridge, the base for its refuse, recycling, street cleaning and other environmental operations. At its inception, the Council employed around 1,000 people. This workforce included housing officers, highway engineers, drainage engineers, leisure staff, architects and a substantial outside workforce. In 2011 the Council employed around 390 full and part-time staff. In 1989 the Council transferred the entire Housing stock to West Kent Housing Association and in 2004 the Council set up Sencio Community Leisure to manage its leisure centres and leisure operations.

Sevenoaks District Council insignia
The ensign was adopted upon the Council's formation in 1974 and consists of a shield with seven oak trees in silver displayed in parallel lines of four and three on a green background and an indented line, with three indents, in blue with silver borders interspersed among the trees. The seven oak trees represent the name of the District and the indents represent the three rivers flowing through the District, namely the ***Darent***, the Eden and the Medway. The ensign is displayed on the council's flag which is flown from the flagpole in front of the council offices on the occasion of full council meetings and when a member dies. The Chairman's Badge of Office is made in silver and was presented to the Council by public subscription in 1976. It consists of a circle with the name of the District inscribed on the inner rim of the circle and with a silver shield attached within the circle containing the Council's armorial ensign engraved on an enamel plate.

Sevenoaks Historical Society
Despite having a rich history, Sevenoaks for many years lacked a dedicated history society, this being left to a 'history section' of the ***Sevenoaks Society***. In 1996 the Historical Society was formed with an inaugural meeting in St Luke's Hall. Within a short time it had more than 150 members. The Society was involved in a millennium exhibition on Christian faith in the area, which was subsequently published as a book.
Killingray (2004)

Sevenoaks Hospital Millennium Panel
The Millennium Panel hanging in the Outpatients department was started in 1998 and presented to the Hospital in 2000, the work of eight local embroiderers. The design celebrated the history of ***hospitals*** in Sevenoaks, with a border of medicinal plants. Worked in glowing colours and metallic yarn, the plants represented all have medicinal properties – Blackberry, Hop, Poppy, Periwinkle, Oak, Celandine, Foxglove, Primrose, Honeysuckle, Violet, Nasturtium, Rose, Hollyhock and Hellebore. The flowers are set into free machine embroidered hand-made felt, with each medallion framed in a shape

inspired by the gable ends at Knole House. The main panel shows three very different hospitals that have helped and healed the citizens of Sevenoaks: the medieval ***St John the Baptist Hospital***, the ***Emily Jackson*** Hip Hospital, and today's out-patients department. These buildings are set against a background showing seven oaks with the ***North Downs*** behind.
To appeal to children visiting the hospitals, the group added separately worked animals – sheep, a red squirrel, a hedgehog, a badger, rabbits, an owl, a fox, a woodpecker and deer, all hidden among the foliage, a sort of embroidered I-Spy.

Sevenoaks Literary and Scientific Society
Formed in 1849 to encourage enquiry into new ideas and developments, its first meeting was held in the rooms over the Old ***Market House***. By 1852 there were 355 members which had grown by 1854 to 718 (in a town of *c*.5,000). The Society had an expanding library of over 1,500 volumes. In 1854 there were 18 talks on subjects ranging from geology to the French language, and the Society's income totalled £170 5s. 10d.

Sevenoaks Local Plan
The first Local Plan for Sevenoaks was the Sevenoaks and Area Local Plan in 1990 which contained policies to protect the historic character of the town and the surrounding countryside. The ***Green Belt*** around Sevenoaks was confirmed, thereby setting a future boundary to urban development. The Plan also defined the extent of the town centre, shopping and business areas, with policies to protect their vitality and viability, including designating ***Bligh's Meadow*** for redevelopment as a future town centre. In 2000 this was replaced by a Sevenoaks District Wide Local Plan which built on previous ideas including maintaining the Green Belt boundary. The 2011 Local Development Framework – Core Strategy, deals with future development of the District to 2026 with an emphasis on safeguarding the high quality and character of the environment.

Sevenoaks Museum
The Museum started as a collection of ***Gordon Ward***'s objects in cases around the walls of the old ***Library*** in The Drive. Later they were put in a room upstairs which was 'unlocked at visitors' request'. It was closed in the mid-1960s when the library needed more space, and the objects were dispersed around Kent museums. There was no museum until 1985 when the 'new' library opened in Buckhurst Lane with a museum upstairs with objects retrieved from the Kent museums. When the Library was refurbished and renamed Kaleidoscope, the museum space was reduced so there was no longer room for some of the larger objects. The Victorian school room was transferred to the Museum of Kent Life. The present collection still has the ***Second World War*** embroidery made by evacuees, the brass fire helmet from the Sevenoaks 'Readies' voluntary ***fire service***, the ***Pett*** cricket bat from 1745, and other well-known items. Efforts have also been made to acquire post-1960 items.

Sevenoaks parish
The boundaries of most Kent parishes were established by 1200. The parish was an ecclesiastical division, the boundaries drawn so as to

provide sufficient income for the maintenance of a church and a priest. The boundaries of the ancient Sevenoaks parish extended south from the river ***Darent*** in the ***Vale of Holmesdale***, up the chartland, and down into the ***weald*** to Hale Oak. In this way, and similar to neighbouring parishes, Sevenoaks included three different kinds of land which reflected an old system of transhumance with livestock being driven south to feed in the dens of the wealden area. The original parish of 6,804 acres was five miles long and little over two miles at its widest point. For hundreds of years parishes served not only as a unit of pastoral care, but by producing tithes and parish ***rates*** as the system of ***local government***. Reforms in the 1530s increased that role as the parish took responsibility for the poor, highways, and petty law and order. These functions were modified in the decades 1830s-80s, and in 1894 Sevenoaks parish became part of ***Sevenoaks Urban District Council***. By then the boundaries of the old Sevenoaks ecclesiastical parish had been altered by new parishes with their own churches being carved from it: ***Weald*** in 1861, ***Riverhead*** in 1864-71, ***Kippington*** in 1877, and ***St John's*** in 1878. Weald and Riverhead formed civil parish councils from 1894.

Sevenoaks Park

The Park came into being after 1500 when 100 acres of common land between ***Oak Lane*** and the future Solefields Road and Hopgarden Lane were 'emparked', reputedly by John Wildgoose. Sevenoaks Park was later owned by Thomas Potkin who sold it to the ***Lone family*** of Rumshed Manor in 1559. During the ***Civil Wars***, George Lone was a Royalist and the estate was sequestrated. In 1654 it was acquired by ***Thomas Lambarde*** then living at Squerries, Westerham. He pulled down the old brick house and replaced it with a large Palladian-style ragstone house. By 1655 Sevenoaks Park consisted of 146 acres of which 71 acres were meadows, 48 pasture, 18 arable and eight woodland including a home farm known as ***Park Farm***. The south side of the Park was bordered by ***Sevenoaks Common***. Multon Lambard II improved the house beyond recognition and in *c*.1789 it returned to its original name, ***Park Place***. It remained in the Lambard family until 1837 when they sold Park Place estate for £15,000 to Colonel Thomas ***Austen*** of Kippington, and moved to their other property, ***Beechmont***. Austen promptly demolished most of the house.

Sevenoaks Poetry Society

The first meeting of the Poetry Society was in 1910 for the purpose of reading poetry and discussing poets and their works. In October 1927 ***Vita Sackville-West*** and Harold Nicolson were present and took part in readings from 'The Land'. The poet W.H. Davies was a founder member and Society members also met Sir Alfred Noyes at a special gathering in 1931. Meetings continued regularly throughout the war years. In 1961 two groups were formed called Alpha and Omega; since then a third group has been formed. The 1,000th meeting was held in September 1994 with a special programme and guests.

Sevenoaks Preparatory School

There is some uncertainty about the very beginnings of the School, but tradition has it that in 1919 Mrs Garrod, wife of the headmaster of ***Sevenoaks School***, brought together a class of six boys who were too young

80 ***Sevenoaks Park*** or Park Place: an early 19th-century print. Large houses came and went. In the past there was less sentiment about preserving old homes, and more emphasis on displaying status by new and better buildings. Later, in the 20th century, many large houses were demolished with little thought as to 'heritage'.

to attend the main school. She taught them in the Cottage Block until they were ready to move up into the main school. In 1921 the Rev. C.G. Holland became headmaster of an already expanding 'prep' school and bought 4 Vine Court Road, moving there with 35 boys. In 1928 M.N. Jukes bought the School, inheriting 30 boys and by 1938 there were 102. On his death in 1957, Mrs A. Lang became headmistress and maintained the School until it was bought by K.C. Ely in 1958. Ely developed the School to meet the increasing demands of education with up to 150 boys until he had the opportunity to take over the tenancy of Fawke Cottage at ***Godden Green***, so gaining more outdoor space. Here the school grew into a co-educational prep school of 380 children under two further heads, Edward Oatley (1977-2005) and Philip Oldroyd.

Sevenoaks Savings Bank

The ***bank*** was established about 1820 and was later housed in a stone building, now a restaurant, in London Road opposite the former Lady Boswell's School. Such Trustee Savings Banks were becoming common, often sponsored by local benefactors like *Lord* ***Amherst*** from ***Montreal Park.*** They could only invest in government securities and were supposed to be safe for small investors. But government supervision was light. The Post Office Savings Bank, founded in 1861, soon became a major rival. A big political scandal in 1887 started when the Cardiff Savings Bank collapsed with big losses to savers. This provoked a series of investigations. Next year it emerged that the Actuary (manager) of the Sevenoaks bank, Henry Sutton, who was also landlord of the Royal Oak, and a respected Sevenoaks citizen, had been siphoning off cash. The Trustees, led by the Rector of Sevenoaks, stepped in and, although not strictly required to do so, repaid the losses; depositors' accounts were transferred to the Post Office Savings Bank; the Savings Bank was closed; and Sutton, who pleaded guilty, was sent to prison for 18 months. The building was sold and has since been used for many different local businesses.

Sevenoaks School

Sevenoaks School is one of the oldest lay foundations in England. It was endowed as a free Grammar school for boys by ***William Sevenoke***, a wealthy merchant, in 1432, although the school could have been functioning from as early as 1418. The school was granted a new constitution in 1560 by Elizabeth I, following representation from Ralph ***Bosville*** of ***Bradbourne***. This established a Corporation to run the school and at the same time granted it the right to call itself 'Queen Elizabeth's Grammar School'. In the early 18th century, the Corporation sold its Thames-side property between Billingsgate and the Tower to the Crown to enable them to build a new Customs House. The money was used to build an imposing ***ragstone*** two-storey School house, flanked by two rows of ***almshouses***. The building, which was completed in 1732, was based on an original design by the eminent Palladian architect, the Earl of Burlington, although he took no part in its completion. The School remained very small for the next 200 years. Its pupils were drawn mainly from the town and local parishes, although at some point the Master supplemented his income by taking in a few boarders. In the mid 19th-century tradesmen in the town protested that their sons were not being considered for the School. Its fortunes improved in the early 20th century assisted by a number of benefactors; the most important of whom was ***Charles Plumtre Johnson***. After the ***Second World War*** the school became fully independent, although it had an arrangement to provide free places for local boys who had passed the 11+ examination. The school grew steadily, taking girls into the sixth form in 1976 and then becoming fully co-educational in 1984. It opened two international boarding houses and established a national reputation for educational innovation. It was one of the first schools in the country to introduce the International Baccalaureate Diploma programme. By 2010 the School had a thousand students, one third being boarders. A Performing Arts Centre, known as the Space, opened in 2010, built at the cost of £13m. To the south of the gate house of the School a 20-metre tunnel under the Tonbridge Road was built in 1992 to give access to the boarding houses opposite. In order not to disrupt traffic the tunnel was constructed by utilising pre-cast square concrete box elements 3.6 metres x 3.6 metres which were progressively pushed under the highway by hydraulic jacks as the tunnel face was safely excavated by hand-working from within the boxes.
Scragg (1993); Taylor (1965)

81 *Sevenoaks School.* School house with its additional floor, which spoiled the once neat symmetry of the ***ragstone*** building. A statue of ***William Sevenoke*** occupies the niche.

Sevenoaks Social Club

The Club was built in 1974 in ***Bligh's Meadow***, replacing the old wooden structure of the Services Club which had opened in 1921 as a meeting place for those who had served in the Services. The new building was an office block and incorporated the old Services Club bar with a club lounge and rooms for indoor games such as snooker.

Sevenoaks Society

A Sevenoaks Society existed in 1781, details which come from a label in a volume of Pliny, but no more than this is known. The present Sevenoaks Society had its origins in The Sevenoaks Town Planning Association which existed between 1930 and 1939. In 1944 the Sevenoaks Civic Society was formed, being re-formed eight years later in 1952 as the Sevenoaks Preservation Society. In 1967 the Society changed its name to The Sevenoaks Society with the sub-title 'for the preservation and improvement of the town'. In 1996 'preservation' was changed to 'conservation' to make the title more contemporary, though without any real change of emphasis. By 2012 the Society had nearly 800 members making it one of the largest civic societies in Kent. Its primary role was to monitor planning developments, to protect the ***Green Belt***, and to maintain the character of the architectural heritage of the important buildings in the Town Centre. This was assisted by publication on-line of a regularly updated Town Centre Survey.

Sevenoaks Town Council

Sevenoaks Town Council was formed in 1974 when the old ***Sevenoaks Urban District*** and Rural District Councils were divided to form the ***Sevenoaks District Council*** and the Sevenoaks Town Council. The Council offices were originally housed in an old wooden hut in a former sand quarry, known at the Arthur Barnard Hall (on the A25), until new Council offices were built in 1991 on the same site, part of which is leased to the British Red Cross. The 16 elected members represent the six wards of Sevenoaks.

Sevenoaks Town motto

The motto of Sevenoaks is *Floreant Septem Quercus*,'May the seven oaks flourish'.

Sevenoaks Urban District Council

The UDC was established as a result of the Local Government Act 1894; it took over the functions of the Sevenoaks Local Board created in 1871. At the same time ***Weald*** and ***Riverhead*** each became civil Parish Councils. The Urban District Council was incorporated into ***Sevenoaks District Council*** in 1974 after the Local Government Act of 1972. The original 12 elected members of the UDC were Rear Admiral ***Henry Miller,*** the first Chairman, John Carnell, magistrate and solicitor, Arthur Hickmott, a socialist with an outfitter's shop on ***St John's Hill,*** Frederick Hooker, the Revd ***John Jackson,*** Thomas Killick, dairy farmer, George Oldfield, Thomas Potter, William Stepney, solicitor's clerk, ***Henry Swaffield,*** Herbert Thompson, solicitor's clerk, and Frederick Wells, a beer retailer. The UDC had wide powers including control over adequate housing standards, purchasing land for Council housing and for recreation, sewage and drainage, refuse disposal and street maintenance.

William Sevenoke (1373-1432)

According to legend, William Sevenoke was a foundling brought up by William Rumpstead (or Romschedde), a local landowner. He was tutored privately and initially apprenticed to an ironmonger in London, although he subsequently joined the Grocers' Company. He made his fortune trading in cloth, salt and wine. Sevenoke's commercial success was accompanied by his steady rise to political influence in the City. As an Alderman he acted as a magistrate and tax collector and served on the Court of Aldermen and the Common Council which governed the City. His growing importance was reflected by election to the post of Sheriff in 1412 and representation of the City in Parliament five years later. Finally, in October 1418 he was elected Mayor of London in a ceremony at the Guildhall. He also profited from a number of contracts from the Crown and was appointed to serve on several commissions by Henry V. There is no evidence that he fought in France or received a knighthood. Sevenoke seems to have retired from public life around 1426, although he continued to advise on repairs and financial matters to the Trustees of Rochester Bridge. He was buried at St Martin's Church, Ludgate Hill. Sevenoke made six separate wills bequeathing most of his wealth to a number of churches in the City, but he also left a wharf and several warehouses by the Thames near the Tower to endow the Grammar school and ***almshouse*** for the town where his uncertain start to life began.

The Shambles

At one time known as Middle Row in the centre of the medieval ***market*** area, the oldest part of Sevenoaks with its narrow passages, courtyards and shops. The passages which open into the High Street, London Road, Dorset Street and the Market Place, have been there since the mid-15th century when they contained fish and meat stalls. In 1650 there were three butchers; in 1741 a ***slaughter house*** as well as a butcher's shop. The area became more than just a market and by the 19th century various tradesmen lived in the Shambles where they ran their businesses. At the London Road entrance to the Shambles there was an inn which has had several names. At one time it was the Swann, later called the Pied Bull, then the Dorset Arms and is now a Thai restaurant. The small square in the Shambles has had its appearance improved in 1999 when local artists Tom Cusins and Juliet Simpson designed murals depicting scenes of former market activities.

Terry (2000)

82 ***The Shambles,*** a drawing by ***Vincent New.*** The oldest surviving building in the town is now a small gift shop in the Shambles. The building, originally detached with a jettied front, had a crown post roof, and is believed to have been built in 1450.

shops
Little information exists on shops in Sevenoaks before the 18th century. Clearly people bought goods of different kinds and required the services of men and women who traded their various wares and skills. In *Bailey's British Directory* for 1784 a number of tradespeople are listed: sometimes just as 'shopkeeper', but also as 'currier' (dressing and colouring leather), 'bookseller and stationer', 'cooper' (making barrels), 'ironmonger', 'shoe-maker', 'fellmonger and glover', 'gingerbread baker' and 'cutler'. By 1840, according to *Pigot's Directory*, the town had many more tradespeople: nine boot and shoe makers, five butchers, three fishmongers, four fruiterers and greengrocers, 13 grocers and cheesemongers, two hairdressers, five hatters and clothes dealers, three ironmongers, seven linen drapers, five milliners and dress makers, three nursery men, three saddlers, eight tailors, six watch and clock makers, two wheelwrights, four wine and spirit merchants, and one tallow chandler. Wares could be displayed in shop windows of small glass panes. Assistants wrapped purchases in brown paper tied with string. This was a pattern that survived to the mid-20th century, although increasingly shops sold mass-produced goods, ready packaged and bearing well-known names. For example, Boots Cash Chemists opened in the High Street in 1912. By then one of the largest stores, ***Young's***, was becoming a department store. Technology made it possible for shops to have plate glass windows. Until the 1920s most shops were concentrated in the centre of the town, gradually spreading further north in the 1930s. The great transformation in food shopping came as a result of the domestic refrigerator, the ***motor car***, and ***supermarkets***. As personal incomes increased, diet changed and a wider range of foodstuffs appeared in Sevenoaks's shops. Eating out also became more common and many new restaurants appeared in the area, including French, Italian, Chinese, and Indian cuisines. Fish and chips, that essentially English 'take away' food, was joined by curry and pizza.
Humphries (1999)

Six Bells Lane
Originally known as Parsonage Lane this pretty, winding, cobbled lane descends steeply from the upper High Street to meet ***Rectory Lane***. Its 17 houses are mostly 18th-century and Grade II Listed, and many of them have typical Kentish weatherboarding. The name Six Bells was derived from the six bells which ***St Nicholas church*** had before the 1750s, when the six were replaced by eight new bells. There is a courtyard behind numbers 1 and 2 which used to belong to a bakery; a pump in the courtyard was in use at the bottom of the lane until piped water reached Sevenoaks. On the east side of the courtyard there is a very good example of a cat-slide roof with dormers which were intended to lighten the roof space underneath.

Thomas Skinner (1855-1925)
Skinner was a Member of the ***Sevenoaks Urban District Council*** with a zeal for clocks and public lavatories. He successfully campaigned for the redundant ***Market House*** to be turned into a public lavatory in 1924, known locally as 'Skinners Palace'. When he lost his seat on the Council in 1925, he committed suicide.

83 *Six Bells Lane.* Vernacular building materials are evident in the Lane: timber-framed and timber-clad houses, brick, tile, and ragstone, with ironstone on the path to provide a non-slippery grip for shoes.

slaughter houses

In medieval times there was a slaughter house in the ***Shambles***, a place where animals would be taken to the butchers' slaughter house and, after slaughtering, the blood would run down the alleyways and drain into the earth. In a lease of 1530, a John Worseley was identified as Yeoman of the Slaughterhouse. A Government slaughter house, opened in 1921, stood at the southern end of Prospect Road, in ***Hartsland***. After 30 years of putting up with the smells which emanated from it, 116 local residents successfully petitioned the ***Sevenoaks Urban District Council*** to close it down. In 1961, plans to open a slaughter house adjoining the Cattle Market by the station were dropped because of local objections.

smells

Personal tolerance of smells has changed over the years. The medieval ***Shambles***, with its sound of dying animals, blood and offal, would not have been acceptable to people in 1850,and certainly not in the modern post-sanitary age of hyper-cleanliness. The most common smell in early 21st-century Sevenoaks is perhaps cooked food being prepared in the many cafes and restaurants. Before ***main drainage*** in the 1880s human waste often went in to middens or soil pits, while other waste lay in the streets, leading to frequent letters of complaints to the press. In an earlier age the smell of wood smoke, the result of open fires for heating and cooking, would have been common. By the 19th century wood was being increasingly replaced by ***coal*** for domestic heating, and commercial machinery, for the manufacture of ***gas*** at ***Hartsland*** and its successor on the Otford Road, and for the ***railways***; the smut and smell of ***coal*** smoke pervaded Sevenoaks. The tannery at ***Riverhead*** could be smelt in the town when the wind blew from the north. Likewise the three ***breweries***, two in the high street, gave off a distinctive smell. Many ***public houses*** held the odour of stale beer and tobacco smoke. Cattle and horses were frequently driven through the town and manure fell in the streets, getting on to people's shoes and the bottom of women's long dresses. Until the advent of modern medicine most people believed that foul smells were a cause of disease. At the time many houses in the town lacked running water, people bathed and washed less frequently than today, and dirt was brushed off woollen and worsted clothing. The better-off social classes tended to stigmatise as 'smelly' the poor and working class who lived and worked in surroundings lacking modern sanitary means. Chemical dry cleaning became more common in the 1930s, drip-dry clothing more widespread after 1950, and domestic washing machines in many homes by the 1970s. From the 1930s the smell of diesel fumes and the emissions from vehicles became a more common smell in the streets. The local Board of Health, founded after 1858, identified noxious smells as nuisances and local and national regulations gradually sought to control them. Health and Safety regulations in the 20th century have contributed to reducing smells by controlling the handling and sale of food, extending street cleaning and removal of waste, and imposing sanitary standards that most people today accept as standard.

Henry Smith (c.1548-1628)
Born in Wandsworth, Surrey, Smith was a salt merchant and successful businessman who invested in land. In 1617 he bought ***Knole*** from the cash-strapped Richard Sackville, 3rd Earl of Dorset, and then leased it back to the family for £100 per year. Smith was a benevolent man and his lands, including Knole until it was redeemed in 1661, were the basis of the Smith Charity which still exists. Often known as 'Dog' Smith, because he was likened to a beggar with a dog on a lead, he is commemorated by a plaque in Wandsworth parish church.

Social Democrat Party (SDP)
Sevenoaks SDP was born, along with the national launch by the 'Gang of Four' in 2001, and attracted over 200 members from across the Sevenoaks district. They included converts from other political parties, and many prominent local people new to politics.

The new party fought the 1983 District Council elections in alliance with the Liberals. It played a role in the election of John Gorton (Liberal), the first Alliance County Councillor in Sevenoaks, for Sevenoaks East in the County elections of 1985. The 1987 local elections saw two SDP district councillors elected, and two town councillors. By the early 1990s all its councillors joined the ***Liberal Democrats*** – a merger of the SDP and Liberals. They won an overall majority on ***Sevenoaks Town Council*** in 1991, and led ***Sevenoaks District Council*** from 1995 to 1999.

social housing
Almshouses were the first form of social housing for the elderly. Later, Victorian philanthropists set up charities such as the Peabody and the Rowntree Trusts to provide affordable homes. In Sevenoaks, when the Sevenoaks Tenants Association planned to build houses at an affordable rent, the ***Rodgers*** family gave the land in Weald, and ***Frank Swanzy*** contributed financially. Swanzy and ***Henry Swaffield*** both gave money to the ***Sevenoaks Artisans Dwelling Company*** to build houses for the working classes.

The ***Sevenoaks Urban District Council***, formed in 1894, was given powers to provide and maintain adequate housing standards. The first social housing, often termed 'council housing', was built in 1903 at Smart's Hill, near Penshurst. At the time many people were living in cramped insanitary dwellings with no ***main drainage*** or adequate toilets; in 1899, 65 per cent of local houses lacked a flush toilet. The Council embarked on a policy of clearing these houses and building new homes. It did not prove easy to find suitable land to buy. Their plan in 1947 to build 400 houses at ***Blackhall*** caused a massive outcry and eventually the plan was turned down. When the ***Greatness*** estate was sold in 1914, the Council purchased land to build the first Council houses in Greatness Lane. More houses were built when they acquired further land from the sale of ***Wildernesse*** estate in 1924. By 1939, the Council had provided 115 housing units. After the war, in 1946 the Council pursued a policy of buying land from the various estates which were being or had been broken up. An extensive programme of building resulted in Lea Road and Shendon Close at Solefields, Westwood Way, The Meadway and part of Betenson Avenue at Bradbourne, Grange Road and Julians Way at Kippington. Hillingdon and Greatness estates were also extended. By 1963, there was a stock of over 800 council houses. The Conservatives' 'Right to Buy' policy of 1980 resulted in many council houses being transferred into private ownership. In 1989, the remaining houses were transferred to West Kent Housing Association.
Sevenoaks Society (1994)

Solefields
The name probably comes from the Anglo-Saxon word Sole or Saal, for a pond, old maps showing a pond at the junction with the main Tonbridge road. Solefields is first recorded as the site of the 'Battle of Solefields' during Jack ***Cade's rebellion*** in 1450. A big house with this name was later built near that corner. By 1900, Solefields Road contained several large Victorian villas. When the original house was sold to ***Sevenoaks Urban District Council*** in the 1940s, along with other nearby estates, new social housing was built on the site.

sounds

What sounds could people hear in Sevenoaks in the past that are no longer be heard? Historians are interested in these changes and so they are worth recording and analysing.

The sound of the bell on the horse-drawn fire engine has long gone to be replaced by the siren on modern emergency vehicles and police cars. Many sounds are peculiar to previous ages: ox-drawn wagons grinding up a hill; a stage coach at full gallop; the cries of street vendors; the noise and vigour of men battling on The Vine during the hustings of 1868; the distinctive call of the corncrake, a bird which disappeared from Kentish fields in the late 19th century; the shrill whistle as an express steam engine passed through ***Tubs Hill*** station bound for the coast is now replaced by the amplified sound of directions to passengers. For many it might be the frightening wail of the air raid warning siren during the ***Second World War***; or the steady throb of hundreds of propeller driven aircraft flying in formation en route to bomb Germany. In the 1820s McAdam's road surfaces reduced the noise of traffic. Eighty years later the motor vehicle brought new sounds and public demands for noise abatement and quieter streets. Radio broadcasting, which began in 1922, brought entertainment and education but it also resulted in intrusive sound from insensitive neighbours and later on from car radios. Since 1970 there have been new sounds: the incessant hum of traffic on the motorways and the Sevenoaks by-pass, and the varying sounds of motor- and electrically-driven garden tools. Familiar office sounds have gone, for example the clack of typewriters or flat bed printing machines. Attitudes to sounds have also changed over time; barking dogs were a common sound in 19th-century Sevenoaks, a noise less tolerated today. There are modern legal restraints on excessive noise, and sound levels can be accurately measured. Many older people have distinctive recollections of sounds no longer heard.

South Park

This road was laid out in 1864. Formerly a narrow lane known as Brands Lane, the ***Post Office*** moved there in 1897.

squatters

As population increased from the late 16th century onwards landless families built cottages on the edge of commons and forests. Areas such as the wooded chart lands of the sandstone ridge at Ide Hill and Toys Hill became home for squatters whose temporary cottages could turn into permanent and larger homes. ***Enclosure*** of land made squatting more difficult and the rural poor were increasingly pushed off to find work in towns.

Stag Community Theatre and Arts Centre

The Stag Theatre was initially built as the Majestic ***cinema*** in 1937 later becoming the Odeon. The Odeon ultimately became the answer to Margaret Durdant-Hollamby's dream for Sevenoaks to have its own theatre. In December 1983, after many years of campaigning, and with the help of ***Sevenoaks District Council***, the building finally completed its transformation into a community theatre. The Plaza Suite, a conference centre, was created in 1993. After various attempts to run the theatre and cinema, it was taken over by the Sevenoaks Town Council on a 25-year lease in 2009. The Theatre houses one of the largest stages in the South

East as well as a modern two-screen cinema and a conference centre at the rear of the building. Margaret Durdant-Hollamby was awarded an MBE in 1994 for her services to the arts.
Durdant-Hollamby (1998)

Stanhope family (1673-1721)
Major-General James Stanhope successfully fought in the war with Spain and became Chief Minister to George I. He purchased the ***Chevening*** estate in 1717, and in the next year was ennobled as Earl Stanhope of Chevening. The 7th Earl Stanhope, James Richard (1880- 1967), was commissioned into the Grenadier Guards and fought in the South African War and the ***First World War,*** after which he turned to politics and served in several Conservative Governments. He died in 1967 without an heir.

Stidulph's Place and Farm
Hasted's *History of Kent* mentions Robert de Stidulfe, who was alive in 1327, as being the proprietor of Stidulfe's Place in Seal. The Stidulph (or Stidulfe) family were then recorded in 1433 when William Stidulph sold Stidulph's Place to William Quintin. The house was on the site of the present Dorton House, formerly ***Wildernesse House,*** in Seal and it must have been substantial as, in the 1664 ***Hearth Tax*** returns, it had a total of 18 hearths. The estate consisted of the house and a farm (Stidulph's Hoath Farm) on the site of the former ***Wildernesse School,*** and the area around the farm and across Seal Road was known as Stidulph's Heath. In 1669 the estate was sold to Sir Charles Bickerstaffe who built a new house and named it Wildernesse House. The farm became the home farm for the ***Wildernesse estate.*** In 1803 the 2nd Earl ***Camden*** enclosed the area of the heath which now includes Hillingdon Avenue to make a new drive and entrance lodge to Wildernesse House, avoiding the poor road near the millpond at ***Greatness.*** Gradually the name vanished as the rest of the heath was built on or became parts of other farms.

street lighting
The first street to be lit at night was the High Street with oil lamps. ***Gas*** lighting came in the 1840s, and ***electricity*** in 1959 with 25-foot standards. Other roads were slowly added to the electric system and gas lighting was phased out in the 1970s.

Suffolk House
The original Suffolk House was a large mansion which stood at the crossroads where Suffolk Way joins the High Street. Its lands stretched down to the 'Hole in the Wall', the gate into ***Knole Park,*** on Seal Hollow Road and along the eastern part of the High Street to the Tesco site of today. The house was built by John Bloome, a mercer from Penshurst in 1585. In 1717 ***John Fermor*** of Middlesex bought the house and 36 acres of land which included Knole Paddock. He built a wall in front of the house, ten rods in length and a footpath six feet wide between the wall and the road. John died of smallpox in 1722 and his brother Sir Henry Fermor inherited the estate. He developed the garden and added a deer park on a large area now known as Knole Paddock. Later stables, a granary and lodge, hop kilns, hop grounds and a cart lodge in the orchard were added. John

Shirley Fermor inherited in 1780. When he died, his wife Catherine sold the estate to the Dowager Countess of Dorset and her second husband, the Earl of Plymouth, in 1807. In the early 19th century it was rented by the Earl of Suffolk and acquired the name Suffolk House. The house was demolished in the 1820s and Robert Comfort, founder of ***Youngs*** store, took over. He converted the stables into a ***brewery*** and completed the building of ***Suffolk Place*** which had been started by the previous owner, Benjamin Saunders, a local auctioneer, undertaker and cabinet maker.

Suffolk Place
Suffolk Place, built *c.*1836-47, was a terraced row of handsome private houses with smart railings and steps up to front doors, homes to doctors, dentists and, at one time, a small school for the children of 'gentlefolk'. In 1936-37 the houses were converted into shops with flats above.

supermarkets
In 1930, the South Suburban Co-operative Society opened a store in the High Street selling groceries and provisions, drapery, footwear, butchery and outfitting. The 'Co-op' was remodelled as a 'supermarket' in the 1970s. Tesco opened a supermarket in the High Street in 1978 to the south of ***Suffolk Terrace***. Five years later Waitrose built a new store in the High Street on the former site of ***Redman's Place***, Guest Yard and Hills Yard. The store was demolished in July 2010 to make way for a new multi-million-pound redevelopment, including Sevenoaks's first escalator, completed in Autumn 2011. Out of town supermarkets with large car parking areas became popular in the 1990s. Sainsbury's 'superstore', built on the Otford Road in 1992, was extended and remodelled in 2011. Tesco opened a 'superstore' in Riverhead in 1999 despite strong opposition from the ***Chamber of Commerce***.

Henry Swaffield (1834-1912)
Born at St Austell, Cornwall, Swaffield came to London in 1856 and moved to ***Granville Road***, Sevenoaks in 1876. He was a generous benefactor giving the ***bandstand*** (1894), shelters in Vine Gardens, and the band practice room in 1902. He had the ***Market House*** equipped as a reading room and social centre for the YMCA in 1900, and gave the site for the ***library*** in The Drive in 1904. A keen Methodist, he gave the site and most of the money for the Methodist Church in The Drive, and provided the ***Cornwall Hall*** and the Retreat ***almshouses***. He was elected to ***Sevenoaks Urban District Council*** in 1894 serving for 15 years, became a JP and Governor of ***Sevenoaks School***. He made his money on the stock market, east European stocks being his specialty. It was not until 1934 that Swaffield Road was so named.

Francis Swanzy (1850-1920)
The Swanzy family came from Co. Monaghan, Ireland, and from the late 18th century were merchants in West African trade. As a result of plural and inter-racial marriage, there were white and black Swanzys on the Gold Coast. During the 19th century the family fortunes came first from palm oil and then increasingly from gold concessions and general trading. Andrew Swanzy (1817-70) created the tight knit family firm of F. & A.

84 ***Suffolk Place*** in Sevenoaks High Street, an early 20th-century photograph. Many people look at the modern shop fronts and fail to view the line of roofs above. The demand for more shops increased in the town during the 1930s, and the once splendid houses found a new purpose as 'retail outlets'. The road has a fairly good surface, but it is not to the metalled standard later required for faster moving motor traffic which on such a surface would have raised clouds of dust.

Swanzy, which became part of Unilever in 1929. Leaving the Gold Coast in the 1850s, he came to live in Sevenoaks, at 'The Quarry', Kippington, a house demolished before 1930. On Swanzy's death, control of his commercial interests passed to his son Francis who lived in Granville Road. Francis was a Liberal, and elected to ***Sevenoaks Urban District Council***, becoming chairman in 1914. He was a strong supporter of an improved water supply, a benefactor to the town (paying half the cost of the Holly Bush Recreation Ground) and also by his will to ***Sevenoaks School*** (the Swanzy Block opened in 1926) of which he was a governor. A portrait of Swanzy hangs in the Sevenoaks Town Council chamber.

swimming pools

There was a centuries-old tradition of swimming in mill ponds. At ***Greatness***, the main mill pond was turned into an open-air swimming pool in the 1870s. Known as the Sevenoaks Open Air Swimming Pool or Greatness Lido, it was 76 feet by 32 feet, with a depth from 3 feet 6 inches to 6 feet 6 inches. At Longford Mill, Dunton Green, a lido or open-air swimming pool was built by a Mr Killick in 1930 fed by the ***Darent***. The pool was popular and attracted families from a wide area. There were deck chairs to sit on and teas were served on the lawn. The pool was closed in 1952 when the mill changed from water power to electricity. In Brasted the Darent Swimming Pool was opened in 1914 by the Earl of ***Stanhope***. It was fed by the Darent and was reputed to be the coldest in Kent.

The indoor Eardley Road Baths, opened in 1914, were presented to the town by ***Edward Kraftmeier***. Bob Tonge, captain of the Swimming Club, was the first person to enter the 25 by 17-metre pool which held nearly 100,000 gallons of water, and had room for 200 swimmers. The Eardley Road baths were closed in 1984 and the new ***Sevenoaks District Council Offices*** built on the site in 1985. A new pool was built on ***Lady Boswell's School*** field, next to the ***Library***, to replace the Eardley Road baths. This pool was replaced in 2000 with the current ***Leisure Centre*** which includes a 25-metre swimming pool, toddlers' pool and teaching pool.
Newman (2008)

Swing Riots
A period of agricultural depression followed the end of the Napoleonic Wars, and led to what local magistrates in 1829 called 'unprecedented distress among farm workers'. It was this which led next year to the 'Swing Riots' (named after the mythical Captain Swing, who signed letters to local farmers, demanding the destruction of threshing machines which reduced winter employment, and threatening the firing of ricks). Although the main centre was further east, there were outbreaks as near as Otford and Greatness. The *Maidstone Journal* reported that in Sevenoaks 'scarcely a night passes without some farmer having a cornstack or a barn set on fire' (at least 14 incidents are recorded), the London Insurance Company suspended cover locally, and an 'Association for Detecting Incendiaries and Protecting Property' was set up in the town. The riots died down the following year and there were few prosecutions in Sevenoaks.

T

telegraph
The electric telegraph system began in 1837 and first came to Sevenoaks with the railway in 1862. A great step forward was made in 1870 when the different telegraph systems were nationalised and placed under the control of the Post Office. From then on local post offices, including those in Sevenoaks and the surrounding villages, were steadily linked into the national and international telegraph system. A line from London to Tunbridge Wells was installed in 1883.
Wilson (1988)

telephone
The telephone was developed from the 1880s, coming to Sevenoaks in the mid-1890s. The first subscriber to the new service was Alfred ***Laurie*** of ***Rockdale***. In 1897 the telephone exchange was situated in ***Post Office***

Yard, behind the Old Post Office in the High Street, and the next year the first telephone was erected in the town centre. Telephone cables on poles became a common sight. In 1975 a new modern telephone exchange was built in South Park.
Wilson (1988)

temperance
Heavy consumption of alcohol and drunkenness was common in 18th- and 19th-century Sevenoaks. Christian and other reformers campaigned to regulate the sale of alcohol and the opening hours of pubs, and to promote temperance or total abstinence. The temperance movement, which began in the 1830s, had the support of ***Methodists***, most other nonconformist churches including the Salvation Army, and also some Anglicans and ***Roman Catholics***. The British Association for the Promotion of Temperance, founded in 1853, aimed to convert ***public houses*** into useful, pleasant and respectable places instead of mere drink shops. The Temperance Hotel and coffee room in ***Lime Tree*** Walk offered an alternative to the pub. In the 1890s the Sevenoaks United Temperance Council opposed extending licences to pubs. Father ***Ignatius Lazzari*** founded in Sevenoaks a branch of the Catholic Total Abstinence League of the Cross in an effort to stem what he called 'the tide of evil and dissipation caused by the great sin of drunkenness' that 'brought ruin to the body and soul'. By the early 20th century there were several branches of the Band of Hope in Sevenoaks, one which met at ***St Mary*** Kippington. *Salmon's Directory 1910* lists a branch of the Women's Total Abstinence Union which met monthly at the YWCA in Argyle Road, and the Sevenoaks Temperance Silver Prize Band which played weekly in the town. In that year there was in England one pub for every 400 people. Locally produced mineral waters were often advertised as an alternative to alcohol.

tennis
In the late 19th century tennis was a game for the well-to-do. It was not uncommon for large houses in Sevenoaks to be advertised as having a 'tennis lawn'. The first recorded club in the town was the Park Lawn Tennis Club in 1920. The Clarendon Tennis Club began soon after the ***First World War***, accounts existing for 1921. The club enjoyed the use of three courts in a disused quarry between Clarendon Road and the town's main ***railway*** line. The clay surface of the courts required a degree of maintenance, including dragging with an old carpet secured to a piece of wood pulled by a rope. The Club hut in the southern corner of the grounds originally featured a flat roof where members could stand to observe matches being played, but this was later roofed over. Members took their lives into their hands to access the club via steep wooden steps that grew increasingly rickety over the years. Membership had something of a colonial feel with a proportion of players returning to this country from overseas postings. When the land was sold for housing, the club merged in 1979 with their old rivals, Sevenoaks Tennis Club. Registered in 1929, the Sevenoaks Tennis Club had leased some land in Bradbourne Vale Road from the Outram family. This too was sold for housing. The merged club was named

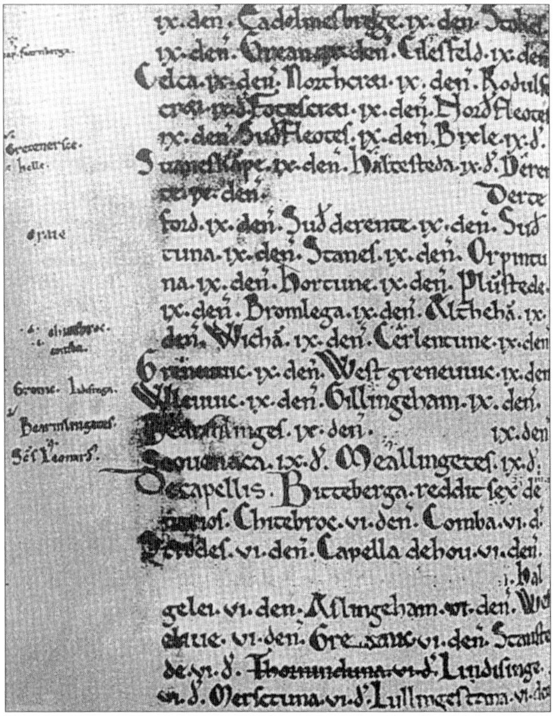

85 *Textus Roffensis* *c.*1120. A page from this thousand-year-old document showing the entry for 'Seouenaca', the earliest record of a parish church at Sevenoaks.

the Sevenoaks Clarendon Lawn Tennis Club. After a brief spell playing on ***Sevenoaks School*** courts, they moved in 1988 to a new site at Raley's Field on land leased from ***Sevenoaks Town Council.***

Textus Roffensis
A list drawn up in *c.*1120 for the diocese of Rochester (Roffensis is a latinised form of the Anglo-Saxon 'Rochester') to record the names of churches in the diocese which were required to make certain payments to the bishop and chapter. ***St Nicholas*** Sevenoaks appears as 'Seouenaca', and owed nine 'denarii' (pence) for chrism oil every Maundy Thursday.

William James Thompson (1817-1904)
William Thompson, owner of ***Kippington*** estate which he bought in 1864, was a wealthy tea merchant and a prominent public figure and benefactor in Sevenoaks. A Justice of the Peace and High Sheriff of Kent, founder and chairman of the Sevenoaks ***Water*** Company, he also helped set up the Cottage ***Hospital*** and donated the ***Drill Hall.*** At one time churchwarden at ***St Nicholas church,*** his evangelical views were at variance with those of the rector, the Revd Thomas ***Curteis.*** He therefore successfully applied to the Archbishop of Canterbury to endow and build his own church, ***St Mary's,*** on his estate at Kippington. After his death his family continued to own the estate until 1946.

time
Much of the modern world is governed by precise time, but this was not the case throughout most of Sevenoaks's past. In medieval times the agrarian seasons of the year, plus the annual calendar of the Christian church, with Christmas, Easter, and Pentecost, dictated a more leisurely sense of pace. By the late 16th century many people in Sevenoaks were probably aware of the year and perhaps the month and even the day of the week on which they were born or married, as this was recorded in baptismal and marriage registers. In 1752 Parliament decreed a change from the Julian to the Gregorian calendar which meant the loss of 11 days, with 25 March becoming 6 April. Until then, 25 March, also known as Lady Day, was one of the Quarter Days, on which rents were annually due to be paid. The move to 6 April then marked the beginning and end of the financial and tax year. A notion of daily time was conveyed by church bells, which called people to divine service. A few large houses had sundials which told the hour but only on sunny days. By the 17th century an increasing number of 'middling' people in Sevenoaks could afford spring powered mechanical clocks in their homes The town had several clockmakers and repairers in the mid-18th century. Six watch and clockmakers are listed in *Pigot's Directory* 1840.

The great change in public awareness of time came in the late 18th century with the advent of industrial time. The London-Sevenoaks stage and the mail cart bringing the post were advertised to arrive and depart from Sevenoaks at specific times. The General Post-Office 'Time Bill' for the London to Hastings route in the 1790s stated that 'the Time must be punctually observed'. Local ***carriers*** also advertised the time of their schedules. Work places, particularly those dependent on power supplies and production lines, such as the silk mill at ***Greatness*** and the ***brick*** works on the Otford Road, laid down working hours, often starting at 6 a.m. until 6 p.m. Workers' demands for a shorter working day were gradually conceded after 1850, and the model of an eight-hour day was attained for many people by the early 20th century. Schools also started and concluded at a specific hour of the day and children became aware of school bells, lesson time-tables, and penalties for being late.

The advent of ***railways*** after 1835 set a more precise sense of industrial time. Trains travelling at 20-35 mph were dangerous and needed to be kept apart from other trains. Thus was born the timetable, the timed arrival and departure from a station, the railway clock, and the official with his watch. The expansion of the railway network led to the adoption of a standardised national 'railway time', although this did not become officially uniform across the country until 1880. Postal services, expanded after 1840, were also based on a timed schedule of collection and delivery of mail. Shops and retail premises also opened and closed at specific times, and licensed hours, standardised in 1874, were officially imposed on beer shops and ***public houses***. The new ***police*** force, which by 1860s had largely replaced the parish constable and the night 'watchman', also worked to timed rosters, as did the navy and army. Drill, an essential part of all training for uniformed forces, involved precise adherence to time.

By the mid-19th century many middle-class people had pocket watches which they might set to a public clock. ***Knole*** had a clock, and a bell that struck the hours (*c.*1745), on Bourchier's tower. A dim imitation was on the stables at ***Maywood***, installed in 1873 along with a bell to chime the hours. A clock hung on platform one at Tubs Hill Station between 1900 and 1975, originally given by Lord Sackville, which is now in the ***Sevenoaks Museum***. Other public clocks were installed above Warren's the opticians in the High Street (1903), on the tower of ***St Nicholas*** parish church (1910), on the Old ***Market House*** (1977), and on ***St Mary's Riverhead*** and also the new market house in Bligh's Meadow.

After 1860 the industrial manufacture of watches reduced the price of a pocket watch; by 1912 one could be bought for five shillings, and the supply of manufactured interchangeable parts meant that it could be locally repaired. By then there were seven watch repairers in Sevenoaks. One indication of the significance of time-keeping was the practice, which became common by the late 19th century, of presenting watches or clocks to workers and public servants to mark a period of faithful service. By the early 20th century most people's daily lives were governed by close adherence to time, aided by the mass production of cheap wrist watches after 1920. Public radio broadcasting from London, begun in 1922, also provided accurate time.

Tithe Redemption Commission
Tithes were an ancient tax levied on the value of all property or its agricultural output within a ***parish*** to provide revenue to support the church and clergy. They were therefore greatly resented by many farmers and also farm labourers who felt that they put downward pressure on their wages, but also by nonconformists. Eventually the new Whig government which came to power in 1832 introduced a new system. The Tithe Redemption Act of 1836 required all properties to be revalued, and imposed a tithe redemption annuity based on these values, intended to extinguish the liability over a hundred years. To do this every parish had to be surveyed. The Sevenoaks survey with its map and schedule was undertaken in 1841. It lists every building and every field, distinguishing arable from pasture, and every plot of woodland. It provides a very important and detailed picture of ***agriculture*** in 1841.
Kain (1974)

tokens
When Oliver Cromwell's government failed to mint enough coins to go round, local traders and merchants issued their own coins or tokens. In Sevenoaks, ***Nathaniel Owen***, a prosperous wool and linen merchant, issued his own tokens. One of his halfpenny tokens is displayed in the ***Sevenoaks Museum***.

'Top of the Town'
A term widely used in the mid-20th century for the Upper High Street part of Sevenoaks, that area between the old Market Place and south towards ***St Nicholas***, which was the highest point of the town. In the same period, and perhaps earlier, local people talked of 'the town'.

Tourist Information Centre
Sevenoaks Town Council set up the Tourist Information Centre in a small caravan in Buckhurst Car Park in 1981. When the new ***Library*** opened in 1986, the Tourist Information Centre moved into that building. In 2010 it moved again, after a temporary period in the Waiting Room at the Bus Station, this time to the foyer at the Plaza Suite at the ***Stag***.

town crier
Sevenoaks had an official town crier in the mid-19th century, as recorded in the *Sevenoaks Advertiser* for March 1843. He rang a bell in the street and to cries of 'Hear ye', 'Oyez', announced the news or perhaps goods for sale. His role declined as literacy increased and as local ***newspapers*** were printed and circulated more widely. However, the street directory for 1895 notes that Somerton Bateman was the 'town crier & bill poster'.

town-twinning
Modern town-twinning increased after the Second World War, an attempt to develop international friendship and co-operation. Since 1964 Sevenoaks has been twinned with the French town of Pontoise. Mayor Adolphe Chauvin led a delegation from Pontoise as guests of

Sevenoaks Urban District Council. The following year Pontoise hosted a party from Sevenoaks, establishing a regular routine of twinning visits. Local organisations, from Rotary to football clubs, have variously participated in twinning activities. When the Urban District Council was abolished, the twinning administration passed to a new association, 'Friends of Pontoise'. In 2001 and 2002, the Pontoise Mayor Philippe Houillon, and Keith Loney the Mayor of Sevenoaks, signed official charters endorsing the twinning. In 2000 Sevenoaks was twinned with the German town of Rheinbach, following a proposal made to ***Sevenoaks Town Council*** five years earlier. A 'Friends of Rheinbach' was formed and the twinning agreement was formalised at ceremonies in Sevenoaks in June 2000 and in Rheinbach in May 2001. Many educational, sporting and musical exchanges have taken place since then.

trade unions

Little has been written on trade unions in the Sevenoaks area. The earliest known was among skilled paper workers in mills along the ***Darent*** whose activities were banned by the 1799 and 1800 Combination Acts until 1824. Early agricultural unions, formed in the area in the 1830s and in the 1870s, were invariably met by fierce opposition from farmers and landowners. Employers often made it very difficult for men and women to join unions. Also many unions represented small groups of local workers. National strikes called by unions, as in 1911-12 and the end of the ***First World War***, and the General Strike of 1926, inevitably included some union members in Sevenoaks. Union membership increased during the Second World

86 Strikers from the workshops at Fort Halstead. The placard stating 'We've never had it so bad' indicates that this strike probably occurred sometime shortly after Macmillan's optimistic speech in July 1957 when he told fellow Tories that 'most of our people have never had it so good'. An earlier brief strike occurred at the Fort in 1952 when 80 men demanded an end to a pay pause.

War and peaked in the early 1980s, falling to 7.5 million members in 2010. By then many blue and white collar and professional unions had become more active in representing the interests of doctors, teachers (they went on strike in 1984), journalists (who also struck in June 1959), and clerical workers.

transhumance
The seasonal movement of livestock, such as cattle, sheep, and pigs, from one location to another. This was customarily done in medieval times with animals being moved along the ***drove ways*** in from the ***North Downs*** to the ***weald*** where they could graze on the richer pasture or root among the woodlands.

Tubs Hill
Probably derived its name from a pub called 'The Three Tubs' at the foot of the hill. Houses were built on both sides of the hill in the late 19th century. Many of these on the lower east side were demolished in the early 1960s and replaced with a parade of shops, and two large blocks of offices (1964) subsequently converted to apartments.

turnpikes
Turnpikes were major highways built, maintained, and repaired by Trusts established by Acts of Parliament. Traffic, whether wagons, carriages, cattle, or horses, paid a toll to use the turnpike. The pike, or tollbar, usually a gate kept by a keeper, restricted access to the road. One local toll gate, long known as ***Paygate,*** stood at the junction of Seal Hollow Road and the A25; another was at the cross roads at the ***Bat and Ball.*** The Tunbridge Wells-Tonbridge-Sevenoaks turnpike was built after 1709, and extended 40 years later by a realigned and regraded road up the ***North Downs*** (present Star Hill) to Knockholt and on to Farnborough and London. An east-west turnpike from Reigate to Wrotham was created in 1765, following the line of the modern A25 road, which intersected with another north-south turnpike from Farningham to Sevenoaks via the ***Darent*** valley completed in 1766. Turnpikes could be realigned to accommodate the interests of local landowners; for example Thomas ***Lambarde*** diverted the Tonbridge Road to prevent it running straight past his house ***Park Place,*** thus the sharp curve to the present road as it leaves Sevenoaks. In 1764 Lord ***Amherst*** 'turned the road further from his house' at ***Montreal Park.*** Between 1834-38 the turnpike up the steep scarp slope of the Downs was rebuilt to the east at Polhill (the present A21) providing a longer but easier gradient for horse-drawn vehicles. Turnpikes increased the volume of traffic on the roads and the flow of trade goods stimulated economic change, By the 1780s the journey from Sevenoaks to London by coach took less than four hours, and a wagon could deliver goods to the city and return in a single day. After 1840 turnpikes increasingly faced serious competition from the new railways. From 1835 onwards parishes assumed more responsibility for roads and by an Act of 1878 highways were subject to local authorities. *Panton and Lawson (2004); Albert (1972); Keith-Lucas (1984); Black (1984)*

Map 16 Turnpikes and railways.

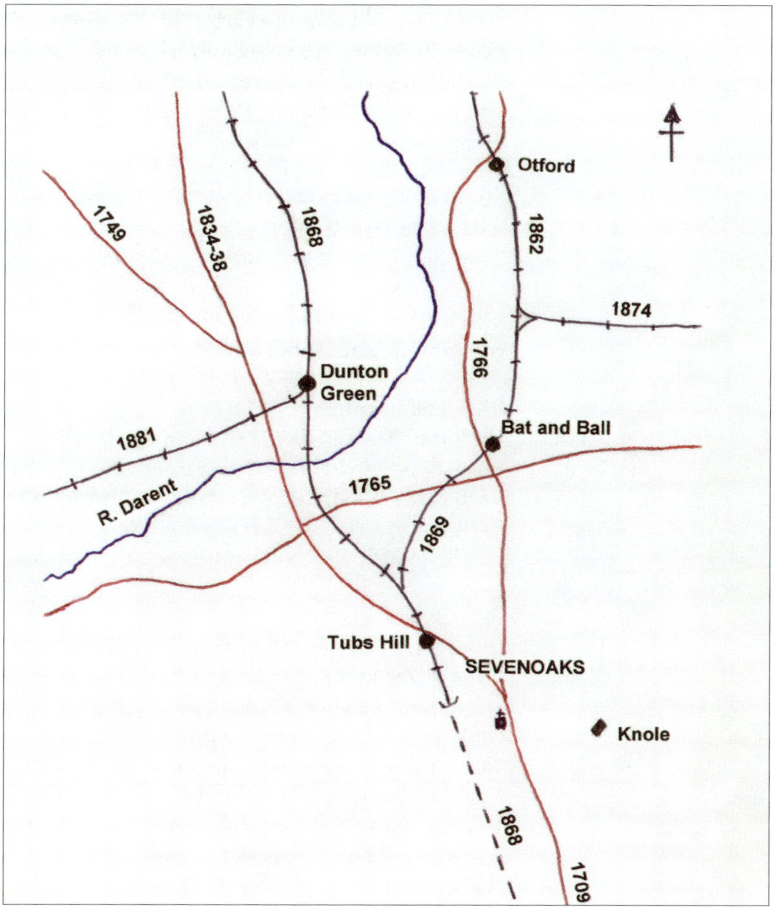

U

Underriver

Underriver is a separate ecclesiastical parish within the local authority parish of ***Seal*** to the south-east of Sevenoaks, below ***Knole Park***. The earliest settlements were Romshedde (Rumshed) and Blakecherl (***Black Charles***) farms mentioned in 13th-century deeds. Great Underriver hamlet consists of buildings which originally serviced the needs of the farms in the area. At one time it had its own forge, wheelwrights, post office, school, pub (*The White Rock*) and church (St Margaret's), but all bar the latter two have now been converted into housing. There was a tannery at Tumbling Bay to the south. Little Underriver below Rooks Hill includes Absaloms Farm and Underriver House, built in 1709, possibly on the site of a Tudor building. By the 1840s, the ***Woodgates*** at Underriver House held over 50 per cent of the land in Underriver, with 30 per cent owned by the Herries of ***St Julian's***. In 1862 the Underriver House estate was broken up with the house bought by John Davison a lawyer and MP. He extended the house and financed the building of St Margaret's Church, designed by George Gilbert Scott. Most of the land in the parish was acquired by the Earl of Derby before the ***First***

World War but was again broken up into individual landholdings. In the 1970s a minor boundary change brought St Julian's into the parish.

Unitarians
Unitarians were a nonconformist sect which denied the Holy Trinity, not accepting the divinity of Jesus Christ. In the 18th century some Presbyterian and General Baptist congregations split over the question of the Trinity, one example being the ***Baptists*** at ***Bessels Green***. The original General Baptist chapel became Unitarian, and remains so today.

University of the Third Age (U3A)
The idea of U3A study groups originated in France in the 1970s and took root in Britain ten years later. A self-help educational charity for those no longer in full-time employment, U3A often also serves as a social group, its activities fostering a strong sense of community. The first Sevenoaks U3A began in 1994 and grew to nearly 900 members in more than 120 study groups; a second group, the Knole U3A, was created in 2009 with 200 members in over 30 study groups.

V

Vale of Holmesdale
The upland vale running east to west between the ***North Downs*** and the sandstone hills on which Sevenoaks is built. It is formed of gault clay with pockets of gravel. A major use has been arable and pasture farming, fruit trees and hops, with some market gardening.

vestry
A room in the parish church where vestments were kept, and which became the meeting place for the Parish vestry which took over the duties of the Manorial or Hundred Courts. At ***St Nicholas church*** the vestry met in a small room, the Parvise, over the south porch. The vestry consisted of the vicar, his churchwardens and about ten appointed officials including the surveyors of highways, the overseer of the poor, constables and the parish clerk. The vestry could adopt various acts, and appoint officials to carry those acts into effect. They were overseen by the Justices of the Peace, men drawn from local wealthy landowners. It provided help for the poor, sick and mentally ill, put the unemployed and orphans in to work and paid for funerals. The vestry's powers declined in the mid-19th century.

Vestry Estate
This large site on the Sevenoaks/Otford boundary was for many years the property of the Vestry (local authority) of St Botolph's parish in London. It was developed as a trading estate after the Second World War. At one time the whole estate was occupied by the Mobil Oil Company.

Veterinary infirmary
This was established in 1895 at Pennard House, Eardley Road, the first veterinarian being D.L. Pugh. He was joined by his son

Leslie Pugh in 1917 and by John Bruford in 1926. Pugh and Bruford traded until 1983 when it became known as the Pennard Veterinary Group. Until 2006 the practice served farms and stables but then became a small animal practice.

The Vine

The Vine is one of the oldest ***cricket*** grounds in the country. It was given to the town as a cricket ground in 1773 by the 3rd Duke of Dorset, John Frederick Sackville, of ***Knole***, who was a great patron of the game. In 1850 the Vine Pavilion was built for Mary Sackville, widowed daughter of the 3rd Duke, who married the 1st Earl ***Amherst***. She let it to the Cricket Club. Before the Pavilion was built, the cricketers used the Cricketing House, which was later turned into two cottages before being demolished to make way for the ***Bandstand***. The ground was taken over by the military for use as a parade ground during the ***First World War***, whilst the Pavilion was used by the YMCA as a canteen for troops.

Vine Court

The house known as Vine Court stood in a triangle of land of approximately 18 acres between Dartford Road, Park Lane and

87 ***The Vine***: modern watercolour. For at least 250 years ***The Vine*** has been a place of assembly and communal activity for the people of Sevenoaks. On this site ***cricket*** and other field games have been played. Town fêtes have been held on The Vine, but also political meetings; strollers have enjoyed hearing the band play, and many residents have enjoyed the extensive views towards the ***North Downs***. Watercolour by Roger FitzGerald.

88 ***Vine Court***: early 19th-century print. Once a splendid 'gentry' house on the northern outskirts of the town. The idea of town planning barely existed in the late 19th century when Vine Court was demolished. The local board had some control over how houses were built, but they largely drew back from regulating what could be done with private property.

Hollybush Lane. Sir ***Multon Lambarde*** owned the property in the early 18th century. When he died in 1758, his widow continued to live in the house. In 1787 it was leased to John Pratt of Wildernesse. Thereafter, the house was lived in by a succession of tenants, with the Lambardes retaining ownership. Among the last tenants was ***James German***. In 1876 the estate was sold to Charles George Hale who demolished the house and all its cottages in order to build houses for the professional classes who were moving to Sevenoaks after the opening of the ***railway***. A condition was put on its sale that 'only genteel houses' were to be built. The building plan proceeded and Vine Court Road and Avenue Road were laid out.

Vine House

Vine House, now 1 Park Lane and situated on the north east corner of ***The Vine***, was built in 1732 by John Mackindor. In 1831, Abraham Peat, a schoolmaster, took a 21-year lease to run a school in the house. According to the 1841 census, there were 25 boys ranging in age from six to sixteen. After Peat left, a new tenant ran a small boarding school. The house was sold in 1874 to the local ***brewer*** Alfred Smith who had his brewery nearby in ***Suffolk Place***. In 1953 a new owner sold the cottage, now known as Park Cottage, together with some of the land from the grounds. Vine House is now a family home.

Vine Lodge
Jane Edwards in *Recollections of Old Sevenoaks* recounts that the elderly Miss Pratt, grand-daughter of Sir John Pratt, Lord Chief Justice of England who owned the ***Wildernesse estate***, lived at Vine Lodge. In 1837 the house and surrounding land was rented by ***John Rogers*** who lived there until he moved to ***Riverhill***. The Tithe map shows the estate extending down ***School Lands*** and along ***Seal Hollow Road*** to what is now Bayham Road. Kelly's *Directory* for 1847 shows Captain W. Brooke ***Northey*** living at Vine Lodge. By 1871, Thomas Rogers, a cotton manufacturer, owned the property, followed by John Spink, a jeweller. The house was put up for sale in 1902; the agent described it as having 12 bedrooms, three reception rooms, billiard room, stabling, coach house and standing in grounds of 22 acres. The property was sold to the Judds in 1919 who sold the estate to Kent County Council in 1948, except for a small triangle of land known as ***Judds Piece***. Kent County Council used the house for a Technical Institute for Boys from 1951 until 1954, when it became a girls' primary school. In 1978 the school was closed and the house used as a teachers' centre. By 1986 the estate was split up and sold. ***Sevenoaks District Council*** bought the old vegetable garden and built the sheltered housing unit Hollybush Court. The house was split into flats and four houses were built in the garden.

Voluntary Aid Detachment
The VAD was formed in 1909 by the St John Ambulance Society and the British Red Cross to provide a nursing force ready for use in event of a war. By the outbreak of the ***First World War*** there were over 70,000 enrolled, two thirds women, and they formed the Voluntary Aid Detachment. They served in Sevenoaks but also overseas; one local woman, Bridget Aurea Lambarde, died in France in early 1919 during the influenza pandemic.

voluntary organisations
Local voluntary organisations and charities have long played a role in Sevenoaks. Many were Christian and extensions of church work. A branch of the St John Ambulance Association was started in the town in 1878. The 20th century has seen a growth of all kinds of voluntary organisations. For example, Age Concern began in 1947 as the Sevenoaks and District Old People's Welfare Committee, holding their first meeting at ***Beatrice Wilson***'s home. The Committee started a small lunch club in the Dorothy Parrott Hall, a wooden hut in Buckhurst Avenue, where 15 people could be served a hot meal by the Women's Royal Volunteer Service. When the Hall was demolished, the organisation moved to Pembroke Road and a small 'pop-in' centre. In 1982, Age Concern moved to ***St John's Church Hall***, and in 1991 to the old ***Cobden Road*** School.

Finally it moved to the Old Meeting House, St John's Road, and in 2010 it was re-launched as Age UK with a Day Centre at Hollybush Court. The Voluntary Service Unit (VSU) began in ***Sevenoaks School*** in 1964 to provide support for young people who wished to volunteer in the community. The Charity grew and expanded to other schools in Sevenoaks, by 2010 drawing volunteers from more than 80 per cent of Kent secondary schools. In 2009 VSU merged with Voluntary Action West Kent to form Voluntary Action Within Kent. The Volunteer Bureau was first set-up in

89 Men of the Sevenoaks volunteers, *c*.1904. In 1899, when the South African War broke out, the Sevenoaks Volunteers were among many of the units that were sent to the Cape. Returning in 1902, they came back to a service and parade held on the Vine cricket ground. Later the Sevenoaks Volunteers became an integral part of the Royal West Kent Regiment and the forerunners of the Home Guard in the ***Second World War***.

1972 with the aim of recruiting local people to volunteer and place them in appropriate voluntary work with individuals or organisations needing help. A Volunteer Transport Group was constituted in 1978 providing transport to medical appointments, at minimal cost, for those unable to use public transport or who could not provide it for themselves. The Sevenoaks Blind Social Club began life in 1947, but no records exist before 1975 when a Miss B. Shewry was the Chairman. Run by volunteers, the Club came under the auspices of the Kent Association for the Blind. The activities of the four ancillary clubs have included crafts, hand bell ringing, and social events. Churches voluntarily support various agencies, such as the Sevenoaks Christian Counselling Service (1983), and the Sevenoaks Area Youth Trust (2002) which provides detached youth workers in the town.

Volunteers

A Sevenoaks ***militia*** regiment was formed in the mid-18th century under the command of Lord Whitworth. Francis Motley ***Austen*** was a captain in the Sevenoaks Volunteer Infantry, later known as the

Sevenoaks and Bromley Regiment of Local Militia. In 1859, following fears of war with France, it was decided by some titled families in Sevenoaks to recruit men for the purpose of home defence. Posters were circulated with the assembly room of the Crown Hotel being the venue for the first public meeting. Chaired by Earl ***Amherst*** and supported by Colonel ***Northey, Multon Lambarde*** of Beechmont and ***Camden*** of Wildernesse. After a disappointing response (only 100 men turned up), a larger number swore the loyal oath, and Multon ***Lambarde*** became the first officer (soon to be succeeded by Sir Nelson Rycroft) commanding the 33rd (Sevenoaks) Company of the Kent Rifles. Training began at ***Bethlehem Farm*** courtesy of ***Samuel Bligh***. All men were volunteers and had to pay 10 shillings for the privilege of joining. Parades were held on alternate days during the afternoon or early evenings. However, issue of the Enfield rifle ensured that at least the men looked the part. At an exercise in ***Knole Park*** in July 1867, volunteers from the district numbered 237. By 1890 the government put on a regular footing all volunteer units. Ten years later the ***Drill Hall*** provided a base for their activities.
Richards (1901), 127-30

W

walls and fences
Walls and fences are so common in modern Sevenoaks that they rarely receive comment unless there is a boundary dispute. Along with hedges they serve to mark out property, and also to restrict access. From early times land ***enclosure*** protected cattle and crops from predatory animals and people. The homes of the wealthy might also be protected by a moat, as at Rumshed and Ightham, or by high walls. In late medieval times deer parks were enclosed to keep in and protect game, for example at ***Knole*** and ***Panthurst***. Privately owned land was often marked by walls or hedges, as at ***Montreal Park***. In the 19th century, when villas and rows of houses were being built in Sevenoaks, the gardens were invariably divided one from another by fences and hedges to identify property rights. Land owned as farms, factories, warehouses and schools is also usually marked by a barrier of some kind.

Walter Smith Ltd
The company, formed by Walter Smith (1876-1943), was responsible for the building and upkeep of many ***roads*** in the district, employing thousands of men over the years. When Smith left school he helped his father in construction work using local stone which gave him the idea of ***quarrying*** stone and gravel. His company had offices on the site of what is now ***Baden Powell*** Road in ***Riverhead***, and was responsible for extracting much sand and gravel from what became ***Chipstead Lake***. Sand and gravel were also brought to Chipstead from quarries at Warlingham and tipped into the Lake from where a dredger extracted it as washed gravel into barges which were then pushed by a small tug to the Riverhead end where Walter Smith had their yard. The firm was sold to Redland Tiles in 1970.

90 ***Walthamstow Hall*** school from a postcard *c.*1900. Probably a succession of girls boarding at the school sent copies of this postcard to their missionary parents overseas with appropriate, possibly tear-stained, messages. Many girls at the school were entrusted to guardians with whom they might stay during the school holidays. Girls could be at the school and not see their parents for several years.

Walthamstow Hall

Walthamstow Hall School was founded in 1838 by Martha Foulger as a school 'to provide for the daughters of Christian missionaries a thoroughly good and liberal education'. Originally located in Walthamstow, the School moved to Sevenoaks in 1882 to enjoy the benefit of clean air and the countryside. The new school built in ***Hollybush Lane***, designed by Edward C. Robins, cost £22,000 and was the largest and most expensive building in the town at the time. Kate Unwin was the first headmistress in Sevenoaks, 1878 to 1898. Described as 'puritanical, inspirational, a good business woman, but also kind and loving', she prepared a few girls to gain entry to universities which hitherto had admitted only men. The School was originally for boarders only, some girls boarding in Knole Cottage, now the ***Quaker*** Meeting House in Hollybush Lane. It was not until the end of the century that day girls were admitted. In 1908, the three remaining acres of ***School Lands*** were purchased to provide a hockey field and vegetable garden. Early in the ***Second World War*** a bomb destroyed the new laboratory, craft rooms and the old gymnasium. The girls were evacuated to Pontesford House, near Shrewsbury, and Walthamstow Hall became a clearing house for evacuees and later an Air Raid Wardens' Post. Walthamstow Hall merged with ***St Hilary's School*** in 1992.
Pike, Currier & Moore (1938; 1973)

war memorials

Most public war memorials date from the ***First World War***, although plaques in churches commemorated men who died in earlier wars. Thought was first given to a town memorial for the dead of the Great War in 1916. A total of £5,663 was raised by house to house collection and public subscription. Final agreement for a statue of a soldier, with his rifle grounded and facing south-east to the Western Front, was not gained until 1919. The memorial, with sculptures by A.G. Walker, commemorated the 226 residents of Sevenoaks who were killed or missing in the First World War, to which were added the 115 dead and missing of the ***Second World War***. The site of the memorial, on a piece of land given by Lord Sackville to the town opposite ***The Vine***, caused controversy when ***Sevenoaks Urban District Council*** decided to create an island by building a short stretch of road from the top of ***St Botolph's Road*** to the Dartford Road. This was to be paid for from the local ***rates*** and was opposed by local bodies such as ***trade unions*** and the ***Middle Classes Union***. A public enquiry resolved the question, and the road was built. Other war memorials were erected: to the dead of Sevenoaks parish in ***St Nicholas*** churchyard, unveiled by children of servicemen who had died in the Great War in December 1919; a ***Kippington*** memorial to men of the parish; at ***Riverhead*** a 'Roll of Honour' along with a Memorial Hall; at ***Dunton Green***, listing the 27 killed in the Great War, and 22 in 1939-45; and at the north entry to Weald village a cross commemorating the 21 men killed in 1914-18 and the nine in the 1939-45 war. Since 1920 each memorial has been the site of an annual Remembrance Day service. Several churches in the area, the former ***Post Office***, and ***Sevenoaks School*** all unveiled commemorative plaques and memorials to those killed in 20th-century wars.

Gordon Ward (1885-1962)
Medical doctor and local ***historian***. Ward was born in south London, studied medicine at Westminster Hospital, and came to Sevenoaks as an assistant to Dr ***Carnarvon Brown*** in 1913. When war broke out the next year he was married and living in Holly Lodge, near the Vine. As an army reservist Ward was called-up and served as an Army doctor on the Western Front and also in Salonika. After the war Ward was elected on a ***Middle Classes Union*** ticket to the ***Sevenoaks Urban District Council*** (1920-23). He also became Carnarvon Brown's partner and helped to establish the first X-ray machine in the town, housed in a wooden building in Pembroke Road. Ward's great interests were archaeology and philately. His contributions, with his friend ***Herbert Knocker***, to researching, retrieving, and writing the history of Sevenoaks were considerable and resulted in *Sevenoaks Essays* (1931), a stream of articles in *Archaeologia Cantiana*, and numerous documents and transcriptions now in the Centre for Kentish Studies. During the inter-war years Ward, along with ***George Bennett*** the town librarian, established the ***Sevenoaks Museum*** in the ***Library*** then in The Drive.
Ward (1931; 1980 edn), 6-13

William Warham (1450-1532)
William Warham, a friend and patron of Erasmus, was scholarly, cultured and much travelled. During the 28 years he was Archbishop (1504-32), he built himself a splendid new palace at ***Otford*** where he entertained King Henry VIII and Katherine of Aragon in 1520. After inheriting ***Knole*** from ***Bourchier*** and Morton, he enlarged it by adding another external layer to the western side of the house, creating the Green Court, and adding a new main entrance.
Sackville-West (2010)

water mills

The river ***Darent*** was ideal for mills with its steady fall of several feet in the Sevenoaks area. Small tributary streams, such as the ***Brad*** and Gunhilder Brook, were also sufficient to provide water power. By the mid-18th century there was on average a mill every mile along the Darent. From the medieval period, the cleansing of new cloth was undertaken in a fulling mill. Water mills were also used for grinding corn, known as grist mills, and by the 19th century for sawing timber. In the Sevenoaks area there were water mills at Sundridge, ***Chipstead, Longford, Bradbourne, Greatness,*** and in ***Whitley Forest.*** There was once a water mill downstream from Spring Hill, and some have claimed that this was one of the original Domesday mills recorded for Otford. This seems unlikely, although there is some hint of a mill in the late 14th century. Clear evidence begins in 1770, from which date records show occupation by a succession of millers, who also farmed several acres of cleared land. At Bradbourne there were possibly three water mills. A deed of 1280 records a fulling mill: 'By Alice relict of Reginald Kempe to Henry de Brutone ... a fourth part of a fulling mill at Bradeburne'. In 1545, the Bradbourne corn mill, powered by the River Darent, was granted by Henry VIII to William Darkenolde. The Andrews and Drury map of 1769 shows quite clearly that there were two mills at Greatness, a corn mill (possibly 1745) and the Nouaille's silk mill. The corn mill had a succession of owners, the last being George Harris who owned the mill for over 40 years. After his death the mill, house and land were sold at auction in August 1927. The mill was bought by George Bennett but in January 1928 it was destroyed by fire. It was rebuilt and continued milling until 1935. Thereafter it became an upholsterer's workshop, and recently was converted into five luxury apartments.

The Greatness farm and watermill was owned by Elizabeth Delamare of Sevenoaks who married Peter ***Nouaille*** III, from another Huguenot family, famous in the Spitalfields silk business. He developed the site as a silk mill and was credited with bringing the over-shot water wheel 'nearer

91 Whitley Mill. There may have been a mill in ***Whitley forest*** since medieval times. This mill was working in 1900 about the time this photograph was taken. The building had a ragstone base, the overshot wheel was iron-framed and housed within a brick structure, and the mill building was timber-clad. A spring 200 yards above the mill, which can still be seen, fed the mill pond, which is now silted and overgrown.

92 A modern watercolour of Greatness Mill, by Roger FitzGerald. In 1816 Peter Nouaille IV, owner of Greatness silk mill, appeared before a Parliamentary Select Committee investigating the employment of children in mills and factories. He employed 80 people, mainly girls from six years of age as their small hands were much better at tying knots in raw silk. They worked long hours with rare days off but he provided them with medical care, clothing, a small school to teach them to read and write, and looked after their welfare as long as they worked for him.

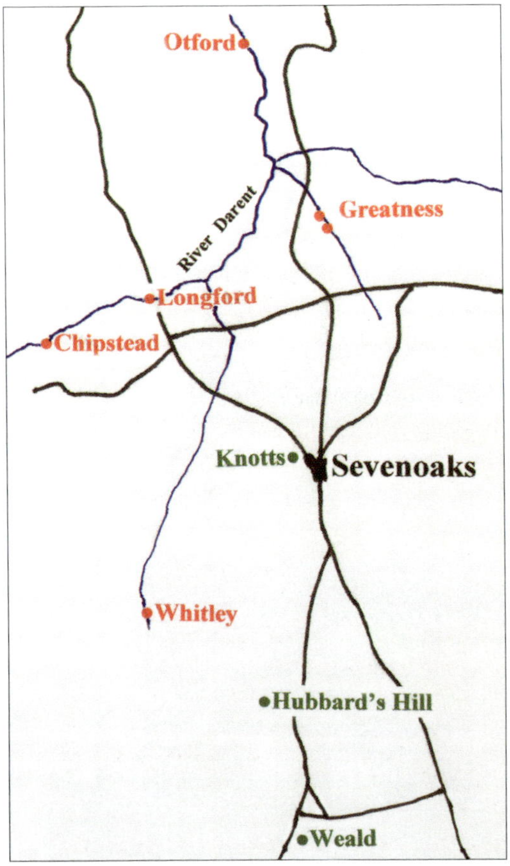

Map 17 Water-mills (in red) and windmills (in green) were a major source of industrial power which continued to be used long after the advent of steam engines. Skilled craftsmen built and maintained engines made of wood and iron that relied on wind and water.

to perfection than any of the others' in improving its efficiency. He was well liked in the community and with his workers, employed more than a hundred people including French refugees. He built two rows of ragstone cottages – which survived until the 1960s – for his workers. Although business was never easy, the silk mill enjoyed times of great success supplying silk to royalty and the nobility. Peter III developed crepe silk – 'bumpy' silk, later much used by the Victorians for funerals. In 1793, George Courtauld, of the famous textile family joined Peter in his business at Sevenoaks. However, the two men argued over George's support for the French Revolution and their relationship foundered in 1797. Peter died in 1809 and his son, Peter IV, took over. There followed a period of decline for the Greatness silk mill, and for the silk industry generally, with the introduction of steam power, the economic slump and the removal of a protective duty on silk. In June 1827 an advertisement appeared in *The Times* for the sale by auction of the estate. The workers were dismissed and the mill fell into ruin. The harvests of the next two years in England were poor, wages and poor relief fell and, in 1830, labourers revolted against landlords and wealthy farmers. Peter Nouaille IV was one of the first recipients in England of a threatening '***Swing*** letter' outlining grievances and calling for reform. He died in 1833, the same year that Joseph Harrison, a former employee, returned to the area and, greatly affected by what he saw, wrote a poem, 'Ode on the silk mills of Greatness'.
Rayner (1997); Seal (2008); Bygone Kent, January 1982; *Stoyel (2008).*

water supply
In the 17th century water supply was restricted to a few springs, one controlled arbitrarily by the vicar on ***glebe land***, from ponds, rainwater from roofs stored in water butts, and a few pumps. In the early 19th century wells to provide water were situated at Tubbs Wells, outside the Rock and Fountain pub, in the yard belonging to the wine merchants, Page and Co, and at St John's Well in the yard of the Bat and Ball Inn on St John's Hill.

Conditions had only marginally improved by the mid-19th century with more private wells and pumps, including public ones in the High Street. There were also a few deep pumps available to the public at ***Six Bells Lane***, London Road, and what is now Bligh's Hotel. The lack of adequate drainage and effective waste disposal (many houses had earth closets) meant that Sevenoaks was a smelly, unhealthy town in the 1850s, the result being water-borne diseases and deaths, as the new Sanitary Authority complained. However, construction of the Sevenoaks ***railway***

tunnel through the sandstone ridge in the mid-1860s revealed a new deep source of clean water for the town. Thereafter access to potable water in the town improved as it was piped to many houses although people in the surrounding rural area continued to rely on traditional sources of supply. The provision of piped water, and the increased demand for improved sanitation and thus expenditure on drainage systems, were political issues involving ratepayers, sanitarians, and those who argued for municipalisation. The introduction of ***main drainage*** in the 1880s was opposed by many ratepayers. In 1910 there was popular concern that continued burials in the St Nicholas's new graveyard were polluting the water supply below in Oak Lane.

Knole had its own private supply, stored in a vaulted tank under the Stone Court built in the days of the 1st Earl; it was re-excavated and recorded by the National Trust in 2010. A small reservoir near the White Hart hotel provided a further supply. This was later supplemented by a deep private well, dug in 1887, which still supplies the house and parts of the estate. A few other large houses, for example ***St Julian's***, drew water from local springs and wells. The Sevenoaks Water Company was established in the1870s with a pumping station at ***Oak Lane*** and two reservoirs, one on the Tonbridge Road holding 300,000 gallons and another higher up on Bayley's Hill with a capacity of 400,000 gallons. These provided the town's main supply, reinforced by further underground reservoirs and pumps built over the next few years. In 1935 this was augmented by new and much deeper wells at ***Cramptons Road*** near the new gasworks. The company had a statutory monopoly of supply over an area which included Seal. A rival supply developed at Kemsing, and disputes over the Sevenoaks Company's monopoly, delayed extensions of supply to several areas north of Sevenoaks.

From 1878 sewage disposal was dealt with by the West Kent and Darent valley drainage scheme in a sewer constructed from Westerham to Dartford. Some local ratepayers opposed this extra burden on the rates. In 1900, 60 per cent of houses in the town did not have flush toilets and relied on privies. A reliable supply of clean fresh water, and a good system for removing human and other waste, was vital to improve public health which can be seen in the falling infant mortality rates in the decades 1880-1920. The Sevenoaks Waterworks Company amalgamated with Tonbridge in 1948 and with Tunbridge Wells in 1973, forming the West Kent Water Company. Sevenoaks is now supplied by the South East Water Company. The water treatment works in ***Cramptons Road*** were built in 1969.
Fox (2007)

Weald

The village of Sevenoaks Weald, or Weald as it is frequently known, is two miles south of Sevenoaks, directly below the greensand ridge on the heavy low weald clay. It occupies a knoll formed by the flow of two streams. Originally part of the parish of Sevenoaks, in 1861 it became a separate parish of about 2,200 acres. The name of the village (akin to the German *Wald*, forest) may derive from it being just inside the immense wooded area that then occupied much of Kent, Sussex and Surrey. It was certainly located on the main ***droveway*** by which animals were brought to the pastures and 'dens' in Penshurst and elsewhere. Weald is not mentioned in

Domesday Book, although 'hurst' place names may indicate Saxon origins. One example is Wickhurst Manor, the core of which is a medieval stone hall. Later medieval structures include the 15th-century rear of the former butcher's shop in Windmill Road. By the 14th century much of the dense local forest had been cleared for mixed agriculture. The pattern of fields and hedges has remained largely unchanged for the past 400 years or more. The ***Hearth Tax*** return of 1664 shows that Weald then had 86 households. By the 19th century most of the area comprised large, gentry-owned estates such as ***Panthurst***, owned by the ***Lambardes***, and Nizells by the ***Glendinings***. Their tenants occupied the farmhouses; the labourers tended to live in village cottages. Although farming remained generally profitable for centuries, it declined dramatically after the ***Second World War***. New residents tended to be car-owning commuters who worked in London or nearby towns, travelling to work by the ***railway*** and by road, principally the A21which skirted the village. At the same time new housing infilled all the orchards and farmland within the village, and house prices rose steeply. After 1980 there was a dramatic fall in the number of shops, pubs and other businesses in the village, which by 2007 had a population of 1,230.

Weald Place

A large house on the sandstone ridge, shown as 'Belle Vue', on the 1869 Ordnance Survey map, then owned or leased by F.J. Underwood (b.1842), landowner and merchant.

weather

Changes in weather frequently occur, and people remember the unusual: the heavy rains of autumn 1968, the hot summers of 1908, 1911, and 1976, the sudden blizzard on Christmas day 1927, the snow falls of January 1940 and 1987, and the harsh winters of 1947 and 1962-63. Great storms are also memorable. The great storm of late November 1703 resulted in over 6,000 deaths in England. The 'high wind' destroyed timber-framed houses and churches, wrecked a large number of ships, and uprooted hundreds of thousands of trees. In the storm's wake the writer and pamphleteer Daniel Defoe (*c*.1660-1731) collected oral evidence of its destructive force from correspondents across the country. His account contains reports from Kent including one from Cudham where the church was severely damaged. The most recent memorable storm was that of the night of 15-16 October 1987. October had been very wet, and the leaves were still on the trees, when a rapidly deepening depression changed course and moved north-east over central Britain, producing gale-force winds on its southern flank. Gusts of up to 80mph were recorded in Kent, where the damage was immense: an estimated 15 million trees were felled, and 19 people lost their lives. National Trust properties were badly affected, and villages cut off for many days. Technically, the storm does not qualify as a hurricane, and Michael Fish, the BBC duty weatherman, famously forecast that there would not be a hurricane that night. Even today, in places such as Knole Park, there are twisted and fallen trees, reminders of the power of nature that night.

On 25 June 1980 a great thunderstorm which lasted for about three hours in the afternoon, produced some of the heaviest rain ever recorded in such a short period in this area. It was a localised storm with just under

93 Trees felled on the *Vine* by the storm of October 1987. Sevenoaks captured the imagination of the national media, after losing six of its seven celebrated oak trees on the Vine in the great storm which occurred in the early morning of 16 October. More people died during the clearing-up operations than in the storm itself.

five inches of rain recorded at ***Sevenoaks School***, while to the north half that fell, and no rain fell at Shoreham. The storm was accompanied by much hail, and banks of hail were still visible on the road to Ide Hill the following morning. The main railway station was flooded to platform level.

The night of 3-4 December 2010 was the coldest recorded in Britain for at least 110 years, and Sevenoaks shared the appalling conditions, which began in the last week of November. By 3 December, snow lay 18 inches deep and there had been eight successive days in which the temperature failed to get above freezing. Under clear skies on the evening of 3 December, temperatures fell, resulting in a new record minimum temperature of -14.5C, yet later in the night warmer air arrived, raising the temperature to +2.5C but also producing no less than 0.26 inches of rain! This reduced the snow cover considerably, but the improvement was only short-lived with six more days that month when temperatures failed to exceed freezing (including Christmas Day), and further heavy snowfalls.
Ogley (1987)

Frederick Wedmore (1844-1921)
Wedmore was the chief art critic for the *London Standard* for 30 years. He also did much to build up a collection of Impressionist paintings at the National Museum of Wales. For the last 19 years of his life he and his wife and daughter lived at 'White Mill End', a comfortable Arts and Crafts house built for them in 1900 at the junction of South Park and Granville Road. After his death his wife and daughter continued to live in the house. All three are buried in St Nicholas's new graveyard.

Elizabeth Weller (1671-1721)
Elizabeth Weller, the great-grandmother of Jane ***Austen***, was the daughter of a lawyer. She grew up in Tonbridge, married John Austen of Horsmonden in 1694, and bore seven children before he died unexpectedly 11 years later, leaving her with considerable debts. In 1708 Elizabeth took employment as housekeeper to the bachelor headmaster of ***Sevenoaks School, Elijah Fenton***, and thereby raised and educated her younger sons free of charge. One of them was William Austen, father of Jane Austen's father, George. Elizabeth is buried at Tonbridge parish church, and commemorated by a plaque at Sevenoaks School.

H.G. Wells (1866-1946)
Writer, philosopher, socialist, visionary: Herbert George Wells was born in Bromley where his father Joseph owned a run-down business selling china, oil lamps and cricket materials. Wells was apprenticed at 13 to a draper, a job he hated and for which he had no aptitude. From this humble and difficult start he developed a desire to widen and improve his life which he did largely by his own efforts. He eventually won a scholarship to the Science School in South Kensington. Wells began his writing career with papers for the Debating Society and he also started on the work which would eventually evolve into his first novel, *The Time Machine*. In 1894 Wells left his wife of three years and moved to 'Tusculum Villa', 23 Eardley Road with his former student, Amy Catherine Robbins, whom he called Jane, and her disapproving mother, scandalising his landlady at the impropriety of the relationship. He married Jane after his divorce

in 1894 but he wrote about his landlady's continuing hostility in *An Experiment in Autobiography* (1934) when he described sitting downstairs in the lamplight on a warm August evening with the window open, trying to shut out the sound of his landlady complaining loudly to a neighbour over the fence that people with lodgings to let in Sevenoaks ought to know the sort of people that might take them. Wells said he 'wrote on grimly' and that 'somehow amongst the gathering disturbance of those days the Time Machine got itself finished'. A blue plaque now marks the house in Sevenoaks where he completed his work on *The Time Machine*.
Wells (1934)

West Heath School
A girls' boarding school which moved to ***Ashgrove*** in 1932. Diana Spencer was a boarder at West Heath. The school ran into financial difficulties in the 1990s due to a falling number of pupils, and went into receivership in 1997. It was bought by the Al Fayed Charitable Trust and opened as the New School in 1998.

West Kent Storage
For 50 years a site on Rye Lane, ***Dunton Green***, was occupied by the complex of large refrigerated buildings of the West Kent Storage company. It stood on the former site of the Dunton Green Brick, Tile and Pottery works with its 80 feet deep eight-acre lake. Bill Davison bought the site, drained the lake, and filled it with rubble from the London blitz, a process completed by 1961. In 1953 the first cold storage buildings were erected. Davison sold out to the Mitchell Cotts group in 1967, and he retired to Australia. The plant storing meat, frozen foods and poultry covered 17 acres and employed 400 people. In 2011 the storage plant closed and building began of 500 houses on the site, renamed as Ryewood.

West Kent Yeomanry
There had been yeomanry forces raised in Kent during the Napoleonic wars, but they were run down after 1815. A small unit survived, but, as its members were required to provide their own horses and equipment, they tended to be farmers or members of the richer local families. The force was reorganised in 1908, alongside the reconstruction of the (infantry) ***volunteers*** into the Territorial Army as part of the Royal West Kent Regiment. At the start of the ***First World War***, the Yeomanry left Sevenoaks, in horse-drawn brakes, for a secret destination. They later served in France.

White Hart Estate
A triangle of land bounded by the Tonbridge Road, Gracious Lane, and Weald Road, developed for housing after 1937. ***Sevenoaks Urban District Council*** considered buying the land in 1930 in order to build houses which could be let for ten shillings a week, but decided the site was not viable for the purpose as it was too far from the town. In Burntwood Road many of the first houses were built on plots of more than one acre and designed by various architects; there was some uniformity of style but houses varied in character. Most gardens were designed with a pond. There has been some redevelopment, extension and infilling mostly dating from the 1990s.

White House
The White House stood opposite the ***Red House*** in the Upper High Street. A Listed Grade II building, it may have been formerly two cottages, the Georgian front being added in 1810. ***Knocker*** and Foskett, the solicitors, had their office in the White House before they moved in to the Red House, and later antique dealers occupied the building for many years. Despite an appeal, the House was demolished in the early 1970s, condemned by a building inspector as a warren of staircases and passages suffering from the ravages of death watch beetle and dry rot.
Ogley (1999), 100

Whitley Forest
During the Middle Ages, Whitley was the hunting forest of the Archbishops of Canterbury, Lords of the Manor of Otford. It remained part of the Manor until sold to James ***Stanhope*** when he purchased the ***Chevening*** estate in 1717. Common rights attached to parts of the forest conferred rights for local people to gather fallen wood for firewood. This led to ***squatters'*** settlements on the periphery of the forest, at Whitley Row and Goathurst Common. An area of chart land, it was never particularly productive. In the mid-19th century, a reasonable period for British ***agriculture***, the current mill tenant farmed 24 acres, and a new farm, of 70 acres, had appeared above Spring Hill. However, the agricultural depression from the 1870s led to decline, and alternative projects were attempted – hops, spring bulbs, watercress – none of which lasted. Meanwhile, ownership had passed to the ***Montreal*** estate, by the 1930s in the hands of John Jaques. The latter hoped to develop the forest for housing, but was prevented by the outbreak of the ***Second World War***, during which the army requisitioned Whitley in preparation for the D-Day landings. By the time Jaques regained possession, the ***Green Belt*** had made development impossible and he returned the area to traditional forestry.

Charles Whitworth (1752-1825)
Soldier, diplomat, and politician who, among other posts, served as ambassador to Russia. In 1801 he married the widowed Arabella, Duchess of Dorset. He was Lord Lieutenant of Ireland 1813-17, and a major benefactor of Sevenoaks, particularly ***Lady Boswell's school*** and ***St Nicholas church***.

Wickenden estate
Wickenden's Wood was on the east side of ***St John's Hill***. By the 1920s a nursery owned by R. Neal and Sons Ltd adjoined the Hill. This was sold for housing development in the 1930s by a local builder, L. E. Jones & Son. Further land was also bought and by the end of the decade semi-detached houses formed Wickenden and Swaffield roads.
Thompson (1994)

Wildernesse estate
An enclosed deer park at Wildernesse was first established in 1680 when Sir Charles Bickerstaffe bought ***Stidulph's Place***, on the site of the present Dorton House, and built the first Wildernesse mansion there. When first enclosed it was 364 acres and covered an area between Seal, Godden

Green and Seal Hollow Road, including Chance Wood and bisected by Park Lane. In 1705 Wildernesse was bought by John Pratt, the Lord Chief Justice and later Lord ***Camden***, who extended the estate as far as Sevenoaks Hospital and also to the north of Seal Road. At its peak it covered more than 500 acres. Camden created Wildernesse Avenue as the principal drive for Wildernesse House; it extended down what is now Hillingdon Avenue. In 1795 the 1st Marquis Camden had been Lord Lieutenant of Ireland and Arthur Wellesley, later Lord Wellington, had been his ADC. In 1815, just before the Battle of Waterloo, Wellington visited Camden at Wildernesse and the great avenue with double rows of limes, known as the Waterloo Limes, was planted in Wildernesse Avenue to commemorate the occasion.

By the middle of the 19th century the Wildernesse Estate included most of the land bounded by Seal Road, Seal Hollow Road, Bayham Road, Quaker's Hall Lane and St John's Hill. In 1866 the 2nd Marquis ***Camden***, the owner, died and his son decided to move to Bayham near Tunbridge Wells where he had another estate. He considered disposing of Wildernesse piecemeal for building purposes to take advantage of rising land values. One plan shows the area described above divided into about a dozen large plots, up to 10 or more acres, for the building of mansion houses. Nothing came of this and Camden leased the estate in 1860 to ***Charles Mills***, later Lord Hillingdon, who in 1885 bought the estate. Mills was a great benefactor locally, providing the land for Sevenoaks ***hospital*** and many buildings for ***Seal*** village.

After the ***First World War***, it was the turn of the Hillingdons to consider how to develop the estate when they decided to sell up and move away from Wildernesse. In August 1921, 550 acres of the estate was put up for auction at The Royal Crown hotel in Sevenoaks. Lots 54 to 64, approximately 115 acres, were described in the sales brochure as 'An Ideal Freehold Garden City Site'. In the event, nobody took up the development challenge and the lots were sold separately: houses and land in Seal village were sold to the tenants; land to the west of Seal Hollow Road was sold off to private developers who built ***Wickenden*** and Swaffield Roads, Pinewood Avenue and the bungalows on Hillingdon Avenue, and to ***Sevenoaks Urban District Council*** who used it for ***social housing, allotments***, and left much as woodland. The mansion and ***golf*** course were turned into an impressive country club; and the rest of the original 760 acres of the Wildernesse estate was sold for residential development. It was bought in 1924 by Percy Harvey, a developer. He sold many of the buildings and plots on the existing roads in Seal village but retained a core acreage around Wildernesse House bounded by Seal Road, Park Lane, Blackhall Lane and Seal Hollow Road. Except for the mansion house and the home farm (the site, later, of ***Wildernesse School***) he divided the area into approximately 160 building plots of half to six acres and established two new roads, Parkfield and Woodland Rise; this area of exclusive houses on large plots is now known locally as 'The Wildernesse Estate'. Many of the houses in Wildernesse Avenue, mostly built between 1925 and the ***Second World War***, were in the Arts and Crafts style; three have been identified as being designed by ***M.H. Baillie Scott***. Tylers Barn, a near copy of a Baillie Scott house, was first owned by a notable plant collector, Arthur Edward Rogers, who acquired three plots with a total of nine acres which he planted with many unusual specimens of rhododendrons and azaleas. The stables of

94 Wildernesse house *c.*1820. J.P. Neale drew many views of the 'seats of noblemen and gentlemen' in Britain. This copper engraving shows Camden's house as a picture of genteel refinement and pastoral comfort.

Wildernesse House at the Seal end of Wildernesse Avenue were used as a hospital in the ***First World War*** and after the war were acquired by a laundry business. After the ***Second World War***, when the mansion house was used by Guy's Hospital with 120 beds, the country club floundered; in 1954 the house was bought by the Royal London Society for the Blind for a school and renamed Dorton House. Between 1926 and the Second World War some 34 houses were built in Woodland Rise with another four post-war. Six of the houses in the road have been identified as having been designed by Baillie Scott and another 14 by prominent architects while many others were by well-known local builders such as L.A.G. Hawkes and T. Woodhams to their own design. Two of the houses had gardens designed by ***Vita Sackville-West***. Parkfield was established on the line of an ancient footpath which crossed the estate from ***Knole Park*** (the stone steps over the park wall) towards Bitchet Green. Some 25 houses were built between 1925 and the Second World War on substantial plots of between one and four acres. Many of them were built in Arts and Crafts style. One, originally called High Winds, was built by Basil Jones, the owner of Sevenoaks Brickworks. After the war it was acquired by the chairman of the Reed Paper Group who had strong connections with the Norwegian royal family, no doubt through the paper business. A cottage was built in the grounds for King Haakon VII for his use on visits to the UK which had a direct telephone line to Harrods! Although in recent years some houses in Wilderness have been demolished and rebuilt, the existence of restrictive covenants and a conservation area mean that the road still retains a rural feel and, despite the ravages of the 1987 hurricane, the trees

95 Wildernesse house, photographed after 1880. The *Mills* family bought the Wildernesse estate in the 1880s, and it remained the family 'seat' for the next forty years.

96 Workers on the Wildernesse estate, *c.*1890s. Bowler-hats and waistcoats for work, the dress of the men depicted the hierarchy of the staff who maintained the gardens and estate of ***Charles Mills***. The man in the three-piece suit, sporting a watch and chain, is probably the estate manager.

and other foliage mean that few houses overlook each other.
Fox, Williams, and Mountfield (2007; Neale (1821)

Wildernesse School
A secondary modern school for boys built, following the 1944 Education Act, on land of the former ***Wildernesse estate*** Home Farm. It opened in September 1951, with 12 teachers and 274 students. Wildernesse Boys School and Bradbourne Girls School amalgamated in 2010 to become ***Knole Academy.***

Wildernesse Sports Centre
The Centre opened in 1974 at the back of the ***Wildernesse School*** building. The facility, run by SENCIO, included courts for badminton, basketball, volleyball, netball, five-a-side football, three squash courts and an all-weather hockey pitch.

Wildlife Reserve, Bradbourne
The site that is now the Wildlife Reserve was excavated between 1935 and 1980 for sand and gravel, first by the Kent Sand and Ballast Company and later by Redland Aggregates. James and Jeffery ***Harrison*** gained the agreement of Kent Sand and Ballast Company to develop the lakes and surrounding countryside as a nature reserve. In

97 The Kent Wildlife Reserve showing one of the 'hides' for bird-watchers. The character of the Wildlife Reserve is almost entirely man-made, all the lakes deliberately dug and most of the trees planted by hand to create a natural looking landscape. The Reserve was originally called the Sevenoaks Gravel Pit Reserve, then the Jeffery Harrison Reserve before being named the Wildlife Reserve.

1956, the banks of each lake were landscaped to form bays, spits and islands to provide shelter and nesting sites for wildlife and birds. The Wildlife Reserve extended over 55 hectares and comprised roughly equal proportions of water and land. It included five lakes and a mixed habitat of ponds, seasonally flooded pools, reedbed and woodland. Over 2,000 species of flora and fauna have been identified at the Reserve. It was the first example in Britain of a former commercial gravel pit being developed for the benefit of wildlife and conservation.

Beatrice Wilson (1897-1980)
Beatrice Wilson was a gifted physiotherapist with a vision to improve the quality of older people's lives. She trained at Guy's Hospital, but showed her commitment to Sevenoaks by opening the town's first physiotherapy centre, the Vitasan Clinic in South Park (1937 to 1964). In 1948 she realised her ambition of improving the care of older people in the town by setting up the Sevenoaks and District Old People's Housing Association (later to become ***Rockdale*** Housing Association) and opened Rockdale House a residential home in 1953. She was also a founder member of the Soroptomists in Sevenoaks.

In 1963 she married Dr Lawrence Lockhart and moved to Cambridge. The physiotherapy services at the Vitasan Clinic were taken over by the National Health Service. She remained President of the Housing Association for many years and continued her interest until her death.

98 Knotts windmill, the last surviving machine, a weather-boarded smock mill, stood in ***Covell's Farm***, Eardley Road, and was demolished *c*.1890.

windmills
Windmills were sited to catch a good and regular flow of wind which turned sails and drove machinery. A windmill is shown on a military survey of the area in 1755, but it has long since disappeared. There were probably several others around Sevenoaks, but most had gone by the late 19th century, by which time corn was usually taken to watermills like the one at ***Greatness***, or to steam mills, the nearest of which seems to have been at Farnborough. Earlier mills stood at ***Hubbards Hill*** (17th century) on ***Sevenoaks Common***, in ***Whitley forest***, on Bayley's Hill, and at Sevenoaks ***Weald*** (working 1880).
Finch (1976; Weald History Group (1999), 97-98

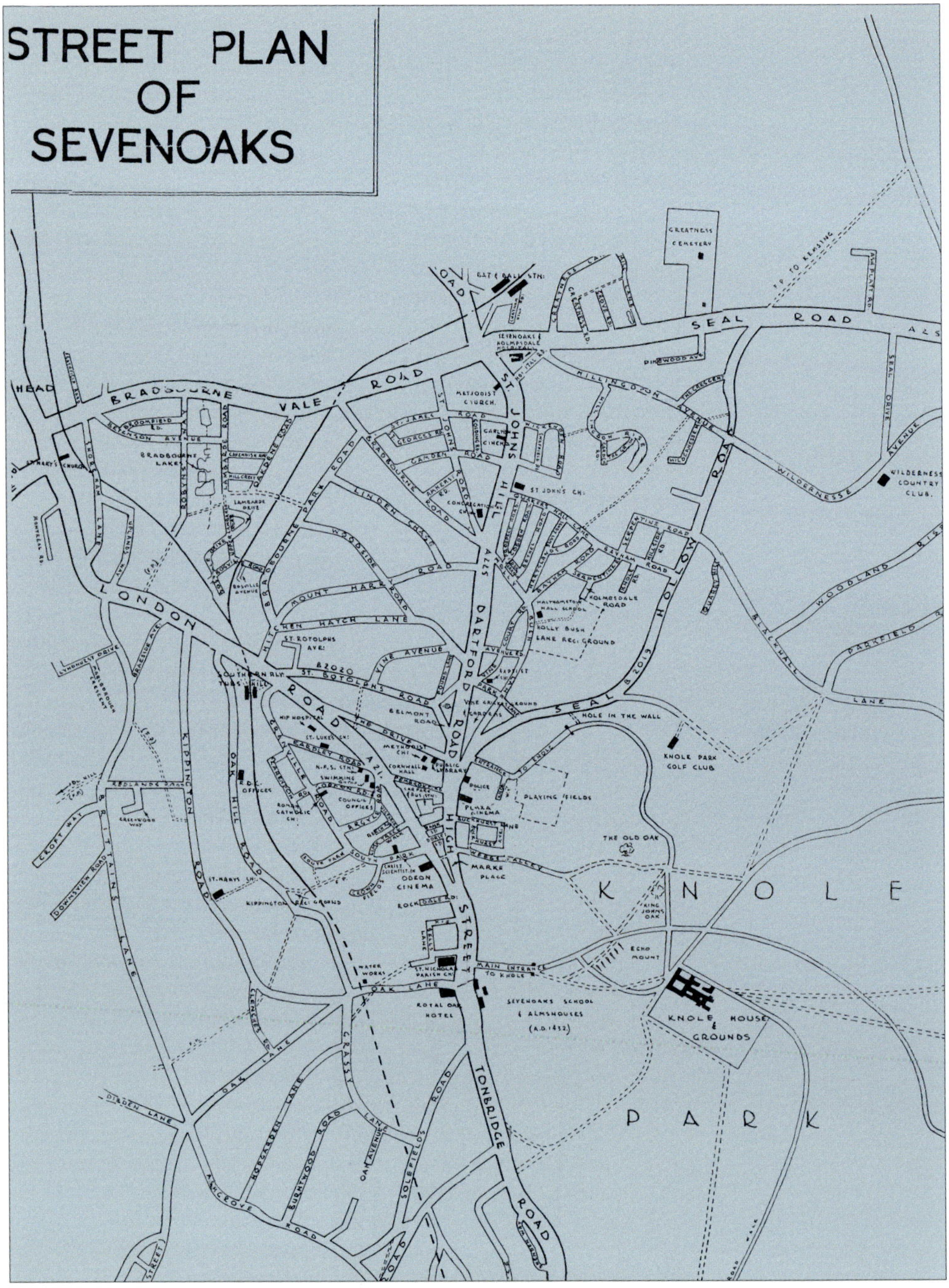

Map 18 Sevenoaks in 1957, from Salmon's Guide and Directory. The ***Montreal***, ***Bradbourne***, and ***Wildernesse*** estates had gone and been replaced with housing. Other major housing developments east of ***St John's Hill***, at ***Greatness*** and ***Hillingdon***, and in the area to the south of ***Oak Lane*** had further enlarged the town. Many newer houses, including semi-detached properties, had a garage for a car. Population increase and increasing ownership of motor cars was steadily changing the Sevenoaks' townscape.

women's organisations
For more than 150 years women in Sevenoaks have been active in a variety of local religious, social, and political organisations, many with a charitable concern. Three such bodies established in the 19th century, with branches in the town were the inter-denominational Young Women's Christian Association (YWCA), the Sisterhoods, and the Mother's Union of the Church of England founded in 1876. An early branch of the Mother's Union was founded at St John's church in 1897. At one time the YWCA ran a hostel within the town. The National Council of Women of Great Britain was founded in 1895 under the title of The National Union of Women Workers. It was joined by other industrial and philanthropic societies working for the benefit of women, changing its title to National Council of Women of Great Britain. A Sevenoaks branch was formed in 1947 to carry on the work of encouraging women to take an active interest in all matters of government appertaining to the advancement of women. Its main aim is still that it should not be a disadvantage to be born a girl. The ideals of the Women's Institute (WI) of truth, justice, tolerance and fellowship remain as strong and important now as at its foundation in 1915. The WI is the largest voluntary women's organisation in the United Kingdom. It exists to educate women to enable them to provide an effective role in the community, to expand their horizons and to develop and pass on important skills. The afternoon Sevenoaks Women's Institute began in 1916 with 15 members, and the Sennocke WI which meets in the evenings was founded in 1968. The Women's Voluntary Service was founded in 1938 in anticipation of a war, and thousands of women were active members in wartime. The Sevenoaks branch continued after 1945 and prepared Claridge House as a receiving station for Hungarian refugees coming to Britain in 1956.

The Soroptimists, a professional ladies luncheon club, was formed in Sevenoaks in 1937, the founding members including the headmistress of Walthamstow Hall School, Dr Abelson a local GP, ***Beatrice Wilson***, and the pianist Ethel Breething. Members were active in setting up ***Rockdale*** as a home for the elderly.

Woodgate family
This family lived at Somerhill, near Tonbridge, and owned land within the Sevenoaks parish, including ***Riverhill House*** from 1781 to 1842. Francis Woodgate bought ***Underriver*** House about 1820 and he became the main landowner in that corner of ***Seal*** parish; his initials appear on several farmhouses and cottages in that area. Many Woodgates married into families around Sevenoaks. One daughter Frances (later Allnutt) kept a diary in 1830 recording that no fewer than 11 large houses in the 12 miles between Seal and Penshurst were owned by her brothers, sisters or cousins, an illustration of the way such families formed a closely-knit network across the area.
Woodgate (1910)

workhouse
Sevenoaks workhouse, with its two acres of gardens, was built *c.*1730 on ***St John's Hill***. Under the old poor law which continued until the late 1830s,

99 Sale notice of parish workhouse 1846. The old parish workhouse stood on the west side of ***St John's Hill***, at the junction with Camden Road. It was sold when the new Union workhouse at Sundridge opened. The sale notice mentions that new owners would be required to put up fences and hedges to mark the boundary of each lot.

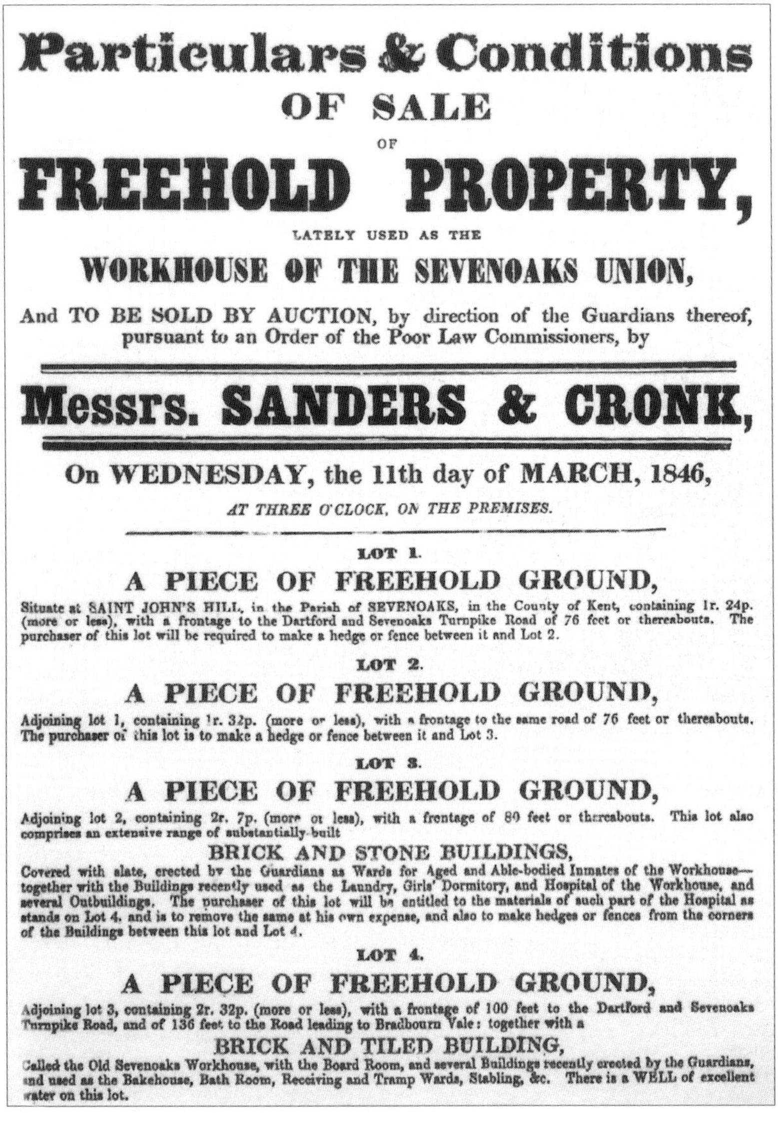

Particulars & Conditions

OF SALE

OF

FREEHOLD PROPERTY,

LATELY USED AS THE

WORKHOUSE OF THE SEVENOAKS UNION,

And TO BE SOLD BY AUCTION, by direction of the Guardians thereof, pursuant to an Order of the Poor Law Commissioners, by

Messrs. SANDERS & CRONK,

On WEDNESDAY, the 11th day of MARCH, 1846,

AT THREE O'CLOCK, ON THE PREMISES.

LOT 1.

A PIECE OF FREEHOLD GROUND,

Situate at SAINT JOHN'S HILL, in the Parish of SEVENOAKS, in the County of Kent, containing 1r. 24p. (more or less), with a frontage to the Dartford and Sevenoaks Turnpike Road of 76 feet or thereabouts. The purchaser of this lot will be required to make a hedge or fence between it and Lot 2.

LOT 2.

A PIECE OF FREEHOLD GROUND,

Adjoining lot 1, containing 1r. 32p. (more or less), with a frontage to the same road of 76 feet or thereabouts. The purchaser of this lot is to make a hedge or fence between it and Lot 3.

LOT 3.

A PIECE OF FREEHOLD GROUND,

Adjoining lot 2, containing 2r. 7p. (more or less), with a frontage of 80 feet or thereabouts. This lot also comprises an extensive range of substantially-built

BRICK AND STONE BUILDINGS,

Covered with slate, erected by the Guardians as Wards for Aged and Able-bodied Inmates of the Workhouse—together with the Buildings recently used as the Laundry, Girls' Dormitory, and Hospital of the Workhouse, and several Outbuildings. The purchaser of this lot will be entitled to the materials of such part of the Hospital as stands on Lot 4, and is to remove the same at his own expense, and also to make hedges or fences from the corners of the Buildings between this lot and Lot 4.

LOT 4.

A PIECE OF FREEHOLD GROUND,

Adjoining lot 3, containing 2r. 32p. (more or less), with a frontage of 100 feet to the Dartford and Sevenoaks Turnpike Road, and of 136 feet to the Road leading to Bradbourn Vale: together with a

BRICK AND TILED BUILDING,

Called the Old Sevenoaks Workhouse, with the Board Room, and several Buildings recently erected by the Guardians, and used as the Bakehouse, Bath Room, Receiving and Tramp Wards, Stabling, &c. There is a WELL of excellent water on this lot.

a system of parish relief was administered by the *vestry* through elected overseers. Much of this was outdoor relief enabling people to stay in their own homes supported by payments for food, clothing, rent, medical care (including midwifery) and funerals. On other occasions relief was either refused or left to the discretion of the officers, and some families were admitted to the workhouse. The rising costs of poor relief led to the Poor Law Amendment Act 1834. Parishes were amalgamated into unions with a central workhouse, to be administered by an elected Board of Guardians, and supervised by Commissioners in London. Local residents in December 1834 agreed to form a Sevenoaks union, eventually of 16 parishes, with a Union workhouse at Sundridge. Local landowners, including Lord ***Amherst***, Lord ***Stanhope***, and the Revd Thomas ***Curteis*** opposed the new Act. Frequent meetings attended by 'so many secret enemies and so many

100 Union workhouse, Sundridge. This photograph was taken in the late 1990s when the former Union workhouse, which became Sundridge hospital, had closed. Union workhouses were often substantial and imposing buildings. Regimes were frequently harsh with the aim of deterring all but the desperately poor from seeking relief.

prejudices and jealousies' resulted in inaction. Instead it was decided to extend the existing Sevenoaks workhouse, which was stated to be capable of taking 120 people. The enlarged workhouse was estimated to be capable of holding 300 inmates, but by 1841 there were 347. The children's accommodation was seriously overcrowded and unhealthy, highlighted in a medical report of July 1841. In November that year *The Times* condemned the 'scandal' in the Sevenoaks workhouse, leading to official demands for the construction of the new workhouse at Sundridge. The old premises were sold for £1,046 3s. 10d. including fixtures and fittings, and eventually demolished.

A new workhouse for the Sevenoaks Union, designed by A.R. Mason, was built in an isolated area south of Sundridge, which opened in October 1845. An infirmary was added three years later. In accordance with the 1834 Poor Law Amendment Act, the members of families were segregated with separate accommodation provided for men, women, the aged, the infirm, boys, and girls. The intention of the Act was that entering the workhouse was a last resort only for the truly destitute; conditions were designed to be worse than those of the poorest labourer. Thus the food was very basic and monotonous, the uniform rough and uncomfortable and inmates slept in dormitories, often sharing a bed, with inadequate washing and lavatory facilities; there was a supervised bath once a week. The able-bodied had to work; the men broke stones or picked apart oakum – tarred rope – whilst the women assisted with domestic work and nursing. Mothers spent perhaps one hour a week with their children. Over time, the workhouse guardians also became responsible for registration of births, marriages and deaths, compulsory vaccination against diseases such as smallpox, and public sanitary matters.

The children had to be given at least three hours' tuition a day in reading, writing, arithmetic and the basics of the Christian religion, these tasks supervised by a poorly paid schoolmaster and schoolmistress. A basic training in trades such as tailoring, boot making and perhaps carpentry was given to the boys, the girls being taught house work and sewing in order that they might later go into ***domestic service***. Despite considerable pressure from the authorities to remove the children from Sevenoaks Union Workhouse, away from the perceived bad influence of the adult inmates, no action was taken until 1908. In that year some were sent to cottage homes including Rock House in ***Chipstead*** Lane. The following year a further 20 went to Ide Hill village school, after an inspector reported that the workhouse school was unsatisfactory.

From 1 April 1930 the Boards of Guardians were abolished, union workhouses were renamed public assistance institutions, and administration was handed to local authorities. They continued in this form (in many cases workhouses under another name) until 1948, when they were abolished. Some were demolished and others converted to various types of hospital under the National Health Service. Sundridge became a hospital for the elderly; it finally closed in July 1998, and was converted to luxury apartments.
Curteis (1842); Keys (2009); Reynolds (1987)

Worships Hill
The Hill is part of the busy A25 road in ***Riverhead***, named after a local medical practitioner, John Lucas Worship (b.1825). Worship was born in Suffolk and practised medicine in Riverhead from the early 1850s. In 1922 villagers petitioned for 'some means of moderating the constantly recurring accidents and damage caused to property by excessive motor traffic' on the Hill.

Wyatt's rebellion
In January 1554 Sir Thomas Wyatt led an abortive rebellion against Queen Mary, fearing her proposed marriage to Philip of Spain would lead to Spanish domination. The rebellion, centered on Allington and Rochester, was supported by William Isley of Sundridge. He was hanged at Maidstone; the Knevett brothers and one of the Martell brothers were tried at the Sevenoaks ***Market House*** and executed at ***Gallows Common*** the next day.

Y

Hilton Young (1879-1960)
Conservative member of Parliament for Sevenoaks 1929-35. Young studied at Cambridge, and although called to the bar in 1904, he became a financial journalist. He was close to the 'Bloomsbury set'. While on active service with the Royal Navy, Young was elected Liberal MP for Norwich in a by-election. He continued in the war, losing his right arm in the raid on Zeebrugge. In Lloyd George's government Young's financial skills were

applied to post-war economic issues. He married Kathleen Scott, widow of Captain R.F. Scott, the polar explorer. In 1926 Young joined the Tory party and three years later was elected MP for Sevenoaks. During the early years of the 'slump' he was Minister for Export Credits, and then Minister of Health, 1931-35, with responsibility for housing, slum clearance, and town and country planning. Young retired from politics in mid-1935, rewarded with a peerage as Lord Kennet.

Young & Sons store
Youngs department store was founded in 1780 by 16-year-old Robert Comfort (1764-1852) when he opened a drapery shop on the eastern side of London Road. His nephews, Charles and Joseph Palmer, took over from him, and were joined by Stanford Young in 1845. The shop then became known as Palmer and Young. When Palmer retired in 1876, Young continued the business, his son Stanford J. Young joining him in 1883. They opened a second store in 1899 on the western side of London Road. The final expansion was into the old ***Rose and Crown*** site in the High Street after the hotel was demolished in 1936, where they sold furniture and electrical goods. The Palmer name was eventually lost as more and more Youngs entered the business. Alec Young, the last Chairman, sold the shops when he retired in 1957. The business was taken over by Allders who in 1976 closed all three stores. Over the years Youngs, the only department store in Sevenoaks, had provided local people with many of their clothing and household needs.
Shorey (1988)

youth organisations
Early youth groups in Sevenoaks were often attached to churches. Some were uniformed, for example, the Church Lads' Brigade at ***St John's*** church by 1907, the Boys' Brigade (founded 1883) which had a company at Sevenoaks Congregational church from the 1920s, and the Campaigners jointly run by ***St Nicholas*** and the St John's URC church. Non-uniformed groups often grew from Sunday schools, for example, ***temperance*** Band of Hope classes, and youth groups for teenagers. There were also Bible classes run by Christian Endeavour, the Covenanters, and also the Crusaders which aimed to reach teenagers who had no church contacts. The Young Men's (and Women's) Christian Associations catered for young adults, both being active in Sevenoaks. Youth work has continued to be provided largely by the churches through the Sevenoaks Area Youth Trust, founded in 2002. An alternative was the Raley's youth club which was linked at some time to the Voluntary Service Unit.

The Boy Scouts was uniformed and sometimes attached to a church. Founded in 1907 by Robert Baden-Powell, the First Sevenoaks (Hicks Own) Scout Group was formed by William Hicks, a teacher at ***Lady Boswell's School,*** in 1909. Members were pupils of the School, and met in the Parish Room of St Nicholas, London Road. In 1928 they moved to their own headquarters in Oakhill Road, calling their new home the Prairie. During the ***First World War*** the Scouts were used to do chores to help the wounded soldiers at ***Cornwall Hall*** and St John's Hall, and to perform guard duties at the Tonbridge Road and Bayley's Hill Reservoirs. The St John's church Scout group was founded by the Rev. F.W. Baggallay in 1911. A similar organisation for girls, the Girl Guides, was started in 1910, the Poppy Patrol in Sevenoaks being registered in July 1910. Scout and Guide rallies and camps were held in ***Knole***, one of the largest in 1953 with 7,000 Guides and a Brownies. A Brownie pack was formed for girls who were admitted long-term to the Cheyne ***Hospital*** for Children in Sevenoaks in the 1940s and 1950s.

The military sought to attract and train young people through the Army Cadet Force and the Air Training Corps (ATC). A squadron of the ATC was formed in Sevenoaks in 1941 at the height of the ***Second World War***. The cadets would parade with gas masks at their headquarters which was a large hut situated where the out-patients department of Sevenoaks hospital now stands. They later moved to the old searchlight hut in Crampton's Road and finally in the 1960s to the ***Drill Hall*** in Argyle Road.

Z

Zulu war 1879

Lt. Francis Holcroft, son of a local solicitor in the High Street, was killed in the Zulu war in southern Africa in 1879. His grieving parents had a stained glass window placed in the north wall of ***St Nicholas church***. Holcroft was part of the badly-led British invading force which was defeated by the Zulu army at the battle of Isandlwana. Twenty years later three other Sevenoaks men died, of disease, in the South African War (1899-1902), their deaths being commemorated by a plaque on the south wall of St Nicholas.

Bibliography

W. Albert (1972), *The turnpike road system in England 1663-1840* (Cambridge University Press: Cambridge).

Peter F. Alexander (1989), *William Plomer: A biography* (Oxford University Press: Oxford).

Gordon Anckorn (1979), *A Sevenoaks camera* (Ashgrove Press: Bath).

Gordon Anckorn (1984), *Sevenoaks memories* (Ashgrove Press: Bath).

Anon (1979), Sevenoaks Scout group. The first seventy years: a history of the 1st Sevenoaks (Hicks) Scout group (Ashgrove Press: Bath).

Anon (1994), *W. Davis & Sons. The first 75 years* (Davis: Sevenoaks).

Anon (1998), *Baptists in Sevenoaks – our story* (Vine Baptist church: Sevenoaks).

Anon (2002), 'The place name of Riverhead & its implications', *KAS Newsletter* 54, pp. 6-7.

Alan Armstrong (1995), ed., *The economy of Kent 1640-1914* (Boydell: Woodbridge).

Alan Armstrong (2001), 'Agriculture and rural society', in Nigel Yates, ed., *Kent in the twentieth century* (Boydell: Woodbridge), pp. 60-67.

John Attenborough (1975), *Living memory: Hodder and Stoughton publishers, 1868-1975* (Hodder & Stoughton: London).

Griselda Barton and Michael Tong (1995), *Samuel Palmer's golden valley* (Froglets: Westerham).

Hugh Barty-King (2000), *The New Beacon 1900-2000* (New Beacon School: Sevenoaks).

Margaret Bates and David Killingray (2003), 'The Herries family and the building of St Julians, Underriver, 1819-1837', *Archaeologia Cantiana*, 123, pp. 273-90.

Christopher Bell (1996), *The Catholic church of St Thomas of Canterbury. A centenary history 1896-1996* (Author: Sevenoaks).

Shirley Burgoyne Black (1984), *Farningham Crossroads: a history of two Kentish turnpikes* (Darenth Valley Publications: Otford).

Shirley Burgoyne Black (2001), *A scholar and a gentleman. Edward Hasted, the historian of Kent* (Darenth Valley Publications: Otford).

D.R. Boe (1989), *The story of Knole Park Golf Club 1924-1989* (The Club: Sevenoaks).

E.G. Box (1927), 'Sevenoaks and adjoining parishes', ts. Sevenoaks Library.

Peter Brandon (2005), *The North Downs* (Phillimore: Chichester).

John Bridgman (1821), *An historical and topographical sketch of Knole* (London).

Robin J. Brooks (1982), 'When silk was made at Sevenoaks', *Bygone Kent*, 3, pp. 465-67.

Robin J. Brooks (1989), 'Sevenoaks goes to war', *Bygone Kent*, 10, pp. 391-93.

Robin J, Brooks (1987), 'Francis Crawshay of Bradbourne', *Bygone Kent*, 8, pp. 465-67.

Vernon C. Brooks (1989), 'An evacuee in Sevenoaks', *Bygone Kent*, 10, pp. 685-88.

G.L Brown and A.U. Peek (1944), *A diary of D Company 20th Battalion Kent Home Guard, 1940 -1944* (Privately published: Sevenoaks).

Jane Brown (1985), *Vita's other world: a gardening biography of Vita Sackville-West* (Viking: London).
Jeremy Burchardt (2002), *The allotment movement in England, 1793-1873* (Boydell: Woodbridge).
Jeremy Burchardt and Jacqueline Cooper (2010), eds, *Breaking new ground: nineteenth-century allotments from local sources* (Chesham: FACHRS Publications).
Phillip Burgess (2001), ed., *Then and now: Sevenoaks* (Tempus:Stroud).
Ruth Butterfield (1993), '"The Royal Commission of King Jesus". General Baptist expansion and growth 1640-1660', *Baptist Quarterly*, XXXV, 2, pp. 56-80.
Julia Cameron (1999), *St Nicholas Sevenoaks: The church that went under* (Paternoster: Carlisle).
Dennis Clarke & Anthony Stoyel (1975), *Otford in Kent* (Otford and District Historical Society: Otford).
D.J.H. Clifford (1990), ed., *The Diaries of Lady Anne Clifford* (Sutton: Stroud, 1990).
Carolyn A. Conley (1991), *The unwritten law: criminal justice in Victorian Kent* (Oxford University Press: New York).
Elizabeth Crawford (2006), *The Women's suffrage movement in Britain and Ireland. A regional survey* (Routledge: London), 'Kent', pp.189-94.
David Cufley (1998), 'Dunton Green and Otford brickfields', *N.W. Kent Family History Society Journal*, 8, 3, pp.103-06.
Thomas Curteis (1842), *A Letter to the Right Honourable Sir Robert Peel, Bart., on the Principle and Operation of the New Poor Law, With an Appendix* (London: Hatchard, 1842).
Davis (1996), *W. Davis and Sons: The first 75 years* (Davis: Sevenoaks).
H.G. Dines (1969), *et al.*, *Geology of the country Around Sevenoaks and Tonbridge* (Geological Survey of Great Britain: HMSO, London).
Mary J. Dobson (1978), 'Original Compton Census returns – the Shoreham Deanery', *Archaeologia Cantiana*, 94, pp. 61-73.
Archie Donald (1992), *The posts of Sevenoaks in Kent: a history of postal services of the Sevenoaks district* (Woodvale: Tenterden).
Gillian Draper (1993 and 1995), 'The first hundred years of Quakerism in Kent', *Archaeologia Cantiana*, Part 1, 112, pp. 317-40, and Part 2, 115, pp. 1-22.
Katharine Draper *et al.* (1999), *A history of the parish of Chevening* (Chevening Parish History Group: Chipstead).
F.R.H. Du Boulay (1961), 'Denns, droving, and danger', *Archaeologia Cantiana*, 76, pp. 75-87.
F.R.H. Du Boulay (1964), ed., *Documents illustrative of medieval Kentish society* (Kent Records: Maidstone).
F.R.H. Du Boulay (1974), 'The assembling of an estate: Knowle in Sevenoaks, *c.*1275 to *c.*1525, *Archaeologia Cantiana*, 89, pp. 1-10.
John Dunlop (1964), *The pleasant town of Sevenoaks* (Caxton and Holmesdale Press: Sevenoaks).
Margaret Durdant-Hollamby (1998), *Life's not a rehearsal: the autobiography of Margaret Durdant-Hollamby* (The author: Sevenoaks).
Jacqueline Eales (2001a), 'Kent and the English civil wars, 1640-1660', in Frederick Lansberry, ed., *Government and politics in Kent, 1640-1914* (Boydell: Woodbridge).

Jacqueline Eales (2001b), *Community and disunity. Kent and the English civil wars, 1640-1649* (Oyster Press: Whitstable).
Jane Edwards (1985), *Her Recollections of old Sevenoaks 1792-1868* (Sevenoaks Society: Sevenoaks).
Simon Evans (1999), *Stopping Places. A Gypsy history of south London and Kent* (University of Hertfordshire Press: Hatfield).
Alan Everitt (1966), *The community of Kent and the Great Rebellion, 1640-60* (Leicester University Press: Leicester).
Alan Everitt (1985), 'Country carriers in the nineteenth century', in Everitt, ed., *Landscape and Community in England* (Hambledon Press: London), pp. 279-307.
Alan Everitt (1986), *Continuity and colonization. The evolution of Kentish settlement* (Leicester University Press: Leicester).
Alan Everitt (1995), 'The Harvest is past' (1995, unpub. ms.).
Benjamin Field (1862), *Sincere devotion exemplified in the life of Mrs C.E. Martin of Sevenoaks* (London).
William Coles Finch (1976), *Watermills and windmill: a historical survey of their rise, decline and fall as portrayed by those of Kent* (1933; Arthur Cassell: Sheerness).
Simon Fowler (2003), *Researching brewery and publican ancestors* (2nd edn, Family History Partnership: Bury).
Jean Fox, David Williams, and Peter Mountfield (2007), *Seal. The history of a parish* (Phillimore: Chichester).
H.S. Franklin (1945), *History of the 20th (Sevenoaks) Battalion of Kent Home Guard* (Privately printed: Sevenoaks).
Victoria Glendinning (1983), *Vita: The life of Vita Sackville-West* (Weidenfeld & Nicolson: London).
David Gould (1999), *The Westerham valley line* (Oakwood Press: Usk).
Maureen Green (2011), 'Hayle Mill: how a small papermaking company thrived in the nineteenth century', PhD thesis, University of London.
Duncan Harrington, Sarah Pearson and Susan Rose (2000), eds, *Kent Hearth Tax assessment – Lady Day 1664* (British Record Society: London).
Jeffery Harrison (1974), *The Sevenoaks Gravel Pit Wildfowl Reserve* (Wildfowl Trust Experimental Reserve: Chester).
Edward Hasted (1797-1801), *The history and topographical survey of the County of Kent*, Volume III (1778-99; reprint EP Publishing: Wakefield).
Keith Hetherington (1986), 'Some prominent Kent Brewers', *Bygone Kent* 7, 9, pp. 529-30.
Patricia Hollis (1987), *Ladies elect. Women in English local government 1865-1914* (Oxford University Press: Oxford).
Hollybush Residents Association (2000), *Hollybush on the Map* (HRA: Sevenoaks).
Brian Hornsey (nd. 2011), *Thirtyfive years of cinema -1929 to 1965 - in Kent* (The Author).
P.L. Humphries (1999), 'Tonbridge families remembered: a study of life in south-west Tonbridge, 1918-39', in C.W. Chalklin, ed., *Tonbridge in the early twentieth century* (Tonbridge Historical Society: Tonbridge), pp. 97-107.
Roy Ingleton (2002), *Policing Kent 1800-2000. Guarding the garden of England* (Phillimore: Chichester).

Basil Jackson (1950), *Recollections of Thomas Graham Jackson, 1835-1924* (Oxford University Press: Oxford).
Simon Jenkins (2003), *England's thousand best houses* (Allen Lane: London).
Journal of the Auctioneers and Estate Agent's Institute of the United Kingdom (1932), 12, 'Old Members', p. 311.
Walter D. Judd (1932), *The record of Wesleyan Methodism in the Sevenoaks circuit 1746-1932* (Bedford: Rush and Warwick).
Roger J.P. Kain (1974), 'The Tithe Commutation surveys', *Archaeologia Cantiana*, 89, pp. 101-18.
Kent Underground Research Group (KURG), *Sand and Sandstone Mines. Available from: http://www.kurg.org.uk/*
Bryan Keith-Lucas (1977), *English local government in the nineteenth and twentieth centuries* (Historical Association, London).
Bryan Keith-Lucas (1983), 'Francis and Francis Motley Austen, Clerks of the Peace for Kent', in Alec Detsicas and Nigel Yates, eds, *Studies in modern Kentish history* (Kent Archaeological Society: Maidstone), pp. 87-102.
B. Keith-Lucas (1984), 'The Kentish turnpikes', *Archaeologia Cantiana*, 100, pp. 345-69.
Bryan Keith-Lucas (1986), *Parish Affairs. The government of Kent under George III* (Kent County Council: West Malling, 1986), ch. III.
John Eric Keys (2009), 'The Care and Education of Children in an Urban and a rural workhouse, Poplar and Sevenoaks, 1870-1914', MA thesis, Open University.
David Killingray (1994), 'Rights, "riot" and ritual: the Knole Park access dispute, Sevenoaks, Kent, 1883-5', *Rural History* 5, 1, pp. 63-79.
David Killingray (2003), 'Tracing peoples of African origin and descent in Victorian Kent', in Gretchen Holbrook Gerzina, ed., *Black Victorians/Black Victoriana* (Rutgers University Press: New Brunswick, NJ).
David Killingray (2004a), ed., *Sevenoaks people and faith. Two thousand years of religious belief and practice* (Phillimore: Chichester).
David Killingray (2004b), 'A London city church estate in Kent: St Botolph's, Sevenoaks, 1646-2002', *Archaeologia* Cantiana, 124, pp. 291-307.
David Killingray (2009), 'Grassroots politics in west Kent since the late eighteenth century', *Archaeologia* Cantiana, 129, pp. 33-54.
David Killingray (2010), 'Influences shaping the human landscape of the Sevenoaks area since c.1600', *Archaeologia Cantiana*, 130, pp. 35-64.
Louis A. Knapfla (1994), *Kent at law 1602. The county jurisdiction: Assize and Sessions of the Peace* (HMSO: London).
W.H. Knocker (1915), 'The valley of Holmesdale. Its evolution and development', *Archaeologia Cantiana*, 31, pp. 155-77.
W.H. Knocker (1926), 'Sevenoaks, the manor, church and market', *Archaeologia Cantiana*, 38, pp. 51-68.
William Lambarde (1576), *A Perambulation of Kent* (Adams & Dart edn 1970: Bath).
Norma Landau (1984), *The Justices of the Peace 1679-1760* (University of California Press: Berkeley, CA).
H.C.F. Lansberry (1988), ed., *Sevenoaks Wills and Inventories in the reign of Charles II* (Kent Archaeological Society: Maidstone).

Frederick Lansberry (2001), ed., *Government and politics in Kent, 1640-1914* (Boydell: Woodbridge).
Terence Lawson & David Killingray (2004), eds, *An historical atlas of Kent* (Phillimore: Chichester).
Tessa Leeds (2000), 'The construction of the Sevenoaks railway tunnel 1863-1868', *Archaeologia Cantiana*, 120, pp.187-204.
Deidrie Le Faye (1989), *Jane Austen: a family record* (2nd edn, 2004, British Library: London).
Dickon Love and Chris Pickford (2002), 'The great bell of Bradbourne House, Sevenoaks', *The Ringing World*, 22 March 2002, pp. 285-86.
A. McCall (1980), *Green Line: the history of London's country bus services* (New Cavendish Books: London).
Ian Macdonald-Smith (2010), *Arts and Crafts master: the houses and gardens of M.H. Baillie Scott* (Rizzoli Publications: New York).
Alan Major (1987), 'The Dunton Green Brick, Tile & Pottery works', *Bygone Kent*, 8, pp. 506-12.
Karl Marx (1867), *Capital, vol. 1* (Penguin Classics edn, 1990: London), pp. 818-19.
Mavis Mate (2010), 'The economy of Kent, 1200-1500: the aftermath of the Black Death', in Sheila Sweetinburgh, ed., *Late Medieval Kent, 1220-1540* (Boydell: Woodbridge), pp. 11-17.
Elizabeth Melling (1980), *Kentish sources. Kent and the Civil War* (Kent County Council: Maidstone).
Marian Mills (1994), ed., *Your most dutyfull servant: the correspondence between Grizel, Countess of Stanhope of Chevening in Kent and John Brampton, her steward, between the years 1764 and 1744* (The author: Riverhead).
Marian Mills (1994), *A Riverhead century 1894-1994* (Riverhead Parish Council: Riverhead).
Ian Mitchell (1997), 'The public markets of some north-west Kent towns 1700-1850', *Archaeologia Cantiana* 117 (1997), pp. 173-87.
Katherine Moore (1989), *A family life 1939-45* (W.H. Allen: London).
J.P. Neale (1821), *Views of the Seats of Noblemen and Gentlemen* (London).
Jean Newman (2008), *Dunton Green*. 2nd ed. (Parish Council: Dunton Green).
John Newman (2003), *Saint Luke's parish church, Sevenoaks – a centenary history* (St Luke's Parish: Sevenoaks).
John Newman (1976), *West Kent and the Weald* (Penguin 2nd edn: London). New edn, *Kent: West and the Weald* (London: Yale University Press, 2012)
W.R. Newton, *The Vine Baptist church Sevenoaks 1748-1948* (Vine Baptist church: Sevenoaks).
David Nunnerley (2000), *A history of Montreal Park Sevenoaks* (The author: Sevenoaks).
Bob Ogley (1976), *Lady Boswell's School 1675-1975* (Lady Boswell's School PTA: Sevenoaks).
Bob Ogley (1987), *In the wake of the hurricane* (Froglets Publications: Westerham).

Bob Ogley (1994), *Kent at War* (Froglets Publications: Westerham).
Bob Ogley (1999), *Kent: a chronicle of the century*. 4 vols (Froglets Publications: Westerham).
Bob Ogley and Roger Perkins (1999), *Sevenoaks chronicle of the century* (Froglets Publications: Westerham).
Oxford Dictionary of National Biography (2004), eds, Colin Matthew and Brian Harrison (Oxford University Press: Oxford).
William Page (1908), ed., *The Victoria County of England. Kent* vol. 1 (Archibald Constable: London), pp. 479-92.
William Page (1926), *The Victoria County History of England. Kent*, vol. 2 (St Catherine Press: London), 'The hospital at Sevenoaks', p. 227.
Frank Panton and Terence Lawson (2004), 'Turnpikes, roads and waterways, 1700-1850', in Lawson and David Killingray, eds, *An Historical Atlas of Kent* (Phillimore: Chichester), pp. 122-23.
R.B. Parish (1999), 'Kent animal pounds', *Bygone Kent*, 20, pp. 663-66.
Monty Parkin (2009), *The Story of Sevenoaks Market. Over a thousand years of history* (Kemsing Heritage Centre: Kemsing).
H. Pearman, et al., (1983), *Sand Mine – Chipstead, Kent. Survey map* (Available from http://www.kurg.org.uk).
Phyllis Pearsall (1990), *A-Z maps. The personal story, from bedsit to household name* (Geographers' A-Z Map Company: Sevenoaks).
Michael Person (1997), *Kent clocks and clockmakers* (Mayfield Books: Ashbourne, Derbys).
Elsie Pike, Constance E. Curryer & U.K. Moore (1938; revised edn, 1973), *The Story of Walthamstow Hall* (Longmore Press: Otford).
Susan Pittman (2011), 'Elizabethan and Jacobean deer parks in Kent', PhD thesis, University of Kent.
William Plomer (1943), *Double lives: An autobiography* (Jonathan Cape: London).
Gordon Raybould (1986), *Combe Bank, Sundridge: a history* (Sundridge: Combe Bank School).
Christopher Rayner (1997), *Sevenoaks Past, with the villages of Holmesdale* (Phillimore: Chichester).
Brian Raynor (2000), *John Frith, scholar and martyr* (Hawthorns Publications: Otford).
Aileen Reid (2001), 'Survival of the smallest: the Sevenoaks tenants estate', *Architectural History*, 44, pp. 401-10.
Sheila Reynolds (1987), 'Poor relief in eighteenth century Sevenoaks', *Bygone Kent*, 8, 1, pp.19-22.
Frank Richards (1901), *Old Sevenoaks* (Salmon: Sevenoaks).
Margaret Roake (1999), ed., *Religious Worship in Kent. The census of 1851* (Kent Archaeological Society: Maidstone), pp. 128-31.
John Rooker (1910), *Notes on the parish church St Nicholas Sevenoaks* (Salmon: Sevenoaks).
Robert Sackville-West (2010), *Inheritance: the story of Knole* (Bloomsbury: London).
Vita Sackville-West (1922), *Knole and the Sackvilles* (Heinemann: London).
Vita Sackville-West (1937), *Pepita* (Hogarth Press: London).
Salmon's Guide to Sevenoaks and the Neighbourhood (1881) (Salmon: Sevenoaks).

Salmon's Directory 1903 - annual to 1968 (Salmon: Sevenoaks).
Anthony C.M.B. Scott (1997), *You Can't Turn the Clock Back* (Multon Books: Nottingham).
Brian Scragg (1993), *Sevenoaks School, a history* (Ashgrove Press: Bath).
Marigold Seal (2008), 'Greatness Mills', Parts 2 and 3', *St John's Parish Magazine* (St John's: Sevenoaks).
Sevenoaks Society (1994), *100 Years' growth in Sevenoaks services* (Sevenoaks Society: Sevenoaks).
Rod Shelton (2002), *The Archbishop's palace – Otford. A history and description of the palace buildings in 1520* (Longmore Press: Otford).
Edna V. Shorey (1988), 'Mr Young's young ladies', *Bygone Kent*, 9, 2, pp. 111-14.
K.J. Smart (1983), *Cricket on The Vine 1734-1984* (Sevenoaks Cricket Club: Sevenoaks).
David Waldron Smithers (1981), *Jane Austen in Kent* (Hurtwood: Westerham).
Perry Snow (2000), *The Search for a Stolen Identity* (Universal Publishers: USA).
H.W. Standen (1958), *Kippington in Kent* (The author: Sevenoaks).
Marilyn Starkey (nd. 1992), *St Hilary's fifty golden years* (St Hilary's School: Sevenoaks)
A.M.W. Stirling, *The Richmond papers from the correspondence and manuscripts of George Richmond, R.A., and his son Sir William Richmond, R.A., K.C.B.* (London, 1926), pp. 108-09.
Anthony Stoyel (1998), 'The Clock House. A Georgian "Trompe-L'Oeil" building', *Sevenoaks Society Newsletter*, Autumn, pp. 5-7.
Alan Stoyel (2008), *Memories of Kentish watermills. The rivers Cray and Darent* (Landmark Publishing: Ashbourne).
Peter Swan (1980), *A short history of library services in Sevenoaks 1905-1980* (Kent County Library: Maidstone).
Sheila Sweetinburgh (2010), ed., *Later medieval Kent, 1220-1540* (Boydell: Woodbridge).
J. N. Tarn (1973), *Five per cent philanthropy: an account of housing in urban areas between 1840 and 1914* (Cambridge University Press: Cambridge).
W.E. Tate (1943), 'A hand list of English enclosure Acts and Awards, Part 17. Open fields, commons and enclosures in Kent', *Archaeologia Cantiana*, 56, pp. 54-68.
Kristin Taylor (2003), 'The development of the park and gardens at Knole', *Archaeologia Cantiana*, 123, pp. 153-84.
L.C. Taylor *et al.*, *Experiments in education at Sevenoaks* (Constable Young Books: London).
Ron Terry (2000), *Old corners of Sevenoaks. The yards, courts and passages of historic Sevenoaks* (Caxton and Holmesdale Press: Sevenoaks).
Joan Thirsk (1993), 'Hasted as historian', *Archaeologia Cantiana*, 111, pp. 1-15.
Edwin Thompson (1994), *Sevenoaks recollections. A photographic perambulation of Sevenoaks and district* (Circa Publishing: Sevenoaks).
Dan Tuson (2007), *The Kent Downs* (Tempus: Chalford).
David Underdown (2000), *Start of play. Cricket and culture in eighteenth-century England* (Allen Lane: London).

Keith Wade (2010), 'Postcards and photographs', *Sevenoaks Society Newsletter*, October 2010.
J.K. Wallenberg (1934), *Place Names of Kent* (Appelbergs: Uppsala).
Gordon Ward (1931; 1980 edn), *Sevenoaks essays* (Ashgrove Press: Sevenoaks).
V. Watts (2003), ed., *The Cambridge Dictionary of English Place* Names (Cambridge University Press: 2003).
Weald History Group (1999), *Sevenoaks Weald. A brief history* (Longmore Pres: Otford).
H.G. Wells (1934), *An Experiment in Autobiography* (Gollancz: London).
Tom West (1993), *Busking with the Band* (The author: Sevenoaks).
West Kent Federation of Women's Institutes (1995), *West Kent within living memory* (Countryside Books: Newbury).
H.P. White (1992), *A regional history of the railways of Great Britain: vol. 2: southern England*. 5th edn (Redwood Press: Melksham).
Wildernesse Residents Association (2000), *The Wildernesse estate; a guide for residents* (The Association: Sevenoaks).
John H. Williams (2010), ed., *The archaeology of Kent to AD 800* (Boydell: Woodbridge).
Henry Williamson (1955), *A fox under my cloak* (Macdonald: London).
Anthony Wilson (1988), 'Improvements in communication: the telegraph and the telephone come to Tonbridge', in C.W. Chalklin, ed., *Late Victorian & Edwardian Tonbridge* (Kent County Library: West Malling), pp. 15-24.
Margaret Wilson (2001), *Jane Austen's Family and Tonbridge* (Jane Austen Society: Chawton).
Frederick G. Wood (1983), *Let's explore the River Darent* (Meresborough Books: Gillingham).
Nigel Yates, 'A Kentish clerical dynasty: Curteis of Sevenoaks', Part I, 1716-1874, and Part II, 1874-1907', *Archaeologia Cantiana* 108 (1990), pp. 1-9; and 117 (1997), pp. 161-71.
Nigel Yates, Robert Hume, and Paul Hastings (1994), eds, *Religion and society in Kent, 1640-1914* (Boydell & Brewer: Woodbridge).
Nigel Yates (2001), ed., *Kent in the 20th century* (Boydell: Woodbridge).
Philip C. Yorke (1931), *The diary of John Baker* (Hutchinson: London).
Michael Zell (2000), ed., *Early modern Kent 1540-1640* (Boydell: Woodbridge).

Index

Note: page numbers in **bold** refer to main entries in the text; page numbers in *italics* refer to illustrations and their captions.

Indexing by Chris Dance